CAMPUS TO COUNTER

Drawing upon multiple oral history interviews with black students who launched the sit-in movement in the Research Triangle in 1960, Brian Suttell provides rich new insights into how these students helped transform race relations in North Carolina.

>—William Chafe, Alice Mary Baldwin Distinguished Professor of History emeritus, Duke University; author of *Civilities and Civil Rights: Greensboro, North Carolina and the Black Struggle for Freedom.*

Written in a manner that would appeal to scholars and the general public, *Campus to Counter* is an exceptional work and makes an important contribution to the scholarship on student activism during the civil rights movement. Brian Suttell aptly underscores the activism of black college students in transforming the civil rights movement and the fight for racial equality and justice in North Carolina. His groundbreaking work further sheds light on the significance of historically black colleges and universities (HBCUs) to black youth activism and the role young people (both black and white) played in shaping the course of the civil rights movement.

>—Thomas L. Bynum, associate professor of History and director of Black Studies Program, Cleveland State University; author of *NAACP Youth and the Fight for Black Freedom, 1936–1965.*

In *Campus to Counter*, Brian Suttell explores North Carolina's civil rights struggles of the early 1960s in granular detail. It was neither the proverbial "outside agitators," nor national leaders like Martin Luther King, Jr., who propelled this movement forward; the driving force, he demonstrates, came from the ground up, students in what Suttell labels the "Protest Triangle" of historically black colleges: Shaw University, St. Augustine's College, and North Carolina College at Durham. In an ironic twist, he shows that while these folks led the way, students and faculty at the better known "Research Triangle"—Duke, University of North Carolina, and North Carolina State—played valuable supporting roles, often in the name of academic freedom. Suttell's work is a nuanced inquiry into the dynamics of desegregation in the Upper South."

>—Ray Raphael, author of *A People's History of the American Revolution*

AMERICA'S HISTORICALLY BLACK COLLEGES AND
UNIVERSITIES series examines the varying role of these
important institutions throughout the Civil Rights
struggle and American history as a whole.

Edited by Quinton Dixie, Duke Divinity School

PREVIOUSLY PUBLISHED

Harry Lefever, *Undaunted by the Fight: Spelman College and the Civil
Rights Movement, 1957-1967*

Bobby L. Lovett, *America's Historically Black Colleges & Universities: A
Narrative History from the Nineteenth Century into the Twenty-First
Century*

Bobby L. Lovett, *A Touch of Greatness: A History of Tennessee State
University*

F. Erik Brooks, *Tigers in the Tempest: Savannah State University and the
Struggle for Civil Rights*

Campus to Counter

CIVIL RIGHTS ACTIVISM IN RALEIGH AND DURHAM,

NORTH CAROLINA, 1960–1963

BRIAN SUTTELL

MERCER UNIVERSITY PRESS

Macon, Georgia

MUP/ P665

© 2023 by Mercer University Press
Published by Mercer University Press
1501 Mercer University Drive
Macon, Georgia 31207

27 26 25 24 23   5 4 3 2 1

Books published by Mercer University Press are printed on acid-free paper that
meets the requirements of the American National Standard for Information
Sciences—Permanence of Paper for Printed Library Materials.

Printed and bound in the United States.

This book is set in Adobe Caslon.

Cover/jacket design by Burt&Burt.

ISBN   978-0-88146-877-9 Print
ISBN   978-0-88146-878-6 eBook

Cataloging-in-Publication Data is available from the Library of Congress

To my family for inspiring me and to the activists who inspired great change in this beautiful nation

MERCER UNIVERSITY PRESS

Endowed by

TOM WATSON BROWN
and
THE WATSON-BROWN FOUNDATION, INC.

CONTENTS

Preface

This book investigates civil rights activism in Raleigh and Durham, North Carolina, in the early 1960s, especially among students at Shaw University, Saint Augustine's College (now Saint Augustine's University), and North Carolina College at Durham (now North Carolina Central University). Their significance in challenging traditional practices regarding race relations has been underrepresented in the historiography of the civil rights movement. Students from these three historically Black colleges and universities (HBCUs) played a crucial role in bringing about the end of segregation in public accommodations and the reduction of discriminatory hiring practices. While student activists often proceeded from campus to the lunch counters to participate in sit-in demonstrations, their actions also represented a counter to businesspersons and politicians who sought to preserve a segregationist view of Tar Heel hospitality.

The research presented in this book demonstrates the ways in which ideas of academic freedom gave additional ideological force to the civil rights movement and helped garner support from students and faculty from the "Research Triangle" schools composed of North Carolina State College (now North Carolina State University), Duke University, and the University of North Carolina at Chapel Hill. Many students from both the "Protest Triangle" (my term for the activists at the three HCBUs) and "Research Triangle" schools viewed efforts by local and state politicians to thwart student participation in sit-ins and other forms of protest as a restriction of their academic freedom. Despite the rich historiography on the American civil rights movement as well as several scholarly works addressing academic freedom, there has been a lack of emphasis on the ways in which civil rights activism and academic freedom were interconnected in the early 1960s.

This book is the result of extensive archival research and the analysis of primary and secondary sources. The author has conducted thirty-one interviews of civil rights activists and members of the Raleigh and Durham communities, in addition to interviews of nationally recognized civil rights leaders such as Andrew Young and Wyatt Tee Walker. Interviewees from Raleigh and Durham were asked to complete surveys, which were utilized to provide a more systematic method for the author to form assertions and analyze patterns of experiences among the activists.

Series Foreword

In 1987 I was an undergraduate student in Darlene Clark Hine's "Black Politics" seminar at Michigan State University. It was there that I was introduced to Clayborne Carson's *In Struggle: SNCC and the Black Awakenings of the 1960s*. Carson's work chronicled the formation of one of the most important civil rights organizations as it confronted the dawning of a new era in African American agitation for full equality in the United States. Since, historians have been compelled to include the stories and voices of African American young people as they engaged their elders in debate about the meaning of democracy, the significance of integration and the usefulness of nonviolence. As a young, impressionable student studying history and public policy, reading Carson's work made me feel as if I had missed out on an important opportunity to take to the streets what I was learning at MSU. For my generation, the Anti-Apartheid movement became our opportunity to test theories of democracy, and the youth engaged in struggle during the 1960s was our model.

While nearly all those young people were students, little has been written about how their experiences as activists informed their classroom learning. Brian Suttell's fresh approach in *Campus to Counter* examines the responses to social activism of the 1960s as co-curricular activity. In that regard, movement activists and their supporters were ahead of their times in asserting the importance of off-campus experiences to making book learning relevant. Additionally, Suttell explores the various ways in which efforts to restrict student involvement were understood as attempts to limit academic freedom. Undoubtedly, his work will enrich the conversation about the civil rights movement as it situates it within debates happening on college campuses then and now.

Our book series *America's HBCUs* seeks to explore what makes these schools important, and in our current political climate, quite a bit rides on the answers. The questions are historical with serious current consequences. For if one concludes there is nothing particularly remarkable about these schools then one might feel it is not worth the economic and political capital necessary to reform or save the HBCUs that teeter on the verge of nonexistence. To the contrary, we believe the histories of black colleges and universities stand as testaments to their ongoing importance. Our thesis is that they endure as symbols of African American institutional development, resilience, self-governance and self-determination in the midst of systemic racial oppression. Additionally, they have been sites of instigation, coordination and development of social activists and activism. *Campus to Counter* progresses our understanding of the critical role HBCUs played in educating, protecting, and propelling forward a new generation of change agents.

Quinton H. Dixie, PhD
Associate Research Professor of
History of Christianity in the United States
and Black Church Studies
Duke Divinity School

Acknowledgments

I would like to thank the civil rights activists whom I interviewed for this project, both for their time and for their contributions to social justice in the United States.

Thanks to Quinton Dixie, Marc Jolley, and the staff at Mercer University Press for the guidance and the opportunity to publish this book.

I wish to thank my friends and colleagues who have helped in my development as a historian, writer, and teacher, including Charles Bolton, Mark Elliott, the late Walter Jackson, Timothy Daniels, Virginia Summey, Jeff Jones, Peter Villella, Linda Rupert, Greg O'Brien, Cynthia Villagomez, Joseph Ross, Jamie Mize, Justina Licata, Jonathan Dent, and Mike and Melissa Bieniek. Thanks for all the excellent perspectives over the years from my students at UNC Greensboro, Ferrum College, UNC Pembroke, Winston Salem State University, and Mac Williams Middle School. I want to acknowledge the assistance I received from archivists, especially Frederick Sills Jr. at Saint Augustine's University, Tom Clark at Shaw University, Andre Vann at North Carolina Central University, and Cynthia P. Lewis at the King Library and Archives in Atlanta, Georgia.

A special thanks to my parents for being a guiding light in my life. To my brothers Chris and Jason for all the fun times and our love of music and sports. To Hope and Lauren for being such good role models for my awesome niece and nephews. Thanks to my Soul Safari music writing brother Andy Stewart and lifelong friends Charlie Hitchings, Dave Fronczak, Greg Korcz, and Bob Toft. And to Elan and Nyra for making me laugh after long days of writing and grading. Thanks to Tara for all the support in every way and for helping me embrace the light, the energy, and the beauty of today.

Chapter 1

Introduction

The scene was festive with a tinge of solemnity as a group of citizens and civil rights activists from Raleigh arrived at the March on Washington for Jobs and Freedom on August 28, 1963. Reverend Dr. Martin Luther King Jr.'s "I Have a Dream" speech was the apogee of a day of speeches and music by the likes of John Lewis, A. Philip Randolph, Roy Wilkins, Floyd McKissick, Mahalia Jackson, and Bob Dylan. But the individuals from Raleigh were not mere *witnesses* to history; they were *participants* in a historic moment that was a public and national display of years of struggle for increased freedom.

The March on Washington was not only a story about a particularly inspiring speech; it was also the 200,000-plus stories of the experiences that participants brought with them, and it was a story about the thousands and thousands of activists whose actions had paved the way for them to participate in this historic event. Whereas A. Philip Randolph brought forth the initial idea for a March on Washington two decades prior, the true force and momentum for the event initiated largely from the actions of students at historically Black college and university campuses in Greensboro, Raleigh, Durham, Nashville, Montgomery, and other cities and towns throughout the South. Through the use of sit-ins and other direct challenges to segregation, student activists had brought significant changes to existing conceptions about race relations in the South and throughout the country prior to the March on Washington.[1]

Students from Shaw University, Saint Augustine's College (now Saint Augustine's University), and North Carolina College (NCC) at Durham (now North Carolina Central University) played crucial roles in shaping the goals, strategies, and outcomes of the civil rights movement in Raleigh and Durham from 1960–1963. Students from these HBCUs took the lead in pushing for changes in policies regarding public accommodations and racial segregation in the two cities. They were part of a broader student movement that applied pressure to local businesspersons and local and state officials to dismantle legal segregation as well as segregation based on social tradition. By the time of the March on Washington in late August 1963, the majority of lunch counters, restaurants, and theaters in Raleigh and Durham had already desegregated, and several establishments had altered their racially discriminatory hiring practices.[2] The March on Washington was a highly publicized event that was in many ways a climax of three years of heightened protest largely initiated in the dorm rooms, courtyards, student council rooms, and auditoriums of the Black colleges in the South and sustained in the streets, lunch counters, restaurants, and theaters of several cities.

For several generations prior to the 1960s, African Americans had recognized the important role of education in helping bring about increased freedom. My research suggests that the student activists in Raleigh and Durham in the early 1960s saw their involvement in civil rights

---

[1] Jon Phelps, "McKissick in Key Role: Number from City in March," *Durham Morning Herald,* 29 August 1963, 1B; "Raleigh 'Marchers' Report on Experience," *Carolinian,* 7 September 1963; Millie Dunn Veasey, phone interview by the author, digital recording, 27 June 2016; Bruce Lightner, interview by the author, Raleigh, NC, 16 June 2016; Carrie Gaddy Brock, interview by the author, Raleigh, 2 March 2016; Vannie C. Culmer, phone interview by the author, digital recording, 26 January 2017; Pete Cunningham, phone interview by the author, digital recording, 21 June 2016.

[2] Jonathan Friendly, "76 Business Firms Here Integrating," *News and Observer,* 6 June 1963, 1; "City-Wide Move: Business Firms Here Drop Racial Barriers," *News and Observer,* 20 June 1963, 1; Durham AP, "Bans Lifting at Durham," *News and Observer,* 5 June 1963, 1; Jon Phelps, "90 Pct. of Durham Eating Facilities Now Desegregated," *Durham Morning Herald,* 19 June 1963, 1.

demonstrations as *part* of their education.[3] The opportunities in a segregated society were not equivalent to the educational attainment of students at historically Black colleges and universities. Thus, the students recognized that creating a more open society without the restraints placed on them through segregation would play a role in increasing their opportunities. David Forbes, who became one of the most important student protest leaders in Raleigh in the early 1960s, recalls that even as far back as elementary school, "Black teachers always said, 'we are teaching you to your possibility because what we are teaching you may not be able to be fully exercised now, but the time will come when you can.' So, there was always that forward view that things were going to change."[4] More so than any other generation of activists, those of the early 1960s pushed for such changes, and they viewed their involvement as part of their education and as a way of opening opportunities for their own future and that of their race.

Since student civil rights activists in Raleigh and Durham viewed the demonstrations as part of their education, they also adamantly opposed any attempts to restrict their rights to protest. In this sense, civil rights activism and an expanded vision of academic freedom that extended beyond the gates of the college were interrelated. Any efforts by city or state officials or college administrators to discourage the protests were perceived by the protestors as well as sympathetic White students from other North Carolina colleges as infringements on their academic freedom.[5]

Some students and faculty from the primarily White institutions of North Carolina State (Raleigh), Duke University (Durham), and the University of North Carolina at Chapel Hill (UNC) also played significant roles in helping to change racial conceptions and defended the students' right to protest. These three universities and their respective cities

---

[3] See survey in appendix.

[4] David Forbes, interview by the author, digital recording, 13 April 2016, Raleigh.

[5] See survey in appendix; Carrie Gaddy Brock, interview by the author, digital recording, 2 March 2016, Raleigh; Stafford Bullock, interview by the author, digital recording, 2 March 2016, Raleigh; LaMonte Wyche, phone interview by the author, digital recording, 29 June 2016; Vivian Camm, interview by the author, digital recording, 27 April 2016, Lynchburg, VA.

comprise North Carolina's "Research Triangle." UNC in particular had a tradition in the decades prior to the 1960s as a strong defender of academic freedom. Many professors from the Research Triangle schools were members of the American Association of University Professors (AAUP), which vigorously defended the idea of academic freedom for professors. While the AAUP periodically issued resolutions on academic freedom that involved issues of race relations prior to 1960, the sit-in movement helped inspire a period in which most of its resolutions dealt with the issue of race and indicated the organization's support of integration. Ideals of academic freedom thus provided a theoretical foundation for the defense of the protests not only by African American students but also by some White professors and students in the region.[6]

In a region often referred to as the Triangle, or more specifically the Research Triangle, another sort of triangle existed in the 1960s at Shaw, Saint Augustine's, and NCC that I refer to as the "Protest Triangle." Students at these Black institutions provided the most active leadership for the sit-ins and other forms of direct action in the region. In Raleigh, students at Shaw and Saint Augustine's worked closely together and would generally meet on Shaw's campus in the heart of downtown before marching to the segregated businesses to stage protest demonstrations or sit-ins. As the first institution of higher learning founded for African Americans in the South, Shaw had a rich educational tradition. Every generation of Shaw graduates had not only symbolized Black progress in education but exemplified its possibilities. But the early 1960s-era students were a special generation of activists who directly challenged a society that had limited the opportunities of its graduates for nearly a century.[7]

Students from the "Protest Triangle" schools provided the backbone of the movements to challenge segregation in Raleigh and Durham. The

---

[6] Robert MacIver, *Academic Freedom in Our Time* (New York: Columbia University Press, 1955), 272; Richard Hofstadter and Walter P. Metzger, *The Development of Academic Freedom in the United States* (New York: Columbia University Press, 1955), 446–50; Charles J. Holden, *The New Southern University: Academic Freedom and Liberalism at UNC* (Lexington: The University Press of Kentucky, 2012), 44–47, 76, 84; Detroit AP, "Professors Rally to Student Aid," *News and Observer*, 10 April 1960, 8.

[7] For analysis of Shaw University's history, see Wilmoth A. Carter, *Shaw's Universe: A Monument to Educational Innovation* (Raleigh: Shaw University, 1973).

theme of "campus to counter" involves a double meaning. On a literal level, student activists went from the campus to the segregated lunch counters to participate in sit-ins in Raleigh and Durham. On a more figurative level, the "campus" acted to counter the established city leadership in the form of business leaders, the mayor, and the city council, as well as state government leadership. The students and most professors and administrators at these Black schools recognized that White leaders would not "bestow" freedom upon them. To push business leaders to integrate or to challenge city, state, or even federal laws to protect their civil rights, they recognized they would have to use direct-action tactics.[8]

Students sought to counter the most blatant supporters of segregation and racial discrimination as well as those who characterized themselves as "moderates" on racial issues. On the local level, they challenged business and municipal leaders. In Raleigh, student protestors targeted the Ambassador Theater, which was managed by Mayor William G. Enloe. By doing so, they sought to bring forth economic and moral pressure for integration. Some protestors viewed Enloe as "part of the status quo," unwilling to take a principled stand for integration.[9] One factor that made the Raleigh movement unique in the state was that the local movement intersected heavily with the statewide movement largely due to the presence of the state capital and the hotel that served as quarters for state legislators. The demonstrations at the Sir Walter Hotel represented some of the tensions between student demonstrators and state legislators, including an incident in which a legislator threatened to "slap hell out" of a UNC student protestor.[10]

Student activists in Raleigh and Durham helped bring about changes to racially discriminatory practices on the local, state, and national levels. Significant desegregation of public accommodations in both cities occurred prior to the March on Washington in August 1963, and overt segregation in restaurants, theaters, and other places of business was mostly a thing of the past prior to the signing of the Civil Rights Act of 1964. NCC

---

[8] See survey in appendix.

[9] McLouis Clayton, interview by the author, digital recording, 2 March 2016, Raleigh.

[10] Bob Lynch, "Negroes 'Sit-In' at Sir Walter," *News and Observer*, 11 June 1963, 1.

students who had been arrested for sit-ins in Durham in 1960 eventually had their convictions overturned by the US Supreme Court. One of those students, John Avent, recalls that "we wanted to pressure everyone in power." While not every student sought arrest when they participated in sit-ins, Avent and those arrested at S.H. Kress in May 1960 had planned for their arrest and welcomed the potential to challenge their convictions in the courts. Avent contends that the sit-in cases, including *John Thomas Avent et al., Petitioners, v. State of North Carolina*, provided the "pillar of the Civil Rights Act." Indeed, the pressure placed on the Kennedy Administration by the various demonstrations, many of which were led by Black college students, had provided the impetus for the legislation that President Johnson ultimately signed in 1964.[11]

The rich historiography of the civil rights movement in the United States has only scratched the surface of the local movements in Raleigh and Durham. In general, the limited historiography of the civil rights movement in Raleigh and Durham and that of individuals who played roles in the local movements in the two cities has often fallen short in addressing the student activists themselves. This is no small oversight considering that the students from the "Protest Triangle" schools were the most influential group in bringing about changes to segregation and racial discrimination in Raleigh and Durham in the early 1960s.

Leslie Brown's *Upbuilding Black Durham: Gender, Class, and Black Community Development in the Jim Crow South* offers poignant insights into Black economic development in Durham, mostly in the first four decades of the twentieth century. She reveals the ways in which African Americans dealt with segregation and how some used it to their advantage. She maintains, "Nationally, black Durham was viewed as a symbol of what African Americans could do on their own when left alone by whites."[12] She addresses the important role of Black businesses in Durham, including

---

[11] John Thomas Avent, phone interview by the author, digital recording, 12 July 2016; Kenneth T. Andrews and Sarah Gaby, "Local Protest and Federal Policy: The Impact of the Civil Rights Movement on the 1964 Civil Rights Act," *Sociological Review* 30, no. S1 (June 2015): 509–27.

[12] Leslie Brown, *Upbuilding Black Durham: Gender, Class, and Black Community Development in the Jim Crow South* (Chapel Hill: University of North Carolina Press, 2008), 14.

the development of the North Carolina Mutual and Life Insurance Company, which became the largest Black-owned business in the world by the mid-1920s. Brown argues that "Durham's black elite emerged within an apartheid system enforced routinely by violence and learned to use segregation to its advantage, believing it could provide a route to autonomy otherwise denied by Jim Crow."[13] In 1925, the famous Black sociologist E. Franklin Frazier dubbed Durham the "Capital of the Black Middle Class." But the veneer of Durham as a thriving place for African American business contrasted with the poverty that existed in the city's Black neighborhoods, particularly among single Black women.[14]

Perhaps the most significant scholarly work on the civil rights era in Durham is Christina Greene's *Our Separate Ways: Women and the Black Freedom Movement in Durham, North Carolina*, although only one chapter directly addresses the direct-action phase that I address in this work. She analyzes some of the civil rights organizing that occurred in Durham prior to the sit-in movement, including the efforts to revitalize the NAACP in Durham by Shaw graduates R. Arline Young and Ella Baker. Greene emphasizes the crucial role women played in organizing and participating in civil rights demonstrations. She points out that at the outbreak of the sit-ins and other forms of protest in 1960, the local NAACP had a majority female membership, and women appeared to have outnumbered men at many of the demonstrations. Yet she acknowledges that sexism existed in the movement and that men spoke more than women at mass meetings. The interviews that I have conducted largely reinforce Greene's assertion that women were often the majority at the protests.[15]

The existing historiography on the civil rights movement in Raleigh is sparse and does not sufficiently address student leadership from Shaw or Saint Augustine's. Historian Peter Ling points out that David Forbes

---

[13] Brown, *Upbuilding Black Durham*, 114.

[14] Brown, *Upbuilding Black Durham*, 252.

[15] Christina Greene, *Our Separate Ways: Women and the Black Freedom Movement in Durham, North Carolina* (Chapel Hill: University of North Carolina Press, 2005), 11, 21, 25. See list of interviews in bibliography. Only two of the student respondents gave a number or phrase that implied that women represented less than half of the demonstrators.

is one example of an activist who "lack[s] a profile in movement studies."[16] Like other activists in Raleigh, Forbes receives occasional mentions for his role in the founding of the Student Nonviolent Coordinating Committee (SNCC) in 1960, but scholars have scarcely addressed his role or that of other movement leaders who attended Shaw, such as Albert Sampson and Mack Sowell, in bringing about desegregation in Raleigh. Forbes was one of the most dynamic leaders of the student protest movement in the city and was among the first group of students arrested for trespassing at Cameron Village in Raleigh on February 12, 1960.[17] He had already established himself as a leader of the local movement prior to his involvement in the Youth Leadership Conference at Shaw in April 1960. Rev. Dr. Wyatt Tee Walker, a close confidant of Martin Luther King Jr., had previously met Forbes at a minister's conference. When Walker came to Shaw for the conference in the spring of 1960, he was not surprised to find that the articulate young student from Raleigh was a leader of the movement to dismantle segregation in the city.[18]

Shaw University was at the heart of civil rights activism in Raleigh during the sit-in movement in 1960, and for three days in April 1960 it served as the epicenter of civil rights organizing on a region-wide level. The historic Youth Leadership Conference organized by the Southern Leadership Conference (SCLC) played a significant role in the growing civil rights movement. The conference and ensuing conferences in Atlanta ultimately led to the development of the SNCC. Much of the scholarly attention given to the conference has focused on the development of the SNCC or on the apparent strategic differences between Martin Luther King Jr. and Ella Baker. In *Ella Baker and the Black Freedom Movement: A Radical, Democratic Vision*, Barbara Ransby describes some of the sources of tensions and disagreements about strategy between Baker and King. According to Ransby, Baker wanted to "preserve the brazen fighting spirit

---

[16] Peter Ling, "Not One Committee, But Several," in Iwan Morgan and Philip Davies, eds., *From Sit-Ins to SNCC: The Student Civil Rights Movement in the 1960s* (Gainesville: University Press of Florida), 89.

[17] Charles Craven, "Police Arrest 41 in Raleigh Demonstrations: Trespassing is Charged in Village," *News and Observer*, 13 February 1960, 1.

[18] Wyatt Tee Walker, phone interview by the author, digital recording, 15 July 2017.

the students had exhibited in their sit-in protests. She did not want them to be shackled by the bureaucracy of existing organizations."[19] Ransby also addresses the impact Baker had on Diane Nash, who had already demonstrated her own leadership in the Nashville movement. But Ransby's work does not directly address the experiences at the conference of North Carolina's student activists. This book addresses the experiences of Shaw students and other students from North Carolina, in addition to examining the perceptions of the conference among "Protest Triangle" students who did not attend the Easter weekend conference.

The extensive use of student interviews in addition to archival research contributes to my emphasis on investigating the connections between Black student activists and Whites who supported their cause in the Triangle. Perhaps the most consistent White supporter of African American civil rights and opportunities in the Triangle was Rev. W. W. Finlator. G. McLeod Bryan's *Dissenter in the Baptist Southland: Fifty Years in the Career of William Wallace Finlator* demonstrates that Finlator took principled stands against racial discrimination even before becoming the pastor at Pullen Memorial Baptist Church in Raleigh in the mid-1950s. In April 1942, Finlator wrote an article in which he questioned whether Americans were practicing Hitler's racism. He also urged Southern churches not to ignore the implications of Gunnar Myrdal's study on race relations, *An American Dilemma*.[20]

Finlator's advocacy of social justice was exhibited in full color in the wake of the sit-ins in Raleigh and demonstrated his connections to Shaw University. The preacher taught classes at Shaw from 1956–1960 and established a friendship with Shaw's Dean of Religion, Dr. Grady Davis. Dean Foster Payne of Shaw commended Finlator for publicly supporting the student sit-ins. In 1962, Finlator gave a speech on the Shaw campus in which he argued that instead of arresting students for wanting to buy a hamburger, public officials should padlock public eating establishments

---

[19] Barbara Ransby, *Ella Baker and the Black Freedom Movement: A Radical Democratic Vision* (Chapel Hill: University of North Carolina Press, 2003), 244.

[20] G. McLeod Bryan, *Dissenter in the Baptist Southland: Fifty Years in the Career of William Wallace Finlator* (Macon, GA: Mercer University Press, 1985), 94–95; Gunnar Myrdal, *An American Dilemma: The Negro Problem and Modern Democracy* (New York: Harper & Brothers, 1944).

that refused to serve Blacks.[21] Finlator's stance in this regard seemed to foreshadow one of the pillars of the Civil Rights Act, which prohibited racial discrimination in public accommodations. His support for integration demonstrated that he was progressive on race issues, but his support of the tactics of the demonstrators made other Whites view him as a radical. To support integration was one thing, but to defend the tactics of the demonstrators to directly challenge unjust laws and social practices demonstrated Finlator's commitment to social justice. One survey in 1961 showed that 84 percent of White Southerners opposed the tactics of the sit-ins, and even among those who supported integration, only 34 percent approved of sit-ins.[22] While some Whites in Raleigh supported integration, Finlator took a leadership role in pointing out that segregation was unjust and that tactics to challenge it were justified. Student activists took notice, and in my survey asking former students to rate individuals on their contributions to improving race relations and opportunities for African Americans on a scale of 1 to 10, the average for Finlator was 9.5.[23]

Allard Lowenstein was another White liberal who took a leadership role in dismantling segregation in Raleigh. Arthur Schlesinger Jr. argues that Lowenstein "was the supreme agitator of his day...a man who touched the consciences of his fellow citizens, educated their sensibilities, and drew forth their capacity for humane action."[24] Lowenstein's contributions to the civil rights movement have been addressed by scholars, but little attention has been given to his interactions with activists in Raleigh, aside from his involvement in an incident in 1963 in which he entered the Sir Walter Café with Angie Brooks, who was a Shaw graduate and Liberian Ambassador to the UN. The group, which included Shaw student Joseph Outland, was denied service, leading the US State Department to issue an official apology to Brooks.[25] From 1962 to 1963, Lowenstein taught social studies at North Carolina State University and became

---

[21] Bryan, *Dissenter in the Baptist Southland*, 101–103.

[22] Morgan and Davies, eds., *From Sit-Ins to SNCC*, 58.

[23] See survey in appendix.

[24] Gregory Stone and Douglas Lowenstein, eds., *Lowenstein: Acts of Courage and Belief* (San Diego: Harcourt Brace Jovanovich Publishers, 1983), xx.

[25] "Seeks Meal: UN Official Turned Away," *News and Observer*, 1 May 1963, 1; "US Agency Apologizes for Incident Here," *News and Observer*, 2 May 1963, 1.

involved with the demonstrations in Raleigh, interacting with Shaw and Saint Augustine's students. Shaw student protest leader Mack Sowell recalls that he and other students visited Lowenstein at his apartment.[26] Ultimately, Lowenstein was representative of the connections between the "Protest Triangle" schools and the Research Triangle schools, a connection that increased during the protest demonstrations in 1963.

While this book focuses mainly on Raleigh and Durham, it will also place the local movements in the broader context of the civil rights movement in North Carolina and the nation. William H. Chafe's *Civilities and Civil Rights* remains one of the most crucial works for understanding race relations in North Carolina in the civil rights era. Chafe points out that despite the state's reputation for progressivism in comparison to other Southern states, much of the evidence demonstrated otherwise. He argues that "North Carolina represented a paradox: it combined a reputation for enlightenment and a social reality that was reactionary."[27] He emphasizes that civility played a role in shaping White North Carolinians' approach to race relations. "Civility," he wrote, "is the cornerstone of the progressive mystique.... Civility was what white progressivism was all about—a way of dealing with people and problems that made good manners more important than substantial action."[28]

While Chafe's arguments apply broadly to North Carolina and to his research on Greensboro, there were expressions among local and state political leaders in Raleigh that lend credence to his assessments. For example, in the wake of the sit-ins, Mayor William G. Enloe remarked that it was "regrettable that some of our young Negro students would risk endangering...race relations by seeking to change a long-standing custom in a manner that was all but destined to fail."[29] Black students indeed sought to endanger existing race relations. They sought to destroy a social system, often supported by local and state politicians, that operated on

---

[26] Mack Sowell, interview by the author, digital recording, 20 April 2016, Raleigh.
[27] William H. Chafe, *Civilities and Civil Rights: Greensboro, North Carolina, and the Black Struggle for Freedom* (Oxford: Oxford University Press, 1981), 5.
[28] Chafe, *Civilities and Civil Rights*, 8.
[29] Charles Craven and David Cooper, "Student Sitdown Strike Spreads to Stores Here," *News and Observer*, 11 February 1960, 1.

paternalism, discrimination, and the denial of economic opportunities and expressions of first-class citizenship for African Americans.

Student activists challenged a segregationist vision of Southern hospitality. Their recollections of that period demonstrate that Raleigh was conflicted between the past and the possibilities of the future. Forbes characterized Raleigh in the early 1960s as a "politely racist city."[30] Wyatt Walker, who had participated in the direct-action campaigns in Petersburg, Virginia, in 1960 and participated in the Youth Leadership Conference at Shaw in April of that year, recalled that the resistance to the movement appeared more intense in Petersburg than in Raleigh. He also pointed out that Raleigh was like a lot of other Southern cities at that time, as it was "trying to be graceful in a time of change."[31] But, unlike many of the so-called White moderate politicians throughout the state, the student activists were more concerned with change than with the perceived grace of a segregated city.

Using oral history, this book seeks not only to include the voices of civil rights participants but to highlight them. The purpose is not merely to reveal the experiences of the mostly unheralded local civil rights activists; it is to analyze their importance to a movement that they helped to foster and sustain. This study incorporates thirty-one interviews conducted by the author, mostly with civil rights activists in Raleigh and Durham in the early 1960s. I have sought to incorporate their experiences as well as their perceptions of the movement into my analysis. Their recollections and insightful anecdotes are a vivid reminder of the human aspect of history. In addition to exposing some of the most unique, painful, and beautiful stories in the challenges to segregation, this work also aims to portray a more systematic approach to history through the use of surveys. Interviewees' responses to the survey questions allow for a more careful presentation of arguments and allow the author to make assertions based on common experiences among those who created historical change.

Student activists in the "Protest Triangle" forced local, state, and national leaders to confront the evils of segregation. They garnered and even mobilized many allies for social justice along the way, including the

---

[30] David Forbes, interview by the author.
[31] Wyatt Tee Walker, interview by the author.

advocates of academic freedom at the Triangle's Black and White colleges. In a segregated society that denied them full opportunities, they realized that dismantling segregation was a step toward employing their full potential. Thus, the special generation of student civil rights activists in the early 1960s recognized their involvement in civil rights protests as part of their education and perceived efforts to thwart the demonstrations as challenges to academic freedom. In response to an interview question asking what role academic freedom played in the movement, Mack Sowell responded, "Probably half has never been told about that."[32] The same could be said for civil rights activism in the Triangle. So, in the pages that follow and with the voices of the activists, I aim to tell it in all its complexity, anguish, and beauty.

---

[32] Mack Sowell, interview by the author.

Chapter 2

Education, Activism, and Academic
Freedom in Historical Context

Education played a crucial role in paving the winding and unfinished road
to Black freedom in North Carolina. African Americans since the Civil
War have recognized the connection between educational improvements
and economic opportunities for people of their race. In 1865, the *Journal
of Freedom*, a pro-Black journal published in Raleigh, declared, "The Free-
man has a disease of learning. It is a mania with him."[1] No other institution in North Carolina was more representative of the connections between education and opportunities for African Americans than Shaw
University in Raleigh. Through its many changes since its founding in
1865, the school has served as a propagator of talent, leadership, and activism in North Carolina.

Shaw fostered the development of a sometimes thriving, but always
striving, group of educated African Americans who recognized the importance of education in bringing about increased opportunities in society.
Shaw graduates made contributions to the development of Black higher
education throughout the state, which became a driving force for further
advancement of opportunities in education, business, religion, medicine,

---

[1] David Perkins, ed., *The News and Observer's Raleigh: A Living History of
North Carolina's Capital* (Winston-Salem: John F. Blair, 1994), 83.

and even politics. Shaw graduates and those they influenced were involved in the consistent efforts to improve opportunities for their race and to increase the challenges to segregation that preceded the height of the civil rights movement in the 1960s.

The institution that became known as Shaw University was the first historically Black college in the South. The school was part of a subregion of the South that became a center for Black higher education, as it was for White higher education. By the mid-twentieth century, the three cities that make up the Triangle (Raleigh, Durham, Chapel Hill) housed the oldest private Black university in the South (Shaw) in addition to another that was founded in 1868 (Saint Augustine's College), the first public school in the nation for graduate students (University of North Carolina at Chapel Hill [UNC]), the nation's first state-supported liberal arts college for Blacks (North Carolina College for Negroes), and what became perhaps the most prestigious private university in the South (Duke University). Quite simply, the Triangle was the heart of higher education in the South for much of the late nineteenth and twentieth centuries.[2]

While there was limited interaction among students and faculty between the Black and White colleges in the region, internal developments at the White colleges in the early to mid-twentieth century portended the more direct challenges to segregation by White university faculty and students in the region in the early 1960s. There were several instances in which principles of academic freedom were utilized to justify discussion of race relations in a more reasonable and less emotional manner. This trend was especially true at UNC and Duke, two institutions that were among the leading Southern advocates of academic freedom. While academic freedom did not necessarily entail progressive ideas on race relations or advocacy of desegregation, it did help those who studied race relations share their findings and ideas even when those ideas were critical of Jim Crow.[3] In a region that often stifled meaningful debate on race relations

---

[2] Earle E. Thorpe, *A Concise History of North Carolina Central University* (Durham: Harrington Publications, 1984), 73; Arnold L. King, *The Multicampus University of North Carolina Comes of Age, 1956–1986* (Chapel Hill: The University of North Carolina, 1987), xi; Clara Barnes Jenkins, "An Historical Study of Shaw University, 1865–1963" (PhD diss., University of Pittsburgh, 1965), 8.

[3] Charles Holden, *The New Southern University: Academic Freedom and*

through legal and social means, the ability to speak critically of segregation and discrimination, within limits, was no small development on the road to exposing the evils of segregation.

The school that ultimately became Shaw University was founded in Raleigh in December 1865 by White former Union Army Chaplain Dr. Henry Martin Tupper in a city that the *Daily Progress* newspaper claimed was a "seething, rushing, boiling cauldron…the streets being entirely filled with soldiers, negroes, men and women, and strangers from the four quarters."[4] After being asked by the American Baptist Home Mission Society to take up missionary work to assist Blacks, Tupper organized a theology class at the Old Guion Hotel in Raleigh. Many African Americans sought educational opportunities in the city. The school was initially named the Raleigh Institute and was the first African American institution of higher learning in the South. By 1867, the school consisted of three buildings, two of which were antebellum cabins. Both Tupper and Elijah Shaw, whom the school was named after in 1870, were White missionaries from Massachusetts. The early development of what became Shaw University was representative of the important role that northern White missionaries played in developing Black educational institutions in the South in the Reconstruction era.[5]

Shaw was a trailblazer in Black education in many respects. In 1870, the school admitted its first boarding female students and thus became the first African American institution in America to open its doors to women. Dr. Wilmoth Carter, the social sciences professor who supported student civil rights activists in the 1960s, maintains that the school stands as a landmark in the higher education of African Americans: "From a national perspective the history of Shaw University replicates the development and growth of Negro higher education, while regionally it parallels the emergence of the 'New South' in which educational rehabilitation became a

---

Liberalism at UNC (Lexington: University Press of Kentucky, 2012), 22, 44–47, 76; James LeLoudis, *Schooling the New South: Pedagogy, Self, and Society in North Carolina, 1880–1920* (Chapel Hill: University of North Carolina Press, 1996), 184.

[4] Perkins, ed., *The News and Observer's Raleigh*, 83.

[5] Hugh Victor Brown, *A History of the Education of Negroes in North Carolina* (Raleigh: Irving Swain Press, Inc., 1961), 19, 25, 67.

major goal."[6]

The establishment of schools for African Americans in the South represented perhaps the greatest challenge to Southern society, which had directly restricted the education of African Americans during the slavery era. It involved the support of Northern missionaries as well as federal programs established in the Reconstruction era. For instance, Saint Augustine's Normal School (now Saint Augustine's University) was established in 1867 with cooperation between the Episcopal Church and the Freedmen's Bureau, a federal program that had as one of its aims the education of freed slaves. Like Carter, fellow 1960s-era Shaw professor Charles Robson understood the historical importance of African Americans who sought education in the post-Civil War era. According to Robson, "Education became synonymous with freedom for the ex-slaves to whom, in the ante-bellum days, any education had been forbidden."[7] Raleigh was not unique in the South in terms of the excitement that many former slaves shared for educational opportunities. But Raleigh was unique in that it had two burgeoning institutions of higher learning in Shaw and Saint Augustine's, while many cities in the state and throughout the South did not yet have one such institution in the years immediately following the Civil War. But where educational opportunities existed for former slaves, they connected those opportunities to a rejection of their enslaved past. In an analysis similar to that of Robson, historian Steven Hahn asserts, "Freed people clamored for schooling because they viewed it simultaneously as a rejection of their enslaved past and as a means of self-respect in the post-emancipation world."[8]

As opportunities for African Americans to pursue higher education expanded, so did political opportunities, and the footprint of Shaw was felt in politics. While North Carolina did not send any Blacks to the US

---

[6] Wilmoth A. Carter, *Shaw's Universe: A Monument to Educational Innovation* (Raleigh: Shaw University, 1973), iii, v.

[7] Brown, *A History of the Education of Negroes in North Carolina*, 27; Glenford E. Mitchell and William H. Peace III, eds., *The Angry Black South* (New York: Corinth Books, 1962), 13.

[8] Steven Hahn, *A Nation Under Our Feet: Black Political Struggles in the Rural South from Slavery to the Great Migration* (Cambridge: The Belknap Press of Harvard University Press, 2003), 277.

Senate in the nineteenth century, four African Americans were elected to
the US House of Representatives in 1875, 1883, 1889, and 1897. All four
represented North Carolina's Second District, a district mostly east of Raleigh that was often referred to as the "Black Second" due to its predominantly Black population. One of the four, Henry P. Cheatham, who was
born into slavery and served in the US Congress from 1889 to 1893, was
an 1883 graduate of Shaw University. The fact that a former slave rose to
the highest lawmaking body in the nation was remarkable. The reality that
political opportunities for African Americans in the South did not improve
on a gradually ascending line from the Civil War to the present is evident
in the stark reality that a Black man who fought in the Civil War had a
greater chance of becoming a Southern congressman than did a Black man
who fought in World War I. While formal Black political power waned
throughout much of the South toward the end of the nineteenth century
largely due to state laws that effectively disfranchised many African Americans, in the 1890s in North Carolina, Populist-Republican fusion tickets
enjoyed some success, including the election of a Republican governor in
1896.[9]

Nonetheless, the 1890s was a period of consistent violence toward
African Americans throughout much of the South. In the period between
1890 and 1917, approximately two to three Black Southerners were
lynched per week. Whites often justified lynching to protect Southern
women from rape by Black men. Historian Leon Litwack asserts, "To endorse lynching was to dwell on the sexual depravity of blacks, to raise the
specter of the black beast seized by uncontrollable savage sexual passions
that were inherent to the race [in the mind of a racist white]."[10] But rape
was overblown as a reason for lynching. As Litwack points out, less than
20 percent of the nearly three thousand Blacks known to have been
lynched in the period from 1889–1918 were *accused* of rape. He points out
that some lynchings took place for the sole reason of punishing a Black
man for achieving economic success. Many lynchings and instances of

---

[9] "Cheatham, Henry Plummer," *Biographical Directory of the United States Congress*, http://bioguide.congress.gov/scripts/biodisplay.pl?index=C000340; Hahn, *A Nation Under Our Feet*, 437.
[10] Leon Litwack, *Trouble in Mind: Black Southerners in the Age of Jim Crow* (New York: Alfred A. Knopf, 1998), 284, 302.

violence toward African Americans had political or economic motivations. In the 1920s, Walter White, a prominent figure in the National Association for the Advancement of Colored People (NAACP) who investigated lynching, concluded, "Lynching is much more an expression of Southern fear of Negro progress than of Negro crime."[11]

The violent response among some Whites to African American involvement in politics was manifest during the Wilmington Massacre and coup d'état in 1898. In a general sense, the violence in Wilmington that year was a White supremacist reaction to the political power wielded by Republicans, largely but not exclusively due to the strong base of African American supporters. Tensions had risen during the summer when Rebecca Felton visited the city. Felton was a Progressive-era reformer who ultimately became a leading advocate of women's suffrage. But the former slave owner was a staunch White supremacist and defender of the lynching of Black men accused of rape. During her visit in Wilmington, she rallied against interracial relations between Black men and White women. In response, Alexander Manly, the Black editor of the *Wilmington Daily Record*, wrote an editorial that discussed the taboo subject of interracial sex. Manly boldly wrote, "Our experiences among poor white people in the country teaches us that women of that race are not any more particular in the matter of clandestine meetings with colored men than the white men with the colored women." He pointed out the double standard that had characterized the South for so long in regards to interracial sex, which often viewed sex between a White man and Black woman as immoral but defensible, while sex between a Black man and a White woman was considered by many Southern Whites as rape, even when the act was consensual. Manly criticized the hypocrisy of Felton and other white supremacists, and he argued that Whites "cry aloud for the virtue of your women while you seek to destroy the morality of ours. Don't ever think that your women will remain pure while you are debauching ours."[12]

---

[11] Litwack, *Trouble in Mind*, 309, 320.

[12] Litwack, *Trouble in Mind*, 282–83; Leslie Brown, *Upbuilding Black Durham: Gender, Class, and Black Community Development in the Jim Crow South* (Chapel Hill: University of North Carolina Press, 2008), 61, 62; Alexander Manly editorial, *Wilmington Daily Record*, August 18, 1898, "The Wilmington Record Editorial," https://www.ncpedia.org/anchor/wilmington-record-editorial.

Democratic newspapers throughout the state, including the *Raleigh News and Observer*, publicized Manly's editorial and pointed out the boldest assertions in capital letters. Newspapers and Democratic Party leaders utilized the Manly editorial as a method of increasing the racial hysteria that surrounded the 1898 elections in Wilmington and other places in North Carolina. Nonetheless, the Fusionists were successful in the November elections in Wilmington. They won the mayor's office and control of the city council. Despite the fact that two-thirds of the council members were White, White supremacists in the city viewed the results as an example of "Negro domination." The day after the election, White Democrats seized the government of Wilmington in what was quite simply a coup d'état. A White mob burned the building that housed Manly's *Daily Record*, and the Black editor was forced to flee the city. After White supremacists terrorized and killed African Americans, hundreds of African Americans fled the city. Historian Leslie Brown avers, "The Wilmington Riot revealed not only whites' determination to forge disorder and to deny African Americans rights, but also their willingness to compromise democracy by violence."[13]

The events in Wilmington were both unique and emblematic of racial politics in the South. The takeover of the government in Wilmington through a coup d'état remains unmatched in American history. But the events were also emblematic of the solidification of White supremacist power in politics in North Carolina and throughout the South. The Wilmington Riot demonstrated that even in cities with heavy African American populations, White supremacy was a winning strategy, whether obtained through legal political means or by intimidation and politically motivated violence. The era of Fusion politics in North Carolina died in the late 1890s. Historian Adam Fairclough asserts, "Fusion might have prevented the South's descent into oligarchy and one-party rule by upholding black voting rights and fostering multiparty competition.... But Fusion was never given a fair test. The Democrats countered the emerging black-poor white alliance by unfurling the banner of white supremacy."[14]

---

[13] Brown, *Upbuilding Black Durham*, 63, 79; Adam Fairclough, *Better Day Coming: Blacks and Equality, 1890–2000* (New York: Penguin Books, 2002), 8–10.

[14] Fairclough, *Better Day Coming*, 8.

At the turn of the twentieth century, more systematic methods were introduced to disfranchise African Americans in North Carolina. In 1899, the General Assembly followed the examples set forth in previous years by the state legislatures in Mississippi, South Carolina, and Louisiana, which aimed for the total disfranchisement of Black voters. Legislators passed an amendment to the state constitution in 1900 that included voting restrictions via poll taxes and literacy tests, combined with grandfather clauses to ensure that African Americans could not vote. In the state that had elected more Black officials than any other state in the South, the opportunity for the election of Black officials became nearly nonexistent in the early part of the twentieth century. George Henry White, the last Black congressman from the South until the election of Andrew Young (Georgia) and Barbara Jordan (Texas) in 1972, stated in 1901 that "at no time in the history of our freedom has the effort been made to mold public sentiment against us and our progress so strongly as is now being done.... I can no longer live in North Carolina and be a man."[15] It was in the context of political disfranchisement of African Americans that segregation was strengthened throughout the South. The 1896 Supreme Court decision in *Plessy v. Ferguson*, which gave sanction to the doctrine of "separate but equal," reinforced the reality that the federal government could no longer be considered a legitimate ally to the rights of African Americans.

Various newspapers supported the solidification of White supremacy and segregation in North Carolina. The experiences and mentality of Josephus Daniels, the editor of the *News and Observer*, offer a window into some of the forces that shaped race relations in the South around the turn of the twentieth century. During the brief period of Fusionist rule in Wake County (1894–1898), a legislator introduced a bill to make representation on the Board of Alderman in Raleigh more equitable. The *News and Observer* characterized it as a measure to "Negroize Raleigh." Daniels supported the White supremacist campaigns in various cities in the late 1890s, most notably that in Wilmington in 1898. In 1941, Daniels reflected that he had been a product of an era that was "torn between forces of progress and reaction." Like many who supported racial segregation, Daniels also supported Progressive-era reforms such as child labor laws, public

---

[15] Fairclough, *Better Day Coming*, 7, 10, 17.

education, Prohibition, and women's suffrage.[16] Indeed, some Whites justified racial segregation as a Progressive reform. At the heart of Progressivism lay a tendency to believe that laws could be used to create a more orderly society. As Litwack points out, "Caught in the age of Progressive reform, some whites preferred to view the restrictions on blacks as reform, not oppression, as a way to use the law to contain both races, resolve racial tension, and maintain the social order."[17]

In the face of disfranchisement and segregation, African Americans in Raleigh and Durham continued to push for improved opportunities for their race. Shaw University graduate and Durham businessman and educator James E. Shepard urged fellow Blacks in 1903 not to be discouraged by the recent worsening of conditions in the state. "Citizenship is not in constitutions but in the mind," he said. "My mind, my soul, and my virtue are ever free."[18] As historian James LeLoudis points out, Black Southerners adapted a subtle strategy to confront the harsh realities of race relations in the early twentieth century, one that "acknowledged the reality of white rule but at the same time searched the crevices of white supremacy for every opportunity for black power and self-determination."[19]

For Shepard, the path toward freedom remained rooted in education. His training as a pharmacist had opened an opportunity to establish a drugstore in Durham. Shepard's most enduring legacy was his establishment of the National Religious Training School and Chautauqua on land donated by White citizens in Durham in 1910. The school grew quickly, and by 1912 there were ten buildings valued at $125,000. By 1923, the state legislature had purchased the school and renamed it the Durham State Normal School, which emphasized teacher training. Ultimately, the school became the first publicly funded liberal arts college in the South and was known as the North Carolina College at Durham during the period of mass civil rights demonstrations in the city in the early 1960s. Like students at his alma mater, students from the institution that Shepard founded would become heavily involved in bringing about integration to

---

[16] Perkins, ed., *The News and Observer's Raleigh*, 119.

[17] Litwack, *Trouble in Mind*, 227.

[18] James E. Shepard, "Message to the Negro Race," *Charlotte Observer*, 8 November 1903; LeLoudis, *Schooling the New South*, 180.

[19] LeLoudis, *Schooling the New South*, 180.

the Triangle in 1960s. Shepard was among many Shaw graduates who played a critical role in the development of African American higher education in the state, joining a list that included Peter W. Moore, the first principal of the State Colored Normal School at Elizabeth City (now Elizabeth City State University), and Ezekiel Ezra Smith, a critical figure in the development of the Fayetteville State Normal School (now Fayetteville State University).[20]

Shepard was part of a thriving Black middle class in Durham. The 1920s are often conceptualized as seeing the emergence of a "New Negro," a term that was not unique to that decade but was popularized by Harvard educated writer Alain Locke in his 1925 edited collection *The New Negro*. The phrase has various interpretations, but at the heart of the concept is an increased assertiveness and sense of race pride that can be seen in the writings and other art forms of the Harlem Renaissance. But in Durham, Black assertiveness and confidence was most forcefully expressed in an economic sense. As Leslie Brown points out, "Harlem may have been the hub of black creative and cultural life, but Durham was the epicenter of its business life."[21] The famous Black sociologist E. Franklin Frazier called Durham the "capital of the black middle class" and noted that "Durham offers none of the color and creative life we find among Negroes in New York City. It is not a place where men write and dream; but a place where black men calculate and work."[22]

No other business represented Black economic power in Durham more fully than the North Carolina Mutual Life Insurance Company. Dr. Aaron M. Moore, an 1888 graduate of the Medical School at Shaw University, was among its three founders. By the 1920s, North Carolina Mutual had grown into the largest Black-owned financial institution in the nation.[23] Many of the leading Black businessmen in Durham and other

---

[20] Carter, *Shaw's Universe*, 50; Brown, *A History of the Education of Negroes in North Carolina*, 970; Jenkins, "An Historical Study of Shaw University, 1865–1963," 117.

[21] Brown, *Upbuilding Black Durham*, 122.

[22] Brown, *Upbuilding Black Durham*, 14; Andre D. Vann and Beverly Washington Jones, *Durham's Hayti* (Mount Pleasant, SC: Arcadia Publishing, 1999), 9.

[23] Christina Greene, *Our Separate Ways: Women and the Black Freedom Movement in Durham, North Carolina* (Chapel Hill: University of North Carolina Press, 2005), 1.

cities did not directly challenge segregation during this period. According to Carter, "The Negro middle class of the South during this period was too busy building its separate world of business, schools, educated children, fraternal and social life, and perpetuating its academic seclusion and its intra-racial social status to destroy its handiwork by demanding an openly integrated world."[24]

Despite the limits segregation placed on African Americans, many Black Durhamites adapted the circumstances to their advantage. The Black elite in the city were both admired and criticized by other Blacks. Black citizens sometimes accused the Black elite in Durham of being agreeable to segregation for their own economic benefit. Leslie Brown asserts that "Durham's black leaders were accused of accommodating segregation. And they did—but not as a capitulation to racism. Rather they viewed upbuilding in the segregated South as a tactic of resistance and as a strategy to outwit Jim Crow."[25]

A palpable pride existed in the Black section of Durham, known as Hayti. In 1920, W. E. B. Du Bois wrote, "There is in this small city a group of five thousand or more colored people, whose social and economic development is perhaps more striking than that of any similar group in the nation."[26] In addition to the economic prowess of the Black elite in Hayti, a vibrant music scene developed where musicians such as Bessie Smith and Count Basie entertained at the Biltmore Hotel. Earl E. Thorpe, who eventually became the first student at North Carolina College to earn a PhD in history and was a faculty member at the school in the period of the sit-in movement, recalled that "Hayti was a symbol of Black aliveness, achievement, activity, and creativity—of Black civilization if you will."[27]

In Raleigh, the heart of Black business operated on East Hargett Street near the Black neighborhoods in the southern and eastern part of the city. According to Carter, Hargett Street contained fifty-one Black and twenty-seven White businesses in 1940. In 1959, on the eve of the sit-

---

[24] Wilmoth A. Carter, *The New Negro of the South: A Portrait of Movements and Leadership* (New York: Exposition Press, 1967), 48.
[25] Brown, *Upbuilding Black Durham*, 19.
[26] Vann and Jones, *Durham's Hayti*, 7.
[27] Vann and Jones, *Durham's Hayti*, 8; Earl E. Thorpe, *A Concise History of North Carolina Central University* (Durham: Harrington Publications, 1984), 76.

in movement in the city, there were forty-six Black and twenty-three White businesses on the street. One of the most important businesses on Hargett Street was the Mechanics and Farmers Bank, which branched out from its roots in Durham and had become one of the largest Black-owned banks in the country. Entertainment options were somewhat limited, but one of the central points was the Lightner Arcade Building, which housed the only hotel for African Americans in the city. The hotel was considered one of the premier hotels between New York City and Atlanta. Like the Biltmore in Durham, the hotel was a hub of social activity, including dances and performances by musicians such as Count Basie.[28]

Despite the examples of vibrant social scenes and economic prosperity among some Blacks in Raleigh and Durham, segregation also limited their opportunities. Audrey Wall, who grew up in East Raleigh, recalled that Blacks could go to the White-owned shops on Fayetteville Street and purchase a dress or a hat but could not try them on. Essentially, once a Black citizen left the Black section of the city, they became second-class consumers. Segregation limited their purchasing options if they sought to maintain their dignity in the face of discriminatory practices. It also limited their mobility. Wall recalled that her family traveled to Nashville and "there wasn't a place we could stop in a blizzard."[29]

Southern hospitality had racial limits, and travel was difficult for African Americans in the South and throughout the country, as many hotels did not extend their full welcome to Blacks. In *Traveling Black*, Mia Bay asserts that "American identity has long been identified by mobility and the freedom of the open road, but African Americans have never fully shared in that freedom."[30] To assist Black travelers in locating hotels that would accommodate them, several publications provided details about such hotels, including the *Negro Motorist Green Book*, which was published from the 1930s to the mid-1960s. In addition to providing hotel information, the *Green Book* included information on restaurants, drugstores, service stations, taverns, and beauty parlors that served Black customers.[31]

---

[28] Perkins, ed., *The News and Observer's Raleigh*, 131.

[29] Perkins, ed., *The News and Observer's Raleigh*, 133.

[30] Mia Bay, *Traveling Black: A Story of Race and Resistance* (Cambridge: The Belknap Press of Harvard University Press, 2021), 3.

[31] Bay, *Traveling Black*, 13, 141–43.

The relative lack of accommodations forced African American trav-elers to be well prepared in advance for their journeys. John Hope Franklin (author of *From Slavery to Freedom*) and his wife traveled with food and drinks packed from Charleston to Raleigh on December 7, 1941, and never learned of the Japanese attack on Pearl Harbor that day until they arrived in Raleigh.[32] On a day that would ultimately lead to tens of thou-sands of African Americans fighting for American freedoms, a man who became one of the most well-respected historians in American history did not want to face the humiliation of being denied service at a restaurant in his own country. The road from slavery to freedom was not fully paved.

One resident of Raleigh recalled two experiences in which she felt the sting of segregation. Vivian E. Irving's family owned a printing company, and after operating in a building on the corner of East Hargett and Blount Street for three months, they were notified that they had to leave the build-ing. The White owner had stated in his will that no "colored" business would operate in the building. She also recalled that when she was a child, her parents would take her down to the capitol to feed pigeons. At the courthouse where the family stopped for a drink of water, she and her sib-lings used the colored water fountain. On the way home, they rode the bus and were forced to sit in the back. In a single day, a child in the segregated South could experience the restrictions that segregation placed on their lives. Feeding pigeons on the lawn in front of the Capitol on a sunny day could very well bring a sense of freedom, a harsh juxtaposition against a building that symbolized a repressive government that had largely disfran-chised African Americans. The same young girl who fed pigeons in the 1920s and 1930s would ultimately become the first Black woman to join the League of Women Voters in Raleigh in 1955. In the 1960s, she joined with student protestors from Shaw University and Saint Augustine's Col-lege as they marched up and down Fayetteville Street, with Shaw to their rear and the state capitol on the horizon.[33]

Just as segregation limited the literal mobility of African Americans, it also limited their opportunities for economic mobility. Despite the

---

[32] Bay, *Traveling Black*, 149–50.
[33] *Let Us March On: Raleigh's Journey Toward Civil Rights* (Raleigh: Raleigh City Museum, 2000), 15–16.

success of the Black elite in Durham for much of the first half of the twentieth century, not all African Americans in the city prospered. For those who worked for White employers, there was always the concern that if economic troubles came, Blacks would be the first to lose their jobs. Single Black women were especially susceptible to poverty, facing both gender and race discrimination in employment and wages. Durham ran the full spectrum of class, from those who lived in deep poverty to some of the wealthiest African Americans in the country. As Brown points out, "Whatever the black elite accomplished in Durham, it was rendered inadequate by the lives that black people had to live in the hollows and alleys of Durham's black neighborhoods."[34]

Despite some of the restrictions that segregation placed on the lives of African Americans, efforts at integration were not always at the forefront of Black activism in the first half of the twentieth century. Many African American leaders emphasized education and creating economic opportunities within the confines of a segregated society. Carter's study of Jim Crow-era Raleigh revealed that many African Americans in the decades prior to the sit-in movement were not focused on dismantling segregation but rather on supporting Black education, patronizing Black businesses, and achieving fairer pay. For instance, a Black maintenance worker at North Carolina State College stated that "the colored ain't got but one real business street and that's Hargett. Negroes ought to use that street and patronize what's there." The man told of how a White man who held the same job as him made more money, despite the fact that the White co-worker took many more breaks than he. He asked his boss for an explanation, and the boss evidently responded that it took more money for a White man to live because he had to pay a maid. The Black man concluded, "But that's why I say the colored got to try to help theirselves." A Black housewife in Raleigh worried that "we just don't patronize each other enough...we just have to learn that to be a race we must stick together and patronize each other and stop being jealous of one another."[35]

Yet another interviewee who worked for a railroad company believed

---

[34] Brown, *Upbuilding Black Durham*, 253, 255.

[35] Wilmoth A. Carter, *The Urban Negro in the South* (New York: Vantage Press, Inc., 1961), 196.

that "sometimes you have to use both colored and white. You can't break down discrimination if you use Negroes only. We got to let the white man know he can't get along without us and we can't get along without him." Another respondent identified as a college teacher (and thus likely from Shaw or Saint Augustine's) argued that White businesses should not discriminate in their hiring practices, but he also believed that "I don't think white people should be discriminated against in any business managed by Negroes, or one operated in a colored business district."[36] The interview responses demonstrate that there was no unified view about how African Americans should approach segregation. In the middle of the twentieth century, there were certainly those who were skeptical of the wisdom of seeking integration. Part of what made the sit-in movement in Raleigh and Durham and other cities in North Carolina in the early 1960s so remarkable was that student protestors and other activists were able to mobilize African American support for integration in a way not seen before.

Direct challenges to segregation were not a new phenomenon in the 1950s or 1960s. In Louisville, Kentucky, in 1871, three Black men sat in the White section of one of the city's streetcars. After being thrown off the streetcar, the men returned. They were ultimately arrested and found guilty of disorderly conduct, but they appealed to a federal court, which reversed the decision. The streetcar company defied the ruling, which led African Americans throughout the city to conduct "ride-ins" and fill the seats. Ultimately, the streetcar company capitulated and allowed mixed seating.[37] In 1896, a group of women led a boycott in Atlanta after a Black man was imprisoned for refusing to sit in the section designated for Blacks. In the two decades of the 1890s and 1900s, African Americans organized boycotts of segregated streetcar companies in at least twenty-five cities and in every former Confederate state.[38]

In Raleigh, five years after the first local Jim Crow law passed in 1898

---

[36] Carter, *The Urban Negro in the South*, 193, 194. The interviews are undated but appear to be from the 1950s.

[37] Maria Fleming, *A Place at the Table: Struggles for Equality in America* (Oxford: Oxford University Press, 2001), 36, 41; Carter, *The New Negro of the South*, 10.

[38] Tera Hunter, *To 'Joy My Freedom: Southern Black Women's Lives and Labors after the Civil War* (Cambridge: Harvard University Press, 1997), 99; Litwack, *Trouble in Mind*, 242.

requiring the separation of races in public transportation, there was a scuffle on a Raleigh streetcar after several African Americans refused to give up their seats to White women. But such instances were rare and did not develop into a citywide mass movement like the sit-in movement of the 1960s. Even as Black business grew in the Triangle, there were always voices adamantly opposing segregation and the discrimination that it fostered and reinforced. At Raleigh's annual Emancipation Day on January 1, 1919, Professor Charles H. Boyer of Saint Augustine's School not only demanded equal opportunities in public education but also protested segregation laws. Boyer's son James would ultimately become the president of Saint Augustine's, which became a hive of student activism during the civil rights protests of the 1960s.[39]

In every generation after the Civil War, there were examples of direct action to oppose segregation and discrimination against African Americans, but most failed to sustain momentum in the face of White supremacist governments in the South. In 1947, the Congress of Racial Equality (CORE), which had been founded in 1942, launched the "Journey of Reconciliation" to challenge segregated interstate bus travel. Specifically, the CORE activists were testing whether states would ignore the recent Supreme Court decision in *Irene Morgan v. the Commonwealth of Virginia*, which had ruled that segregation on interstate buses was illegal based on the Constitution's Interstate Commerce Clause. The interracial group traveled through various cities in Virginia, North Carolina, Tennessee, and Kentucky. After embarking from Washington, DC, the group made a stop in Richmond and then Petersburg, Virginia. Before the Trailways bus left Petersburg for its trip to Raleigh, one of the African Americans in the group was arrested and released on $25 bond. On a trip from Durham to Chapel Hill, two Black men were arrested, including Bayard Rustin, a leading figure in CORE, who eventually played a crucial role in organizing the 1963 March on Washington. James Peck, the White man who was severely beaten during the 1961 Freedom Rides, was also arrested. Ultimately, the three were released without charge when an attorney arrived

---

[39] K. Todd Johnson and Elizabeth Reid Murray, *Wake: Capital County of North Carolina, Volume II: Reconstruction to 1920* (Raleigh: Wake County Commissioners, 2008), 45.

on their behalf. In Chapel Hill, police arrested four of the riders, including Rustin, who later was sentenced to thirty days on the road gang. After the men were released in Chapel Hill, Charlie Jones, a White Presbyterian minister, drove the group to his house. Local residents threatened to burn down his house, but the group ultimately escaped Chapel Hill and continued on to other cities.[40]

The Journey of Reconciliation was in many ways a precursor to the more sustained Freedom Rides in the early 1960s. Likewise, the sit-in movement of the 1960s had predecessors in the years prior to the February 1, 1960, sit-in in Greensboro that sparked a new phase in the civil rights struggle. In the nation's capital, the NAACP college chapter at Howard University helped bring about desegregation at the Little Palace cafeteria in 1943 through the use of picketing and sit-ins. In Durham in 1957, Reverend Douglass Moore led sit-ins at the Royal Ice Cream Parlor, with most of the participants being students at North Carolina College at Durham (NCC), which foreshadowed the important role that students from that college would play in the 1960s sit-ins. The following year, the Wichita Kansas NAACP Youth Council organized sit-in demonstrations that led to desegregation of the Dockum Drug Store and other local businesses. Sit-ins in Oklahoma City also led to the desegregation of major chain stores in the city.[41]

Hence, there were several examples of Black activism in the period between 1865 and 1960. Yet the tradition of Black activism prior to the outbreak of a sustained direct-action movement in the wake of the Greensboro sit-ins should not overshadow the fact that the students from Black colleges in North Carolina and throughout the South in the early 1960s were a special generation of activists. In Raleigh, students from Shaw University and Saint Augustine's College provided the backbone of

---

[40] Bayard Rustin and George Houser, "We Challenged Jim Crow!" Report Prepared for CORE and the Fellowship of Reconciliation, April 1947, General Collection, Greensboro History Museum, Greensboro, NC; Robert Weisbrot, *Freedom Bound: A History of America's Civil Rights Movement* (New York: Penguin Books, 1990), 13; Art Chansky, *Game Changers: Dean Smith, Charlie Scott, and the Era that Transformed a Southern College Town* (Chapel Hill: University of North Carolina Press, 2016), 31.

[41] Thomas L. Bynum, *NAACP Youth and the Fight for Black Freedom, 1963–1965* (Knoxville: University of Tennessee Press, 2013), xvii, xviii.

a local movement (as did those at NCC in Durham) that was emblematic of other movements in North Carolina and the South that challenged segregation in a more sustained, direct manner than had previously occurred. By the 1960s, the scholar who was perhaps the most qualified to address the connection between the history of African American activism and the significance of local activists in Raleigh in the early 1960s was Shaw University professor Wilmoth Carter, a consistent supporter of student activism. In her study, *The New Negro of the South*, Carter points out that the precedent for various forms of activism had been established before 1960 but argues that "the essential difference is that prior to 1960 they were highly localized, and often individual, whereas in the 1960s they became generalized and collectivized."[42]

Nonetheless, there were examples of organizational development that helped establish the roots of a massive movement to resist segregation, many of which originated at Shaw University and NCC. Shaw graduate and NCC president James Shepard, NCC graduate and *Carolina Times* (a Black newspaper in Durham) editor Louis Austin, and North Carolina Mutual president Charles Clinton Spaulding were among the founding members of the Durham Committee on Negro Affairs (DCNA) in 1935. The organization committed itself to the "educational, economic, social-civic, and political welfare of the Negro" and had the motto "A voteless people is a hopeless people."[43] Meanwhile, Shepard and faculty members at NCC advocated for the hiring of Black policemen and fire department personnel and for equal job opportunities in municipal, state, and federal government and private industries in the 1930s. In Raleigh in 1932, fifteen local African Americans founded the Negro Citizens Coordinating Committee, which eventually changed its name to the Raleigh Citizens Association (RCA). Robert Prentiss Daniel, the second African American president of Shaw University, was among the original members. The group mostly focused on increasing Black voter registration and participation.[44]

---

[42] Carter, *The New Negro of the South*, 10.

[43] Greene, *Our Separate Ways*, 21; Brown, *Upbuilding Black Durham*, 336.

[44] Thorpe, *A Concise History of North Carolina Central University*, 19, 52; *Let Us March On*, 4–5; Carter, *Shaw's Universe*, 82, 90. The first African American president at Shaw was William Stuart Nelson in 1931.

Both the DCNA and the RCA were important in organizing Black political activity in the two cities. But their influence in bringing forth direct challenges to segregation should not be overstated. The DCNA did not endorse the 1957 sit-ins at the Royal Ice Cream Parlor in Durham, although it did come out in support of the 1960 sit-ins. By the outbreak of the sit-ins in 1960 in Raleigh, the RCA was mostly dormant and was reinvigorated by the sit-in movement.[45] The key point is that it was the student activism in the form of sit-ins and picketing that provided the impetus for the DCNA and RCA to take stronger and more pointed stands against segregation.

One of the most significant conferences of African American leaders in the South took place on the campus of NCC in 1942. Fifty-nine Black leaders, mostly from the South, met and ultimately issued "A Basis for Inter-Racial Cooperation and Development in the South," which came to be known as the Durham Manifesto. Among those in attendance were Shepard, Daniel, and James T. Taylor, the Dean of Men at NCC. W. E. B. Du Bois, who was teaching at Atlanta University at that time, was not present but offered this comment: "The planning of programs to guide the future of the Negro has not been in vain. On the whole the Durham program is a pretty good document." The conference inspired further meetings that eventually led to the creation of the interracial Southern Regional Council in 1944.[46]

The Durham Manifesto should be understood in the context of its times, which included US involvement in World War II. The statement was accurate in its proclamation that the war "sharpened the issue of Negro-white relations in the United States, and particularly in the South." The group pointed out that African American soldiers who returned from World War I were not met with evidence of respect for the democracy for which they had fought. In the year prior to US entry into the Second World War, NAACP leader Walter White asked members at the annual

---

[45] "Citizens Committee Reactivated in City," *The Carolinian*, 20 February 1960, 1.

[46] "Southern Conference on Race Relations," Durham, NC, 20 October 1942, 5, 12–13, 15, available at the University of North Carolina at Chapel Hill Internet Archive, https://archive.org/details/southernconferen00sout; Greene, *Our Separate Ways*, 15.

convention, "What point is there in fighting and perhaps dying to save democracy if there is no democracy to save?" During World War II, many Blacks recognized the contradiction of members of their race fighting a war against tyranny abroad when they faced intense discrimination in their own nation.[47]

The group who met in Durham in 1942 exhibited their willingness to challenge existing restrictions of African American rights. They advocated for increased funding for Black schools and pay equality for Black and White teachers, as well as equal pay for equal work in other occupations. The group also recognized the obligation of all citizens to serve in the military and advocated for equality of opportunity regarding chances to rise in military rank. In the section under "Political and Civil Rights," the group decried police brutality and suggested the employment of Black police officers. The group also called for the abolition of the all-White primary. Throughout much of the South in the first six decades of the twentieth century, securing the Democratic nomination was tantamount to winning the election. Thus, the all-White primary was another tool utilized to disfranchise African Americans until the US Supreme Court effectively struck down the all-White primary in *Smith v. Allwright* in 1944.[48]

But the Durham Manifesto did not project a pointed attack on segregation. The suggestions made by the group regarding education did not directly challenge segregated schools or suggest that separate schools were inherently unequal. There were instances in which the document seemed to implicitly accept segregation: "In the public carriers and terminals, where segregation of the races is currently made mandatory by law as well as by established custom, it is the duty of Negro and white citizens to insist that these provisions be equal in kind and quality and in character of maintenance."[49] The emphasis on equality of service rather than integration demonstrated a key difference between the goals of the adult leaders

---

[47] David Levering Lewis, *W. E. B. Du Bois: The Fight for Equality and the American Century, 1919–1963* (New York: Henry Holt and Company, 2000), 466.

[48] "Southern Conference on Race Relations," 6–7; *Let Us March On*, 6. Raleigh hired its first Black police officer since the Reconstruction era in 1942, and Durham did so in 1944.

[49] "Southern Conference on Race Relations," 7.

at the 1942 conference and that of the mostly student leaders who met on Shaw's campus in April 1960.

One of the most horrific acts of racial violence in Durham's history occurred two years after the meeting of the group who produced the Durham Manifesto. In early July 1944, a White bus driver ordered a uniformed African American soldier, Booker T. Spicely, to move to the back of the bus. Spicely commented, "I thought I was fighting this war for democracy." As the soldier grudgingly walked to the rear of the bus, he muttered, "If you weren't 4-F [someone deemed unfit for military service], you wouldn't be driving this bus." The soldier then apologized, but his apology was not enough. After the soldier exited the bus, the driver fired two shots that killed Pfc. Spicely.[50]

The Spicely murder was evidence that challenges to segregation could literally be a matter of life and death, even in a city in the Upper South. It also demonstrated that obtaining justice for even the most egregious acts of racial violence was not likely. Two months after the killing, an all-White jury acquitted the man who murdered an American soldier.[51] In the midst of an era in which Americans were fighting fascist regimes in order to ostensibly preserve democracy at home, the implications of the Spicely case were evident: Blacks were systematically denied the rights of first-class citizens in a segregated society. While the federal government deemed Spicely fit for service, a Southern court deemed him unworthy of the most basic of human rights.

In the wake of the Spicely killing, a group of local African Americans met and elected a new slate of NAACP officers, including Louis Austin as president. In the efforts to revitalize the Durham NAACP branch, the influence of people associated with Shaw University was apparent. According to historian Christina Greene, Shaw University Biology Department Chair R. Arline Young was instrumental in revitalizing the Durham branch of the NAACP. Young enlisted the help of a Shaw graduate who was then based in New York City, Ella Baker. Like Young, Baker was concerned that the traditional Black leadership in Durham was an impediment to the development of more aggressive challenges to segregation.

---

[50] Greene, *Our Separate Ways*, 19.
[51] Greene, *Our Separate Ways*, 19.

But some of the more "conservative" Black leaders like Shepard appeared to recognize the move toward a more assertive attack on segregation. Shepard did not object to Young's efforts to establish a college chapter of the NAACP at NCC. Young played a significant role in establishing statewide NAACP youth councils, and in the 1950s, NCC graduate Floyd B. McKissick carried on her efforts.[52] Participation in youth councils and college chapters (especially at Shaw and NCC) of the NAACP was one of the ways in which the student activists who participated in sit-ins in the early 1960s carried on some of the organizing traditions established in previous decades, many of which had been associated with Shaw or NCC.

One of the most striking examples of the involvement of a group from NCC in challenging a segregated society occurred in 1944. Without permission from Dr. Shepard, NCC basketball coach John McLendon organized a basketball game against a Duke medical school team that had previously defeated the Duke varsity team. Much like the NCC Eagles had done in the Colored Intercollegiate Athletic Association (CIAA), the team from Duke had dominated their competition that year. Coach McLendon, who ultimately became the first Black head coach of a predominantly White institution (at Cleveland State in 1965), later recalled, "There was always a little part of you that wondered whether you could really compete with them—white teams—or not. And until you did, there was no way to know."[53]

Early in the game, it seemed the Eagles would lose, as they trailed by twelve midway through the first half. A hard foul nearly resulted in a fight, and the momentum began to shift. After trailing by eight at halftime, the Eagles turned up the pressure and played the fast-paced game that was their trademark. As the Eagles gained confidence, they went on huge scoring runs en route to an impressive 88–44 victory. In *The Secret Game: A Wartime Story of Courage, Change, and Basketball's Lost Triumph*, Scott Ellsworth depicts how many NCC students had come to the gym only to find the doors locked. But a few had worked their way up to the window

---

[52] Greene, *Our Separate Ways*, 21, 25.

[53] Scott Ellsworth, *The Secret Game: A Wartime Story of Courage, Change, and Basketball's Lost Triumph* (New York: Little, Brown and Company, 2015), 299–300, 262.

ledges late in the first half and looked inside. In Ellsworth's eloquent description, "They could not believe what they saw. Nor were they alone. For as the morning wore on, more and more heads began to appear in the windows, wide-eyed witnesses to an unimaginable, brave new world."[54]

In the decade prior to the secret game, an NCC student sought to integrate the state's preeminent public university. In 1933, under the encouragement of Durham lawyers Conrad O. Pearson and Cecil McCoy, NCC student Thomas Hocutt applied to the UNC pharmacy school. After he was rejected based on race, Pearson and McCoy, with NAACP support, filed suit in what became the first legal action to try to desegregate public higher education in the South. Some members of the Black elite supported the challenge, including C. C. Spaulding, but he later advised against the lawsuit, largely for fear of provoking violence. NCC President James Shepard attempted to talk Hocutt out of proceeding and sent faculty member Alfonso Elder to try to discourage Hocutt from continuing the case, to no avail. As the president of a state-supported college, Shepard was concerned with potential funding cuts if he publicly supported integration efforts. Historian Jerry Gershenhorn argues, "While Shepard and Spaulding's visions of the future were based upon a short-term adaptation to segregation, Hocutt's youthful supporters sought an immediate end to segregation and the injustices it perpetuated."[55]

Hocutt's lawyers based their petition to the state superior court on the equal protection and due process clauses of the Fourteenth Amendment of the US Constitution and argued that North Carolina laws did not explicitly mandate segregated universities. Ultimately, the judge ruled against Hocutt on two counts. For one, the court could only order UNC to rule on Hocutt's application in an impartial manner but could not compel UNC to admit a student. Second, the court ruled that the application was incomplete, as Shepard had withheld Hocutt's transcript. As Gershenhorn points out, the incomplete transcript justification was specious since UNC's pharmacy school was an undergraduate program and

---

[54] Ellsworth, *The Secret Game*, 273, 269.

[55] Jerry Gershenhorn, "*Hocutt v. Wilson* and Race Relations in Durham, North Carolina During the 1930s," *North Carolina Historical Review* 78, no. 3 (July 2001): 291, 296, 304.

thus seemingly would have only required a high school transcript.[56]

Various historians have interpreted the case differently, with Christina Greene emphasizing that some NAACP leaders believed that Spaulding and Shepard "sabotaged" the case, while Leslie Brown maintains that "Hocutt lost on a technicality that was engineered by James E. Shepard, president of North Carolina College for Negroes, which intentionally withheld Hocutt's transcript."[57] There is little doubt that Shepard hurt Hocutt's chances of winning the case, but the fact that the judge offered two explanations reveals that the withholding of the transcript was not the only reason for the failure in the case. As would be seen in many later cases, including Joseph Holt's effort at integrating the Raleigh city schools in the late 1950s, denying integration based on a "technicality" could be quite broadly applied in Southern courts that seemed bent on preserving segregation.[58]

Further challenges to segregation in higher education in North Carolina preceded the momentous 1954 *Brown v. Board of Education* decision. Once again, NCC students were at the heart of the battle. In *McKissick v. Carmichael*, NAACP lawyer Thurgood Marshall, as well as Pearson, argued for the admission of Black applicants to the law school at UNC on the basis that the somewhat recently created NCC School of Law was inferior in resources and facilities.[59] UNC attorneys countered by calling representatives from the state's legal establishment to testify. Wake Forest law professor I. Beverly Lake testified that a student could get just as good of a law education at NCC as at UNC. The judge, a North Carolina native, agreed and held that the two law schools offered an equal legal education. Marshall and Pearson appealed the decision, and on March 27,

---

[56] Gershenhorn, "*Hocutt v. Wilson* and Race Relations in Durham, North Carolina During the 1930s," 300.

[57] Greene, *Our Separate Ways*, 21; Brown, *Upbuilding Black Durham*, 312.

[58] See chapter 4 for more analysis on Joseph Holt Jr. and school integration efforts.

[59] In the wake of a 1938 US Supreme Court decision forcing officials in Missouri to either accept Blacks at a White-only law school or create a similar school for Blacks, North Carolina politicians quickly acted to help establish a law school at NCC in order to avert forced desegregation of the UNC law school. See Richard A. Rosen and Joseph Mosnier, *Julius Chambers: A Life in the Legal Struggle for Civil Rights* (Chapel Hill: University of North Carolina Press, 2016), 26.

1951, the Fourth Circuit court in Richmond, Virginia, reversed the deci-sion.[60]

In May 1951, World War II veteran and former NCC student Floyd B. McKissick became one of the first five Black students to matriculate at UNC, after three years of study at the NCC law school while the case progressed. Like the other students, he faced harassment and later recalled that White students put dead snakes in his clothes drawer and rigged water buckets to douse him upon opening his door. McKissick's role in integrat-ing the law school at UNC foreshadowed his civil rights activism in the Triangle and beyond in the coming years. In the early 1960s, he was one of the most ardent supporters of student protestors in the region, including his daughter Joycelyn. Like her father, Joycelyn had blazed a trail for inte-gration by becoming the first African American to attend a previously all-White public school in Durham in 1959.[61]

As African Americans dealt with segregation and discriminatory practices in the century after emancipation, a seemingly disparate view-point about higher education was developing in the Triangle and through-out the country: academic freedom. Connections between conceptions of academic freedom and concerns over the rights of African Americans were intermittent but not insignificant in the period before the height of the civil rights movement in the 1960s. At UNC and Duke, the promotion of academic freedom provided a context for a more reasoned discussion of race relations and the impact of segregation in the Triangle and through-out the South.

Academic freedom is an amorphous concept that has been variously defined in different time periods and locations. One scholar points out, "There is, one soon discovers, no clear and widely accepted definition or justification of academic freedom and no settled account of the way in which claims of violation may be assessed."[62] In 1955, the director of the American Academic Freedom Project at Columbia University, Robert MacIver, declared that "the broad meaning of academic freedom is plain

---

[60] Rosen and Mosnier, *Julius Chambers*, 26–28.

[61] Rosen and Mosnier, *Julius Chambers*, 29–30; Greene, *Our Separate Ways*, 73–74. Note: Durham Catholic School had admitted three Black students in 1955.

[62] Edmund Pincoffs, ed., *The Concept of Academic Freedom* (Austin: University of Texas Press, 1975), vii.

enough. It is the freedom of the scholar within the institution devoted to scholarship, 'the academy.'"[63] While the freedom of a professor to express ideas that contribute to knowledge in his or her field is perhaps the clearest example of academic freedom, the right to express ideas outside of that expertise have been more heavily contested. Additionally, while academic freedom is generally considered the purview of the professor or faculty member, one must consider the impact on students as well. As MacIver points out, "The two freedoms, the intellectual freedom of the teacher, and intellectual freedom of the taught, though certain distinctions must be drawn between them, are closely associated and are interactive."[64]

One factor making the Triangle unique in the South was its commitment to higher education and the prominent role Duke and UNC played in shaping ideas of academic freedom. UNC professor Benjamin Sherwood Hedrick was involved in perhaps the most celebrated academic freedom case dealing with the slavery issue. As word got out that he planned to support Republican candidate John C. Fremont in 1856, public pressure mounted for him to resign. He responded in a statement in which he gave Jeffersonian reasons for his opposition to the extension of slavery and for his support of Fremont. He denied that his students would receive any sort of free-soil indoctrination, and he refused to resign. Despite support from some faculty, Hedrick was dismissed by the school's trustees. This early case in which academic freedom was restricted based largely on an issue related to race relations also demonstrated the intertwined connection between restrictions on civil liberties and academic freedom. As Richard Hofstadter points out, neither civil liberty nor religious liberty are identical with academic freedom; "however, both of these more inclusive rights are at points broadly analogous to academic freedom, and altogether they provided the historical matrix of the concept of academic liberties."[65]

Despite the outcome of the Hedrick case in the antebellum era, North Carolina's two most prestigious institutions of higher learning would generally defend academic freedom, even when the cases dealt with race

---

[63] Robert M. MacIver, *Academic Freedom in Our Time* (New York: Columbia University Press, 1955), 3.

[64] MacIver, *Academic Freedom in Our Time*, 10.

[65] Richard Hofstadter and Walter P. Metzger, *The Development of Academic Freedom in the United States* (New York: Columbia University Press, 1955), 258–62.

relations. In 1903, in the wake of White supremacist campaigns to reestablish Democratic Party dominance throughout the state, a professor at Trinity College (which was incorporated into Duke University in the 1920s) became the victim of verbal attacks and calls for his ouster after writing an article for the *South Atlantic Quarterly* that was critical of prevailing views about racial inequality. History professor John S. Bassett wrote that Blacks were becoming "too intelligent and too refined" to continue to accept their inferior status. Bassett claimed that White men must adopt "these children of Africa into our American life."[66] While not devoid of some of the paternalistic language of the era, Bassett's arguments were radical in a time when the political and social atmosphere in the state was reactionary. His article led to calls throughout the Triangle for his expulsion. *News and Observer* editor Josephus Daniels led the attack on Bassett and called for him to issue a full retraction. As local pressure mounted, Bassett submitted his resignation.[67]

What followed was one of the most glaring examples of the defense of academic freedom in American history. Fifteen alumni petitioned for Bassett to be retained, including one who maintained that a professor from the school "should be allowed to hold and express any rational opinion he may have about any subject whatsoever."[68] Ultimately, the Board of Trustees voted 18–7 to allow Bassett to keep his job. The statement that accompanied the decision declared, "We are particularly unwilling to lend ourselves to any tendency to destroy or limit academic liberty."[69] The statement also defended the decision in light of civil liberties, maintaining that "we cannot lend countenance to the degrading notion that professors in American colleges have not an equal liberty of thought and speech with all other Americans." As historian Walter Metzger points out, "These were memorable phrases and they became notable additions to the *belles-*

[66] Hofstadter and Metzger, *The Development of Academic Freedom in the United States*, 446.

[67] Hofstadter and Metzger, *The Development of Academic Freedom in the United States*, 447.

[68] Hofstadter and Metzger, *The Development of Academic Freedom in the United States*, 448.

[69] MacIver, *Academic Freedom in Our Time*, 272.

lettres of academic freedom."[70]

The Bassett case, especially the statement that defended the decision to retain him, demonstrated the connection between free speech and academic freedom. But his ability to speak on such a controversial topic as racial inequality was not merely a matter of free speech. Bassett was a historian and helped to pioneer the study of African American history in the state. Bassett once stated, "I desire to find out what there is in the negro, what he has done and what he can and will do."[71] Thus, Bassett's article discussing the potential for African Americans in society was not simply a matter of expressing personal views but was also a utilization of his knowledge to discuss a key societal issue. The Constitution protected his right to express his views without legal punishment. But the evolving concept of academic freedom at institutions such as Trinity College, one that had to stand tall in the face of public pressure, was what protected his job.

The Trinity College Board of Trustees' defense of Bassett was indicative of the ways in which academic freedom was used to defend those who sought to explore race relations in a more rational manner. It may have also demonstrated the influence of the Duke family, who had been primarily responsible for the growth of the college. The Dukes were Republicans and were despised by racial conservatives, who viewed them as enemies of White supremacy. Perhaps the most prescient statement in regards to the Bassett case is one that hinted not only at the racial violence of the period but also at the dangers of sacrificing academic freedom in the face of public pressure. In an appeal to the college to retain Bassett, Benjamin N. Duke warned, "There are more ways of lynching a man than by tying a hempen rope around his neck and throwing it over the limb of a tree. Public opinion can lynch a man, and that is what North Carolina is trying to do to Bassett now. Don't allow it. You'll never get over it if you do."[72]

The concept of academic freedom was given more formal description in a founding document of the newly created American Association of University Professors (AAUP) in 1915. The AAUP produced *The*

---

[70] Hofstadter and Metzger, *The Development of Academic Freedom in the United States*, 449.

[71] LeLoudis, *Schooling the New South*, 184.

[72] Hofstadter and Metzger, *The Development of Academic Freedom in the United States*, 450.

Declaration of Principles on Academic Freedom and Academic Tenure, which seemed to echo Benjamin Duke's concerns about public opinion. The group of scholars that created the document warned of the "tyranny of public opinion" and opined that "an inviolable refuge from such tyranny should be found in the university."[73] The *Declaration* emphasizes the premise that the purpose of a university education is not to provide students with ready-made conclusions but "to train them to think for themselves, and to provide access to those materials which they need if they are to think intelligently."[74] Thus, the freedom of the professor in the classroom was linked to student learning.

In addition, the *Declaration* also addresses the "freedom of extramural utterance and action." The *Declaration* offers the view that scholars should not be barred from giving their opinions on controversial questions. Perhaps the clearest establishment of a principle that would have implications for the relationship between academic freedom and the civil rights movement (addressed in later chapters) was the following statement: "It is clearly not proper that they should be prohibited from lending their active support to organized movements which they believe to be in the public interest."[75]

Just as the creation of the *Declaration* impacted conceptions of academic freedom, the tendency among UNC professors to embrace ideas of academic freedom had implications for race relations in the state. In the 1920s, UNC president Harry Woodburn Chase was an ardent defender of academic freedom and presided over the institution in a period when UNC leaders viewed academic freedom as a social good and as a key to Southern progress. Historian Charles J. Holden maintains that "by invoking academic freedom as a necessary function of the modern intellectual's expertise, some at UNC took and defended extremely unpopular positions against segregation and industrial exploitation of workers."[76] Holden also points out how UNC scholars in the 1920s and 1930s treated Southern

---

[73] Matthew W. Finkin and Robert C. Post, *For the Common Good: Principles of American Academic Freedom* (New Haven: Yale University Press, 2009), 172.

[74] Finkin and Post, *For the Common Good*, 80.

[75] Finkin and Post, *For the Common Good*, 178.

[76] Charles J. Holden, *The New Southern University: Academic Freedom and Liberalism at UNC* (Lexington: University Press of Kentucky, 2012), 22.

race relations as an academic issue. Faculty research on the Ku Klux Klan enabled scholars to criticize the organization and expose some of the KKK's false claims. The academic freedom that allowed professors to analyze race issues as a scholarly endeavor helped to produce a much more critical stance on racial violence and segregation.[77] Of course, examining and critiquing the KKK was different than making an all-out attack on segregation, but the academic freedom at UNC provided an avenue for addressing racial concerns in a more open and less emotional manner.

In 1927, UNC welcomed NAACP leader James Weldon Johnson to campus, a daring move in light of the hatred that many Whites had toward the organization. University leaders treated his appearance as a purely academic event, and the *Daily Tar Heel* newspaper even cleverly described Johnson as a "negro poet," taking care not to mention his NAACP affiliation. According to Holden, "UNC's leaders felt confident that their academic freedom to examine the issue of race relations was helping lead the South toward a better racial situation."[78]

In his inaugural address in 1931, UNC president Frank Porter Graham spelled out what academic freedom could mean at an institution such as UNC. For faculty, that involved their right to teach and speak freely as scholars without interference from the university or the state. He also discussed the impact of academic freedom on students, suggesting that it meant "a growing sense of responsibility and student citizenship," as well as the "right of lawful assembly and free discussions by any students of any issues and views whatsoever."[79] By the late 1930s, some UNC students and faculty increasingly criticized segregation itself and viewed racial progress through the lens of ending segregation rather than merely reforming it. The support of academic freedom did not necessarily imply a progressive view toward race relations overall at UNC. The denial of Hocutt's application in 1933 was just one indicator of that reality. But it did provide a context for research on race issues (especially by UNC's famous sociologists) and the problems that African Americans confronted in a segregated

---

[77] Holden, *The New Southern University*, 27.
[78] Holden, *The New Southern University*, 45, 47.
[79] Holden, *The New Southern University*, 84.

society.[80]

In the 1940s, Graham also worked behind the scenes to defend embattled professors in other Southern states like Georgia who risked termination for their "liberal" views on race issues. Graham publicly defended University of Texas president Homer P. Rainey in the mid-1940s when the Texas Board of Regents removed him from the presidency for his liberal views on race and labor. Rainey acknowledged Graham as the leader of academic freedom in the South and commended him for his "fearless and courageous leadership."[81] Thus, the top leadership and some of the faculty at UNC had already established themselves as defenders of academic freedom prior to the sit-in movement of the early 1960s. In some cases, that opened opportunities for better understanding of African American concerns and the impact of segregation. But it was not until the civil rights activism largely emanating from the three HBCU campuses in the Triangle in the early 1960s that the connections between academic freedom and Black civil rights became a powerful force for challenging segregation.

The development of what became Shaw University had established some of the roots of Black higher education that impacted several facets of Black life in the Triangle and throughout the state. Graduates rose to prominent political positions, helped to foster the growth of Black business, and played prominent roles in developing Black colleges, including NCC. Ironically, the very segregated practices that in some respects isolated Black colleges helped produce activists who recognized not only their own talents but also the history of the South that had placed limits on the development of those talents.

On the eve of the sit-in movement that commenced in earnest in February 1960, there were several cracks in the walls of segregation in the Tar Heel state. Challenges by African American students, including those at NCC, to segregated practices at institutions of higher learning had produced initially frustrating but ultimately tangible results by the 1950s. While there had been instances of direct action both in the Triangle and other cities in the South since the Civil War, many Black communities

---

[80] Holden, *The New Southern University*, 88, 102–106.
[81] Holden, *The New Southern University*, 157.

were not united in their resistance to segregation. The tepid response among many African American leaders in Durham to the sit-ins at the Royal Ice Cream Parlor in 1957 was an indicator that some still viewed direct challenges to segregation in the Triangle as impractical or too dangerous. Thus, it would take a special generation of activists who recognized not only the importance of higher learning in paving the long road to Black freedom but also that participating in a movement challenging a segregated society that limited the potential of Black education could be a fundamental *part* of their education. And so, on a cold and snowy week in the Triangle, student activists in Raleigh proceeded from Shaw to the heart of downtown, from campus to counter.

Chapter 3

Academic Freedom and the 1960 Sit-Ins

Tension mounted as students from Shaw University and Saint Augustine's College picketed outside segregated stores in downtown Raleigh on the afternoon of February 16, 1960. A group of White teenagers and a few White men verbally taunted and pushed some of the protestors and reportedly slapped a Black woman. This abuse was mild in comparison to the incident the following day in which a White man struck Shaw student Otis Clark with a chain after Clark confronted another White man who had taken a protest sign from a Saint Augustine's student. Clark reacted to the chain attack with a solid right to the man's cheek and sent him staggering into a parked car. The sit-ins and pickets in Raleigh had begun a week earlier, and these were the first reported incidences of violence.[1] In fact, violence toward the protestors was relatively rare (and by the protestors even more rare), but the taunts and verbal assaults were more common. Thus, the violence of these two days in Raleigh was more anomalous than emblematic.

While the reported physical violence was the most newsworthy

---

[1] "Students Carrying Signs Picket at Raleigh Stores," *News and Observer*, 17 February 1960, 1; David Cooper, "Two White Men Arrested Here after Encounter with Negroes," *News and Observer*, 18 February 1960, 1, 2; Otis Tucker Jr., mail interview by the author, received 5 May 2016; Leroy Cofield, phone conversation with the author, 20 April 2016.

aspect, perhaps the most telling aspect of the February 16 demonstration could be read on one of the protest signs that asserted, "You Just Can't 'Lump' Justice." The sign was an obvious jab at North Carolina Attorney General Malcolm Seawell, who had responded to criticism by the American Civil Liberties Union (ACLU) for his critical position on student sit-ins by saying that "I stand by what I have said—if you like it, well and good—if you do not like it, you may lump it."[2] College students were especially disapproving of Seawell's stance that college administrators could or, in his estimation, should attempt to curb their students from participating in sit-ins.[3]

This chapter addresses the 1960 sit-ins and protest demonstrations in Raleigh, Durham, and other cities in North Carolina and reveals that ideas of academic freedom gave the protest movement support from students and faculty from historically Black as well as predominantly White colleges and universities. In Raleigh and Durham, the sit-in movement was primarily led by students at the historically Black schools of Shaw, Saint Augustine's, and North Carolina College at Durham (NCC), which I term the "Protest Triangle" schools. Activists at these schools viewed their participation in civil rights protests as part of their education and as a way of opening societal opportunities. By extension, they viewed any restrictions on their participation by political leaders or school officials as a restriction on their academic freedom.[4] Protestors received support from some students and faculty at predominantly White colleges, especially the Research Triangle schools of Duke University, the University of North Carolina (UNC), and North Carolina State College. An expanded vision of academic freedom, one that viewed the students' right to participate in civil rights demonstrations as part of their education, was critical in mobilizing support from Black and White students and faculty in the Triangle.

Students from HBCUs provided the backbone for the sit-ins and other civil rights demonstrations in 1960. As chapter 1 makes clear, the Greensboro sit-in of February 1, 1960, was not the first attempt to

---

[2] "Students Carrying Signs Picket at Raleigh Stores," 1; "'Like It or Lump It': Seawell Fires Back at ACLU," *News and Observer*, 13 February 1960, 3.

[3] Charles Clay, "Three Alternatives: Seawell Cites Legal Aspects of Sitdowns," *News and Observer*, 11 February 1960, 1, 2.

[4] See survey results in appendix.

integrate lunch counters in the South, but the action by the "Greensboro Four" of Ezell Blair Jr. (later Jibreel Khazan), Franklin McCain, Joseph McNeil, and David Richmond helped spark a more aggressive phase in the struggle for Black freedom. The sit-in produced an immediate response from students at the historically Black North Carolina Agricultural and Technical College, and by the following day, twenty-nine students had participated in the sit-ins at Woolworth. Within five days, over three hundred students were participating and the protest spread to S. H. Kress. Ultimately, the sit-ins spread to several cities in every state throughout the South, with perhaps seventy thousand students participating in some capacity. According to Adam Fairclough, approximately three thousand six hundred students were arrested in 1960 alone for offenses such as trespassing and disorderly conduct.[5] William Chafe has argued that the Greensboro sit-ins were a "watershed in the history of America."[6] While Black activism in Greensboro and other cities in North Carolina was certainly not born on February 1, 1960, the actions of the Greensboro Four helped give force to a strategy that could directly challenge segregation in the streets and at the lunch counters. One did not need to be a member of any civil rights organization or have any political connections to demonstrate their displeasure with segregation.

In addition to the students at North Carolina A&T, students from the historically Black, all-female Bennett College played a major role in the Greensboro sit-ins. As Chafe points out, Bennett had been a model of racial strength for many years prior to 1960. Since it was a private institution, it did not have to "kowtow to public prejudices" to appease state officials for funding. Chafe argues that president Dr. Willa Player best exemplified adult support for the student movement. In addition to supporting the students, she was the first Black person to turn in her charge card at Meyer's Department Store, which refused to desegregate its lunch counter. When sit-ins returned to Greensboro in earnest in 1963, Player mobilized her staff to support the movement.[7]

---

[5] Adam Fairclough, *Better Day Coming: Blacks and Equality, 1890–2000* (New York: Penguin Books, 2001), 242–43.

[6] William H. Chafe, *Civilities and Civil Rights: Greensboro, North Carolina and the Struggle for Black Freedom* (Oxford: Oxford University Press, 1981), 71.

[7] Chafe, *Civilities and Civil Rights*, 20, 97, 129.

Administrators at state-supported colleges were under pressure from state and local political leaders to curtail student involvement in the demonstrations. After the initial wave of sit-ins in 1960, North Carolina A&T President Warmoth T. Gibbs met with city leaders, who asked him to discourage students from protesting in Greensboro. Gibbs did not take any disciplinary action against the students who staged the sit-ins. When city leaders asked Gibbs to keep the students on campus, he replied, "We teach our students how think, not what to think."[8] While Gibbs hardly took a leading role in promoting the actions of the students, his refusal to take disciplinary action against the students showed an implicit support.

The reaction to the sit-ins in Greensboro and other North Carolina cities by the state's top political leaders was generally one of discouragement of the tactic. No other phrase captured the response of state and local leaders more than the appeal to "law and order." In early March, Governor Luther Hodges stated that "I have no sympathy whatsoever for any group of people who deliberately engage in activities which any reasonable person can see will result in a breakdown of law and order as well as interference with the normal and proper operation of a private business."[9] But those in favor of the sit-ins as a means of challenging segregation could easily point out the flaw of Hodges's reasoning. One UNC student wrote an editorial that asked, "Whose law and order, governor?" He pointed out that the state of North Carolina was not complying with the laws established by the *Brown v. Board of Education* decision of 1954.[10] Another UNC student wrote a letter to Hodges arguing that "Hitler and Stalin probably had law and order enforced, but they did not consider justice or nondiscrimination."[11]

Both segregationists and integrationists appealed to certain laws to advance their cause in the early 1960s. But civil rights activists and those who sympathized with them recognized that law and justice were not the

---

[8] Fairclough, *Better Day Coming*, 243; see also "Key Players—Warmoth T. Gibbs," *Greensboro News and Record*, 2016.

[9] Clay, "Three Alternatives," 1.

[10] Frank Cowher, "Editorial," *Carolina Times*, 26 March 1960, 2.

[11] Thelma Howell to Luther Hodges, 13 March 1960, Box 523, Folder: "Segregation: Sit-Down Situations," Governor's Papers, Luther Hodges, North Carolina State Archives, Raleigh, NC.

same thing. When preexisting laws mandated segregation, civil rights activists challenged them. When no laws existed to mandate segregation, they sought to challenge the social traditions that preserved them.

Local and state political leaders often portrayed the sit-ins as stirring racial problems. On February 10, the same day that the sit-ins spread to the capital city of Raleigh, state Attorney General Malcolm Seawell claimed that the Black college students were doing "irreparable harm" to race relations with their "sit-down strikes."[12] Indeed, he was correct. The sit-ins were a clear demonstration that African Americans were in fact displeased with the current state of race relations. They adamantly opposed the idea that Blacks were content with racial traditions in North Carolina and their respective cities. In response to the sit-ins, Raleigh Mayor William G. Enloe released a statement that said, "it is regrettable that some of our young Negro students would risk endangering Raleigh's friendly and cooperative race relations by seeking to change a long-standing custom in a manner that is all but destined to fail."[13] Enloe underestimated the will of the students to push on and force businesspeople and city leaders to make tough decisions. In February 1960 there was a long road ahead to achieving integration in public accommodations, but the crucial step of making it crystal clear that most African Americans were not content with racial segregation had been taken.

The sit-in demonstrations not only initiated a new phase in the Black freedom struggle but also brought to light competing ideas about academic freedom and the freedom of college students to engage in activities outside the college. On February 10, Seawell said college officials "have the perfect right, and probably the duty, through appropriate action to prohibit any action on the part of students which threatens or is prejudicial to the peace and welfare of the community."[14] Seawell seemed blind to the fact that African Americans were a part of the community in which they lived and that their grievances constituted a problem in their communities. He argued that the college stood in the "position of parents" to the students.[15]

---

[12] Clay, "Three Alternatives," 1.

[13] Charles Craven and David Cooper, "Student Sitdown Strike Spreads to Stores Here," *News and Observer*, 11 February 1960, 1, 23.

[14] Clay, "Three Alternatives," 1.

[15] Clay, "Three Alternatives," 1.

If indeed the college had such a responsibility, the fact remained that many of the protestors' parents approved of their actions, especially when they demonstrated within the limits of the law. The ACLU's response to Seawell appealed to the constitutional guarantees of equal treatment of all citizens: "We hope that rather than invade constitutional freedoms you will defend them."[16] Seawell responded that it was of the "utmost unimportance" to him what the ACLU thought.[17]

The question of whether college administrators should attempt to thwart the actions of students at their colleges became a prominent issue after three White students from Woman's College of the University of North Carolina (UNC Greensboro today) joined the sit-ins in Greensboro on February 4, as did White students from Greensboro College and Guilford College. The three Woman's College students, Ann Dearsley, Genie Seaman, and Marilyn Lott, sat at the counter at Woolworth's and said they did not want to be served until African Americans were. Dearsley maintained that the protests were "being carried out by intelligent college students whose requests should be a natural right under law, not factors which have to be fought for."[18] In response to the students' actions, Woman's College Chancellor Gordon W. Blackwell addressed the Student Assembly on February 9, pondering his own question of "was the sit-down demonstration, even though passively conducted, a wise move given the objectives of the participants? My answer must be an unequivocal 'No.'"[19] Thus it is clear that Blackwell was personally opposed to the sit-ins as a tactic. Whether this stance was due to personal prejudices or not remains unclear, but the important part of his position on the sit-ins dealt with the students' right to protest outside of the campus.

Blackwell's speech was plagued by contradictions as he stated that the college should never tell students what stand to take on controversial issues

---

[16] New York (UPI), "Civil Liberties Union Replies to Seawell," *News and Observer*, 21 February 1960, 3.

[17] "'Like It or Lump It,'" 3.

[18] Greensboro (UPI), "Sitdown at Greensboro: White Students Back Negroes in Demands at Lunch Counter," *News and Observer*, 5 February 1960, 1.

[19] Chancellor Gordon W. Blackwell, "Talk to Student Assembly," 9 February 1960, Box 522, Folder: "Segregation: Lunch Counter (Negro) 1960," Governor's Papers, Luther Hodges, North Carolina State Archives.

or how they should assert their rights as individuals and citizens. "But your responsibility as students at Woman's College goes beyond personal considerations," he added. "Your class jacket is a symbol of the College. On and off the campus you represent this institution. Your actions bring credit or discredit to the College. You are not living in a vacuum unencumbered by duties and responsibilities. The results of your actions may affect many others in a kind of chain reaction as has been painfully demonstrated this week."[20] The irony was that much of this excerpt could indeed have been used to support participation in the demonstrations. The women who joined the sit-ins understood that their responsibilities in society went beyond personal considerations. In an article in the Woman's College student newspaper, *The Carolinian*, Dearsley stated that students participated in order to express their sentiments about equality, freedom, and the rights of the individual as expressed in the US Constitution.[21] Students and others who challenged segregated practices ostensibly challenged Americans to confront one of the key paradoxes of American history: the interplay between a history of discrimination and the idyllic yet unfulfilled notion of "we hold these truths to be self-evident: that all men are created equal...."[22]

Another irony of Blackwell's speech was that he addressed the concern over academic freedom, stating, "A college must consider the matter of academic freedom of students as well as of faculty."[23] The heart of Blackwell's speech was advising students to refrain from participation in demonstrations. But if students were to take Blackwell's words to heart that "on and off the campus you represent this institution," it seemed a clear restriction on their academic freedom to discourage their involvement. The speech may have gone relatively unheralded if Governor Luther Hodges had not promoted it as a model for how college administrators should proceed. Hodges sent the speech to the heads of each of the Black

---

[20] Blackwell, "Talk to Student Assembly."

[21] "Ann Dearsley Reviews Lunch Counter Strike," *The Carolinian [Woman's College of the University of North Carolina]*, 12 February 1960, 1, 3. *The Carolinian* was also the name of a Black newspaper in Raleigh.

[22] Thomas Jefferson et al., "Declaration of Independence," July 1776.

[23] Blackwell, "Talk to Student Assembly."

and White state-supported colleges.[24]

Hodges's support of Blackwell's stance was unpopular among many college students at Black and predominantly White institutions. East Carolina College student Sandra Porter wrote a letter to Hodges that portrayed his appeal to the college administrators as a betrayal of academic freedom. She asserted that Hodges had "left the ethical yardstick behind" for "political expediency" but stated that the real problem she had with Hodges's position was that "instructing students as to why, when, where and over what they may peacefully demonstrate is in direct opposition to any semblance of academic freedom."[25] Porter's letter is one piece of evidence among numerous others showing that many college students in North Carolina viewed restrictions on civil rights demonstrations as an assault on academic freedom.

Blackwell's and Hodges's stance on how college administrators should approach student demonstrators also drew fire from college faculty. In late March, a group of eight NC State professors belonging to the executive committee of the AAUP sent a letter to Governor Hodges criticizing him for his support of Blackwell's speech. The letter stated that Hodges was acting to restrict civic freedom, a "disservice to both educational quality in our State-supported institutions and to development of the human potential of our State." Hodges responded harshly by saying, "I don't know how smart these people are who wrote that letter, but they apparently aren't as smart as they sound."[26] Hodges's folksy and circular logic in his response was characteristic of the anti-intellectual strain that had periodically gripped North Carolina politics, even though Hodges had attended the state's preeminent public university (UNC). The NC State professors also sent a letter to Chancellor Blackwell, which said that his advice to the student body at the Woman's College "to refrain from taking such action (no matter how well-intentioned the advice) appears clearly to

---

[24] Charles Craven, "Governor Asks College Officials to Help Sitdown Protests," *News and Observer*, 1, 20.

[25] Sandra Porter to Luther Hodges, 11 March 1960, Box 523, Folder: "Segregation: Sit Down Situations," Governor's Papers, Luther Hodges, North Carolina State Archives.

[26] Charles Craven, "Professors Attack Hodges' View on Sitdown Protests," *News and Observer*, 25 March 1960, 1, 2.

restrict the civil rights and academic freedom of students."[27]

Whereas many professors and students loathed Blackwell's action, a nuanced look at his role reveals that he did attempt to call together representatives of Woman's College, Bennett College, Greensboro College, North Carolina A&T, and the Woolworth and Kress stores. After students initially refused to halt demonstrations, they agreed to a two-week moratorium. Other negotiations followed, but students resumed protests in Greensboro in early April. In September, Blackwell left Woman's College to become the president of Florida State University. Blackwell took over for Dr. Robert M. Strozier, who had died earlier in 1960. Prior to Blackwell's arrival, six Florida State students had been arrested for taking part in the demonstrations in Tallahassee, and the college placed them on probation with a warning to steer clear of demonstrations. Florida State officials questioned Blackwell on his racial views before hiring him and evidently were satisfied.[28] Blackwell later oversaw the integration of Florida State when the first three African Americans entered the school in the fall semester of 1962.[29] Hence Blackwell may very well not have been a staunch segregationist. Yet the response among students and professors in North Carolina that questioned his discouragement of students from protesting are indicators of the ways in which ideas about academic freedom provided ideological support for student civil rights activism.

While the sit-ins and protests received some support from the Triangle's largest White colleges (UNC and NC State), they also received support from certain segments of the student body at the state's most prestigious private educational institution, Duke University. On April 15, a group of Duke Divinity School students announced the adoption of two resolutions that opposed racial discrimination and expressed support for the student movement. It should be noted that opposing racial discrimination and supporting the tactics of the demonstrators were two different issues. Some Whites favored the former but disapproved of the latter. One part of the first resolution stated that "we identify ourselves with the purpose

---

[27] Craven, "Professors Attack Hodges' View on Sitdown Protests," 1, 2.

[28] Tallahassee UPI, "Blackwell Questioned on His Racial Views," *News and Observer*, 17 August 1960, 22.

[29] Joan Abbott, "Three Negro Students Enroll Here this Fall," *Florida Flambeau*, 5 September 1962, 1.

of the students who are participating in non-violent protestations, and we are in accord with the end for which they are striving, namely the elimination of all racial discrimination."[30] Thus, without explicitly promoting the sit-in tactics, the Duke students nonetheless supported the actions of the student movement to eliminate segregated practices. The second resolution maintained that the "policy of segregated lunch counters, followed by certain local merchants and chain stores is not in harmony with Christian principles." This resolution also recognized the difficult position in which local merchants found themselves and therefore included a pledge to eat at lunch counters that chose to integrate. Not every Duke Divinity School student supported the resolution, but the vote was overwhelmingly in favor of adoption with ninety-one affirmatives, fifteen negatives, and five abstentions.[31] The vote demonstrated that among Whites, support for integration came largely from two segments of the population: college students or faculty, and religious leaders.

Whereas the divinity students demonstrated overwhelming support for integration, the views among the Duke student body were more divided. The *Durham Morning Herald* pointed out that a plurality of undergraduate men (44 percent) favored a continued policy of segregated admissions, or that is to say, no admissions for African American students. The reality was that Duke did not admit an African American student until the 1961 fall semester. Thus, the university itself did not take a leadership role in favoring integration, but certain student and faculty groups did. The most obvious example of White student support at Duke came from those who participated in the demonstrations in downtown Durham. Duke students joined the sit-ins with students from NCC, a historically Black public institution in Durham. A dozen Duke students, in addition to sixty-three NCC students, two students at Durham Business College, and three African American Durham residents were arrested on trespassing charges in May 1960 when they refused to leave segregated lunch counters.[32]

---

[30] "Sitdown Move Commended by Duke Divinity Students," *Durham Morning Herald*, 16 April 1960, 1B.

[31] "Sitdown Move Commended by Duke Divinity Students," 1B.

[32] "Tarheel Polls on Desegregation," *Durham Morning Herald*, 15 April 1960, 4; Durham (AP), "46 Negroes, Whites Face Trial after Durham Counter Reopens,"

The response by one Duke faculty member to the arrest of student Lonnie Benton Chesnutt was particularly revealing about the interplay between student activism and college officials' reactions to direct-action tactics in Durham. In mid-May, Dean of Students Robert Cox dismissed Chesnutt from a housemaster's position for the following academic year due to Chesnutt's participation and arrest for trespassing during sit-ins. Cox made it clear that his action toward Chesnutt should not be interpreted as the official position of the college, an indicator that the college did not have an official policy for its employees. But after consulting with several students and members of the faculty, Cox decided to change his decision and reinstated Chesnutt to his position.[33]

Cox's decision to change his mind reveals several important realities about the situation on college campuses regarding student sit-ins. First and foremost, attitudes about racial discrimination as well as students' right to protest were fluid and being challenged in ways that sparked self-reflection. College administrators throughout North Carolina were being pulled in varying directions by tradition and segregationists on the one side and those in favor of integration and advocates of students' rights on the other. For Cox, an arrested student presented a particularly difficult dilemma and begged an answer to the troubling question of whether a student's pursuit of justice excused his challenge to a segregationist interpretation of the law.

The decision by Cox to reverse his punishment for a student activist was clearly influenced by discussions with faculty members and students, but he also likely considered a recent resolution approved by the Duke chapter of the AAUP. The unanimously approved resolution of April 25 condemned the use of academic authority to discipline, suspend, or expel students for peacefully protesting against racial discrimination.[34] Implicit in the denunciation of the use of academic authority to curb protests was an acknowledgment of the students' expanded conception of academic freedom, one that extended beyond the property limits of the campus.

News and Observer, 7 May 1960, 1.

[33] Ray Lowery, "Duke Dean Changes Mind about Depriving Student Sitdown Participation," *News and Observer*, 19 May 1960.

[34] Lowery, "Duke Dean Changes Mind."

The backbone of the movements in Raleigh and Durham came from the students, and in some cases faculty and administration, of the HBCUs in the cities. NCC president Alfonso Elder had established a tradition of promoting issues related to academic freedom before the sit-in movement developed in earnest in 1960. Even prior to his official inauguration as president in 1949, he made the decision that students needed to become more knowledgeable about democracy. In his fourteen years as president, Elder emphasized the concept of "student self-direction." He maintained that two phases of student self-direction emerged in the late 1940s and the following decades. The first was a concept of independence that emphasized the students' "freedom to initiate and control their own affairs without faculty interference."[35] The second phase emphasized student-faculty cooperation. The two phases overlapped, and by the early 1960s Elder believed that "our experience has led us to conclude that both types are important in an educational institution, that they complement each other, and that they should be provided simultaneously."[36]

NCC student involvement in the sit-ins provided what some might term a dilemma for Elder, but he embraced it as an opportunity. The students had largely acted independent of the faculty and the administration. If Elder wanted to retain any semblance of student respect for his idea that student self-direction and student-faculty cooperation could coexist, he could not discourage them or direct faculty to do so. The students had put the concept of student self-direction into action and demonstrated an expanded concept of academic freedom that extended beyond the campus. Elder had three options for how to respond to the sit-ins. One was to take a strong stand against them and appease Governor Hodges and many state legislators. Such a move would sacrifice ethics for the practical concern of not risking state funding. A second option was to remain silent, which could be interpreted as implicit support balanced against a concern for potential loss of funding. A third option was to take a strong stand in favor of the demonstrations. Elder's speech indicated that he pursued the third

---

[35] Alfonso Elder, "The Evolution of a Concept of Student Self-Direction," 1, 3, undated, Series 3 (Speeches 1960-1963), Folder 228, Alfonso Elder Papers, James E. Shepard Memorial Library, North Carolina Central University, Durham, NC. Although Elder's speech is undated, it is highly likely that it was delivered in 1960.

[36] Elder, "The Evolution of a Concept of Student Self-Direction," 6.

option, one he largely justified through the concept of student self-direction.

Yet to acknowledge the student right to participate and to encourage faculty support were two different things. Elder not only supported the students' right to demonstrate but also gave indicators that faculty should support the students. He warned that "it will be a great pity if we who are teachers do not make use of the convictions, the determination, and the dispositions to act in the interest of an idea which this new development in self-direction had produced."[37] In supporting the students' right to demonstrate, he solidified his adherence to student self-direction. This justified his support of the student demonstrations and their impact on striving for a more democratic society. His actions provide further evidence that an expanding concept of academic freedom provided strong ideological support for civil rights activism in North Carolina.

The student demonstrators in Durham received immediate support from some members of the community. The Durham Committee on Negro Affairs, which stated that it was unaware of the plans of the NCC students to participate in sit-down strikes (a term used by many in the initial stages of sit-ins), officially endorsed the strategy of the students. In a February 12 letter to Hodges, Committee Chairman John H. Wheeler commended the students for the poise they demonstrated while experiencing threats, cursing, and a shower of eggs and stated that the irresponsible elements of the community that had committed such acts "would do well to acquire some of the qualities of good citizenship and understanding which have been shown by those who protest."[38] The letter specifically addressed the concern that the committee had in regards to certain state officials attempting to call upon African American leaders, including college presidents, to use their influence to halt the activities of the students.

Hodges had pressure coming from other elements of society that asked him to take a strong stand against the demonstrations. The segregationist group North Carolina Defenders of States' Rights asked the

---

[37] Elder, "The Evolution of a Concept of Student Self-Direction," 8.

[38] John H. Wheeler to Luther Hodges, 12 February 1960, Box 523, Folder: "Segregation: Sit Down Situations," Governor's Papers, Luther Hodges, North Carolina State Archives.

governor to "take any action necessary through the administrations of the Negro schools whose students are now creating social disturbances in the stores throughout the state to remedy this unwholesome and unhealthy social situation." Hodges responded that there was little he could do about the participation of students at state-supported colleges and noted that "the administration can't tell the boards of trustees what to do in running the schools."[39] Thus, Hodges did not make a concerted effort to use the full force of the governor's office to halt demonstrations. Yet the following week he endorsed the Blackwell speech. On March 11, Elder declined to comment on Hodges's support for the Blackwell speech.[40] Thus in the early stages of the demonstrations in 1960, Elder implicitly supported the students by not supporting the governor's wishes for college presidents to use their influence to halt the demonstrations.

Governor Hodges did not understand, or at a minimum did not appreciate, the goals and aspirations of student demonstrators. In my survey asking respondents to rate a variety of individuals on their influence in bringing about integration and positive changes in race relations on a scale of 1–10, the student participant average rating for Hodges was 2.9.[41] Perhaps no other statement by Hodges demonstrated his lack of understanding of the goals of the student movement more clearly than a comment he made at an industrial meeting in Richmond, Virginia. He stated that African nations seeking independence and African Americans seeking integrated service in the United States were similar in that "they want to get freedom but they don't want the commensurate responsibility."[42] His statement neglected the reality that in addition to the goal of eating at lunch counters at stores in which they were able to shop elsewhere in the store, many students also had broader goals. They sought further equality in a society that denied them the opportunities that they felt their level of education should have provided them. Students from the "Protest

---

[39] "In Lunch Counter Protests: Moderation Will Prevail—Hodges," *Durham Morning Herald,* 2 March 1960, 1.

[40] Bill Frue, "Official Position of NCC Given: Elder Calls for Negotiations in Sitdown Controversy Here," *Durham Morning Herald*, 12 March 1960, 1B.

[41] See appendix for survey results.

[42] Richmond, VA, AP, "Hodges Says: Negroes Seek Freedom But No Responsibility," *News and Observer*, 28 April 1960, 36.

Triangle" schools recognized that increased freedoms meant increased responsibility. They demonstrated their intelligence, talents, and responsibility in the classrooms on the campus of Shaw, St. Augustine's and NCC. But they wanted to be able to utilize those traits more effectively in a society that limited their ability to do so.

Elder had a clearer understanding of the students' aspirations than Hodges and many political leaders. Although Hodges was no longer governor in 1962, a speech made by Elder in February of that year at a meeting of the National Student Association at Duke appears to be a fitting response to state political leaders who concurred with Hodges that African Americans sought freedom but not responsibility. Elder pointed out that there had traditionally been a tendency in institutions of higher learning to distinguish between 1) the acquisition of knowledge and 2) the application of knowledge. In the segregated South, students at Black colleges acquired knowledge without the commensurate ability to apply their knowledge in the form of jobs that met their educational attainment. Elder held that social activism on the part of students fell into the category of application of knowledge.[43] Seeking to integrate the lunch counters was a step toward further employment opportunities. Thus, Elder seemed to appreciate the reality that many student activists viewed the demonstrations as part of their education.

Ultimately, Elder recognized the importance of an expanded concept of academic freedom in providing support for student civil rights activism. He stated that students and teachers had the right to function in a dual role as members of the school community and as citizens of their local communities. He declared that "the second basic right which I shall mention is academic freedom. The one commitment or unalterable position which should be considered the 'proper' commitment for students and teachers in an institution of higher learning is the commitment to open inquiry and to the pursuit of truth 'wherever it may lead.'"[44] Elder took a stand that the students' freedom to protest peacefully should not be

---

[43] Alfonso Elder, "The Responsibility of the University to Society (With Special Emphasis on Student Involvement in Extra-Class Affairs)," 25 February 1962, address delivered at Duke University, Durham, NC, Folder 215, Scan 215, pp. 3–4, Alfonso Elder Papers.

[44] Elder, "The Responsibility of the University to Society," 5.

infringed. Student demonstrators from NCC and other Black institutions protested a system that limited their social and economic opportunities. Alfonso Elder understood that they sought greater opportunities to *apply* the knowledge they had acquired. To restrict their activities would have been a clear repression of academic freedom.

NCC faculty members reinforced Elder's support for student demonstrations. After the first week of sit-ins in Raleigh and Durham, NCC math professor Dr. C. Elwood Boulware endorsed the demonstrations. Even at this early stage, he seemed to appreciate the historic nature of the students' actions and claimed that they had moved out of the philosophy of the 1950s and had "intelligently and lawfully employed the techniques of the new leaders of the sixties who are accomplishing something."[45] Boulware's endorsement was a courageous step, as it was unclear at that stage what impact public support of the demonstrations might have on his job. By April 1960, more unified support emerged from NCC faculty, as 103 faculty and staff signed a statement of support for the demonstrations, which was released by the school's AAUP chapter. Boulware was the chapter president and made it clear that the statement did not represent an official college position. The position on the sit-in demonstrations was quite clear in the statement, which criticized community leadership for allowing the patterns of segregation to continue for so long and explicitly stated that the "orderly protests ought to continue as long as opposition to the granting of equal rights is unyielding."[46]

The NCC chapter of the AAUP's reaction to the demonstrations was symbolic of the broader response from the AAUP. Founded in 1915, the AAUP was always on the lookout for violations of academic freedom, and in the wake of the sit-ins, the organization supported the right of students and faculty to participate in the demonstrations. Just as the AAUP chapter of Durham's most influential state-supported Black educational institution backed the demonstrations, the AAUP chapter at Duke University

---

[45] "Durham College Prof Endorses Demonstrations," *News and Observer*, 15 February 1960, 3.

[46] "103 at Durham School Sign AAUP Statement on Sit-Downs," *Carolina Times*, 16 April 1960, 2; "NC College Profs Back Picketing," *Durham Sun*, 15 April 1960, 9B.

gave similar support.[47] Of course, AAUP support at any given college should not be confused with official support from the college. As previously mentioned, Duke did not allow Black student admission (aside from a few foreign Black students) until 1961. Nonetheless, AAUP college branches often gave an aspect of formal faculty support for the demonstrations or, at the least, an assertion that students should not be punished for their participation in demonstrations. At the heart of these policies was an expanded commitment to academic freedom not only for faculty but for students as well, one that permitted peaceful civil rights activism.

In 1960, for the first time in its history, the AAUP devoted most of its resolutions to concerns over racial discrimination. For example, the association declared that any teacher had the right to belong to any organization working for school integration, a likely response to Southern states that banned membership in the NAACP. The AAUP also passed a resolution condemning the expulsion of students from Southern colleges for their participation in peaceful demonstrations. According to the AAUP, colleges that expelled students for peaceful protests exhibited an abuse of academic authority.[48] In some cases, historically Black colleges in the South had little choice but to expel students when pressured by state political leaders. For example, in late February 1960, the Alabama state board of education accepted a resolution by Governor John Patterson, which essentially ordered Alabama State College president Harper C. Trenholm to expel nine student demonstration leaders or else face the loss of state funding.[49]

The case of the expelled Alabama State College students is important to an analysis of the protest movement in Raleigh and Durham. For one, it demonstrates the power that governors could wield in states that would accept such an infringement upon academic freedom and freedom of assembly. When viewed in contrast with reactionary governors such as John Patterson, Hodges could viably be considered a "moderate" on racial

---

[47] Ray Lowery, "Duke Dean Changes Mind about Depriving Sitdown Participant," *News and Observer*, 19 May 1960, 18.

[48] Detroit AP, "Professors Rally to Students' Aid," *News and Observer*, 10 April 1960, section 2, p. 8.

[49] Diane McWhorter, *Carry Me Home: Birmingham, Alabama: The Climactic Battle of the Civil Rights Revolution* (New York: Simon and Schuster, 2001), 152.

issues. On a more direct level, the expulsion of the Alabama State students had a direct impact on the historic conference at Shaw in Raleigh in April 1960 that ultimately led to the creation of the Student Nonviolent Coordinating Committee (SNCC). Eight of the nine expelled students from Alabama were delegates at the conference.[50]

While there were periodic connections between students from Black colleges in North Carolina and those from other states, students at the local colleges performed the majority of organization and daily planning. In Raleigh, Saint Augustine's College and Shaw University were different from NCC in one crucial aspect. The two Raleigh schools were private, religious-affiliated institutions, whereas NCC was a state-supported institution. Saint Augustine's College was an Episcopal Church-affiliated institution that was the site of an important conference in 1959. Two Episcopal clergymen, John Morris and Cornelius "Neil" Tarplee, called Episcopalians together at the school to form an organization to respond to the nation's growing racial crisis. According to religious historian Gardiner H. Shattuck Jr., Saint Augustine's was chosen because it was one of the few church-related institutions in the South at which a large interracial group could meet without arousing undue attention from local White opponents. Approximately one hundred people met for the conference in late December 1959. They established an organization called "The Episcopal Society for Cultural and Racial Unity," later known by the acronym ESCRU. The participants adopted a statement of purpose calling for an end to racial criteria in the admission of people to schools, camps, hospitals, and other institutions affiliated with the Episcopal Church. The statement also called for support of Episcopalians working for integration.[51] Historian Charles W. Eagles argues that ESCRU immediately took a militant stand against segregation, and he maintains that it was the first national religious organization to endorse the lunch counter sit-ins.[52]

---

[50] "Delegates to the Youth Leadership Conference, Shaw University-Raleigh, N.C., April 15–17, 1960," 2 June 1960, Box 25, Folder 1, SNCC Papers, King Library of the Martin Luther King Jr. Center for Nonviolent Social Change, Atlanta, GA.

[51] Gardiner H. Shattuck, *Episcopalians and Race: Civil War to Civil Rights* (Lexington: The University Press of Kentucky, 2000), 100–101.

[52] Charles W. Eagles, *Outside Agitator: Jon Daniels and the Civil Rights Movement in Alabama* (Chapel Hill: University of North Carolina Press, 1993), 39–40.

While support for ESCRU was not unanimous among Episcopalians, it likely gave the president of the college, James Boyer, an additional basis for supporting student civil rights activism. Boyer was born on the campus of Saint Augustine's College in 1909, where his father taught and later became the school's first African American dean. The younger Boyer served as a professor of English at the college before serving in the United States Navy from 1942–1946. He was the Dean of the College from 1949–1955 before becoming the president, a position he held until 1967. But it was during his time working on his EdD in English at the University of Michigan that we get a glimpse into some of the ideas that would guide his leadership style. In a paper he wrote in 1949, titled "Teacher-Administrative Relationships," Boyer criticized Saint Augustine's first African American president, Dr. Harold L. Trigg, for his apparently autocratic leadership style. Boyer pointed out that the AAUP had challenged at least one of Trigg's decisions for dismissing a teacher without sufficient cause. What is even more telling for how Boyer would approach his eventual role as the president of Saint Augustine's is his criticism of Trigg's relationship with the students. Boyer claimed that under Trigg, students had become frustrated by the constant "Thou Shalt Nots" from the president, which caused them to become apathetic because any deviation from the established norms would lead to severe punishment or expulsion. Boyer cited another scholar, G. Robert Koopman, who argued that an effective administrator should "practice democratic techniques…push others into the foreground of acclaim and believe that as many as possible should have opportunities to take responsibility and exercise leadership."[53]

Even at private historically Black institutions, college presidents faced a dilemma over how to respond to the student-led sit-in movement. On the one hand, Boyer likely wanted to live up to his ideal of practicing "democratic techniques" and the belief that students should have an opportunity to exercise leadership. On the other hand, the sit-ins presented concerns that could potentially result in loss of funding from White donors

---

[53] James A. Boyer, "Teacher-Administrative Relationships," 3, 6, 10, unsorted box labeled "Dr. James Boyer Papers—Mrs. Emma Boyer Correspondence," James A. Boyer Papers, Prezell R. Robinson Library, Saint Augustine's University, Raleigh, NC; G. Robert Koopman, Alice Miel, and Paul J. Misner, *Democracy in School Administration* (New York: D. Appleton-Century Company, Inc., 1943), 3–4.

and African American alumni who may have believed the strategies were too radical. As 1963 graduate and three-sport athlete LaMonte Wyche (Sr.) points out, "It was a fine line" that the college administration had to walk in their response to the demonstrations.[54] One of the people closest to Boyer from a professional standpoint was Millie Dunn Veasey, who was executive secretary to the president during the period of the sit-ins. Veasey had served in the Woman's Army Corps during World War II and attended Saint Augustine's with GI Bill funding. She recalls that Boyer was not directly involved but never made any effort to discourage the students, which is reinforced by other Saint Augustine's former faculty and student interviewees.[55] Veasey was involved in the demonstrations and participated in marches but not sit-ins. She never feared losing her job if she discussed the protests with other faculty or with Boyer. She also discussed the protests with students, including her son Warren Veasey, who became the vice president of the Raleigh branch of the Congress of Racial Equality and a movement leader in the second wave of protests in 1963. Thus, Millie Dunn Veasey had a unique position, being close to both the college president and to one of the student leaders, and she acknowledges that the student-led groups were the most influential in the sit-in movement.[56]

Boyer did not take a strong leadership role in promoting integration in public accommodations, but faculty and students at Saint Augustine's College and Shaw University in the early 1960s gave him generally high ratings on the survey, which asked them to rank him from 1–10 based on whether he did all he could do within his power to improve conditions for African Americans in Raleigh.[57] According to student and faculty interviewees, the dean of the college, Dr. Prezell R. Robinson (who later became president), was more heavily involved. Wyche never forgot

---

[54] Lamont Wyche, phone interview by the author, digital recording, 29 June 2016.

[55] Millie Dunn Veasey, phone interview by the author, digital recording, 27 June 2016; Helen Chavis Othow, phone interview by the author, digital recording, 13 July 2016; Pete Cunningham, phone interview by the author, digital recording, 21 June 2016; Lamonte Wyche, phone interview by the author.

[56] Mille Dunn Veasey, phone interview by the author; Gene Roberts Jr., "A Look at the Negro Student: Thunder on the Campus: Protest on Mainstreet," *News and Observer*, 3 March 1963, section 3, p. 1.

[57] See appendix for composite survey results.

Robinson's reminders that "your first responsibility is to prepare." Whereas Robinson in this instance was not referring specifically to protests, these were words of wisdom that could be applied to the demonstrations. Wyche, who was co-captain of the basketball team, recalls a time when he discussed the student protests and mentioned his goal of a CIAA basketball championship to Robinson, and Wyche said Robinson's response was chilling and still resonates to this day. The dean's response was essentially, "Yes, maybe we will get our freedom and maybe we will win a championship, but if you don't keep your grades up, you won't be here to celebrate it."[58]

Most student protestors recognized that the demonstrations and their education were not mutually exclusive. Wyche recalls that student protestors viewed the demonstrations as part of their education. They would often write position papers in class about the movement and debate civil rights issues in their dormitories. Robinson did not discourage him from participating in civil rights activities or sports but merely reinforced that it all started with education. Robinson was not restricting Wyche's academic freedom, and indeed, according to Wyche, "academic freedom was assumed" among the students at Saint Augustine's. The administration encouraged them to *think*. Students were also encouraged by some famous visiting speakers such as Morehouse College president Benjamin Mays, who told them "You must think for yourself."[59] Implicit in the advice from Black educational leaders was that students must make their own choices about how to improve their own futures and those of their race.

The implicit support that the college administration gave to students at Saint Augustine's was like that at Shaw. On November 16, 1951, Dr. William Strassner was inaugurated as the president of Shaw. At his inauguration, former Shaw president W. S. Nelson stated that "the genius of a private institution of learning is to teach the truth, speak the truth without any fear of coercion."[60] Prior to becoming president, Strassner was the dean of religion. Seeking a replacement for the position he previously held,

---

[58] LaMonte Wyche, phone interview by the author. According to Wyche, he did not participate directly in sit-ins but did participate in a protest march and other civil rights activities.

[59] Wyche, phone interview by the author.

[60] Untitled article, *The Crisis*, 59, no. 1 (January 1952): 52.

in November 1952 he reached out to a twenty-two-year-old Boston University theology student, Martin Luther King Jr. Strassner had previously been a guest minister at Martin Luther King Sr.'s church in Atlanta. King Jr. was recommended to Strassner by Dr. Sankey Blanton, the president of Crozer Theological Seminary in Pennsylvania, from which King Jr. had received his Bachelor of Divinity degree.[61] One can only speculate on how the civil rights movement in Raleigh or Montgomery or Atlanta or, indeed, the United States of America may have been changed had King decided to accept the position of dean of religion at Shaw. King Jr. would ultimately come to Shaw in April 1960 for the conference organized by Ella Baker and sponsored by the Southern Christian Leadership Conference.

Perhaps no other action demonstrates Strassner's willingness to embrace civil rights activism more than when he allowed some of the most important civil rights leaders to meet on the campus. Strassner was given generally favorable responses on the survey asking if he did all in his power to produce positive changes for African Americans.[62] 1960 graduate Vivian McKay stated that the college administration's response to the sit-ins was one of "silent approval," and she felt that "they were just as excited about it as we were."[63] The student interviewees were in agreement that the college administration and most professors at Shaw favored the demonstrations.[64]

Some Shaw faculty members played a significant role in civil rights activism, and the one most mentioned by student interviewees was the eloquent, wise, and personable Dr. Grady Davis. Student leader David Forbes remembers Davis was humorous, and if someone asked him how

---

[61] William R. Strassner to Martin Luther King Jr., 18 November 1952, Box 117, Martin Luther King Jr. Papers Project.

[62] See appendix for survey.

[63] Vivian (McKay) Camm, interview by the author, digital recording, 27 April 2016, Lynchburg, VA.

[64] Camm, interview by the author; Carrie Gaddy Brock, interview by the author, digital recording, 2 March 2016, Raleigh, NC; Otis Tucker Jr., mail interview by the author, received 5 May 2016; David Forbes, interview by the author, digital recording, 13 April 2016, Raleigh, NC; McLouis Clayton, interview by the author, 2 March 2016, Raleigh, NC; Louis Powell, interview by the author, digital recording, 13 April 2016, Raleigh, NC.

he was doing, he might respond, "I am faculty, I have all my faculties, and I am highly functioning." Forbes recalls a time when Davis spoke at a meeting and said, "Folks always ask me what Negroes want...we want everything the white folks got. Even if they got some diseases that we don't have, we want them too."[65] 1962 graduate Louis Powell characterized Davis as a "true activist."[66] But even a highly respected advocate for civil rights like Davis acted more as a counselor and worked in an advisory role when it came to sit-ins. While student respondents do not recall Davis participating in sit-ins, he was at Cameron Village on February 13, 1960, the day after the forty-one students were arrested outside of the F. W. Woolworth store. Students continued their protests that day, resulting in two arrests, and police told Davis and his two passengers that they would have to leave the parking lot or face trespassing charges.[67]

Other faculty members also offered encouragement for the protests, and some even discussed them in class. The topic was most likely to be brought up in social science classes. 1961 Shaw graduate and student protest leader Albert Sampson recalls talking a lot about Black history in Charles Robson's class, in which Robson required students to read John Hope Franklin's classic historical work *From Slavery to Freedom*. Dr. Wilmoth Carter also discussed the protests in her classes and gave support to the student demonstrators. Another graduate reiterated that social science/history professors would discuss the protests and their historic nature. "That was right in keeping with history. They could see the far-reaching changes better than we could."[68]

In some cases, professors gave tangible support to the demonstrators. Education professor Elizabeth Coffield discussed the demonstrations and encouraged the students. Her husband James E. Coffield was a bail

---

[65] David Forbes, interview by the author, digital recording, 13 April 2016, Raleigh, NC.

[66] Louis Powell, interview by the author, digital recording, 13 April 2016, Raleigh, NC.

[67] "Village Official Orders Two More Students Arrested," *News and Observer*, 14 February 1960, 1, 2. The passengers with Davis were Dr. O. L. Sherrill and Rev. John W. Fleming.

[68] Albert Sampson, phone interview by the author, digital recording, 12 July 2016; Carrie Gaddy Brock, interview by the author.

bondsman and would bail the students out of jail.[69] At both historically Black private colleges in Raleigh, students received theoretical foundations, emotional and spiritual encouragement, and even practical support for their actions in the direct-action movement. Yet one point remained clear. This was a student-led movement, and the primary action and leadership remained with the students. As 1960 Shaw graduate McLouis Clayton noted, "Adults were supportive of the movement, but the students were the action people."[70] Just as the students understood that they were ultimately responsible for their own educational success, they also realized that they were the ones who needed to take the leadership role in local civil rights activity.

To understand the relation between civil rights activism and an expanded vision of academic freedom, one must account for the reality that many student demonstrators viewed their involvement in civil rights activities as part of their education. On a survey asking early 1960s "Protest Triangle" students to rate on a scale of 1–10 (with 1 = strongly disagree and 10 = strongly agree) based on the statement "Students viewed participation in the movement as a part of their education, and as a way of opening societal opportunities," the average response was 8.25.[71] The true value of education is not only obtaining knowledge but also developing the capacity to apply that knowledge in a variety of settings, including potential job opportunities. African American job opportunities were limited in both the public and private sector in the South and throughout much of America at the beginning of the 1960s. While the sit-ins were not necessarily directly aimed at improving job opportunities, the challenge to segregated seating at lunch counters was a step toward the destruction of a society deeply rooted in segregation. In some cases, protesting segregated eating facilities coincided with protests against hiring and employee promotion discrimination. Just as a student seeks high grades and a quality education largely to increase their opportunities, so were student demonstrators attempting to tear down barriers to societal and economic

---

[69] Albert Sampson, phone interview by the author; David Forbes, interview by the author; Carrie Gaddy Brock, interview by the author; "Village Official Orders Two More Students Arrested," 1, 2.

[70] McLouis Clayton, interview by the author.

[71] See appendix for survey.

opportunities.

Louis Powell was a Shaw student whose participation in the demonstrations had broader goals than simply being able to eat at a lunch counter. "I just wanted to see change. I wanted to see opportunities open for everyone."[72] He wanted to see further opportunities opened in state employment, as he felt that becoming a teacher was about the only practical option for an African American in North Carolina to obtain a decent job. Powell realized that Research Triangle Park was just opening up at that time. Perhaps no other project in North Carolina better demonstrated the potential that the combined resources of state and local governments, the business community, and important educational institutions could bring for job opportunities in the Triangle. And no other group of people was more influential in eventually opening those types of opportunities than the students who initiated a more aggressive challenge to segregation. Powell recalls that those "industries that were coming in [were] offering tremendous opportunities to people, but those opportunities were not open to blacks. I just felt like we deserved or had earned the right to be considered for activities there also."[73]

For those students at the "Protest Triangle" schools who viewed civil rights demonstrations as part of their education, any attempt to thwart those activities could conceivably be viewed as an attack on their academic freedom. At the two private historically Black colleges in Raleigh with primarily Black faculty and administration, it might be expected that student participation would not be discouraged. Vivian McKay (Camm) said that she "could not conceive of the college telling us not to" participate in civil rights demonstrations.[74] Fellow Shaw graduate Carrie Gaddy (Brock) said that "academic freedom played a big part because the president viewed us as young adults capable of making our own decisions."[75]

The students at the HBCUs who showed tremendous organization and discipline in the 1960 sit-ins were indeed capable of making their own decisions about movement strategies and goals. They had taken the

---

[72] Louis Powell, interview by the author.

[73] Powell, interview by the author.

[74] Vivian Camm, interview by the author.

[75] Carrie Gaddy Brock, interview by the author.

primary leadership role in the local movements, and their actions received support from national groups that defended academic freedom, such as the AAUP. The student protestors' actions also mobilized support from some students and faculty at the Research Triangle schools, many of whom defended the students' right to protest as part of their academic freedom. Whereas the student protestors appreciated the encouragement and counseling from respected professors and college officials on their own campuses and beyond, they realized the movement was student-led. At the historic conference on the campus of Shaw University in April 1960, students from the "Protest Triangle" and many other schools in the South would make important decisions on the future strategy of the movement. For nine weeks, Shaw had been the hub of civil rights activism in Raleigh. And for three days in the heart of spring, it would be the epicenter of a blossoming regional and national movement.

Chapter 4

The "Protest Triangle" and the 1960 Youth Leadership Conference at Shaw University

The late winter of 1960 was an exceptionally cold and snowy time in Raleigh and other parts of North Carolina. Shaw University student Carrie Gaddy (Brock) recalls that the snow and ice did not deter the students from making the trek downtown to participate in sit-ins. She remembers when a White bystander set a few bullets on the lunch counter where the Black students sat.[1] Similar incidents of intimidation toward Black protestors were common, as were verbal assaults. The sit-ins came to Raleigh on February 10, 1960, nine days after the brave actions of the "Greensboro Four" and two days after they had spread to Durham stores. An egg flew across the room at the lunch counter at F. W. Woolworth in Raleigh and splattered on several of the African American students, yet they remained unfazed. According to the *News and Observer*, approximately 150 students from Shaw and Saint Augustine's College participated in the demonstrations that day at seven stores in downtown Raleigh and at the Woolworth store in Cameron Village, a shopping center approximately three miles from the Shaw campus in downtown Raleigh. Students from all three of

---

[1] Carrie Gaddy Brock, interview by the author, digital recording, 2 March 2016, Raleigh, NC.

the "Protest Triangle" schools participated in Raleigh that day, as Samuel T. Gibson, a North Carolina College at Durham (NCC) student visiting a friend at Saint Augustine's, also joined in the protests.[2]

Students from "Protest Triangle" schools were instrumental in pushing the sit-in movement forward in North Carolina in 1960. Several students also participated in the historic conference at Shaw on Easter weekend in April. But the conference that ultimately led to the creation of the Student Nonviolent Coordinating Committee did not represent the beginning of their activism. This chapter shows that a burgeoning student leadership had already emerged at the "Protest Triangle" schools prior to the conference, and that the strategies and philosophies discussed at the conference mostly reinforced those that had already been promoted by student leadership at Shaw, Saint Augustine's, and NCC. Perhaps the most newsworthy aspect of the conference was the presence of several established civil rights leaders, including Martin Luther King Jr., Ella Baker, and James Lawson. But more importantly, the conference was emblematic of the fact that in 1960, it was students from HBCUs who pushed the movement forward most forcefully. The conference was indispensable in establishing connections among activists in North Carolina and throughout the South, and it emboldened student leaders who by April 1960 were already becoming the heart of the civil rights movement.

From an ideological and moral standpoint, students from historically Black college campuses acted to counter established local and state political leadership who generally supported segregation. And in a literal sense, as student participants in Raleigh proceeded from Saint Augustine's College and Shaw University to segregated eating establishments downtown and in Cameron Village, they went from campus to counter.

The lunch counters at all the places in which sit-ins occurred on February 10 in Raleigh were temporarily closed. The students continued their protests the following morning, and downtown stores followed different strategies to get them to leave. At S. H. Kress, about fifteen students sat at the lunch counter, which was in the basement of the larger store. Employees turned off the lights and the demonstrators left. The lunch

---

[2] Charles Craven and David Cooper, "Student Sitdown Strike Spreads to Stores Here," *News and Observer*, 11 February 1960, 1, 23.

counters at F. W. Woolworth, Walgreen's Drug Store, and McLellan's on
Fayetteville Street remained closed from the previous day, and at
Walgreen's a large sign read, "Closed in the Interest of Public Safety,"
mirroring a common sign throughout the segregated South in the coming
months.[3]

Most protest activity in Raleigh in 1960 occurred in the downtown
stores on Fayetteville Street, a street bookended by the state capitol and
the Memorial Auditorium, which is adjacent to the Shaw University campus. But one of the most important events in the history of the sit-ins came
at Cameron Village in Raleigh on Friday, February 12, 1960. Protestors
from Shaw University and Saint Augustine's College had staged sit-in
demonstrations at the F. W. Woolworth store the previous two days, but
the arrests on February 12 came mostly on the sidewalk around the store.
William Worth, the vice president of Cameron Village, Inc., stated that
he asked the students to leave and proceeded to flag down a passing police
patrol wagon. Worth said the group of protestors was orderly, but he asked
them to leave as a matter of public safety. "I simply asked them to leave
the private premises of Cameron Village.... I do the same thing with white
youths when they congregate in front of the drug store."[4] Shaw student
Cornell Adams maintained that he was making a phone call from a phone
booth in front of Woolworth when he was told he had two minutes to
leave the area. Adams was heading toward a street when an officer arrested
him and told him his "two minutes were up." Police arrested forty-one
protestors on February 12, but protests continued the following day with
picketing outside of the segregated stores and two more arrests for trespassing.[5]

The forty-one arrests on February 12 were the first arrests in North
Carolina in 1960 related to student-led civil rights demonstrations. The

---

[3] Charles Craven, "Sitdown Scene Peaceful: Lunch Counters Closed," *News and Observer*, 12 February 1960, 1, 2.

[4] Raleigh (AP), "Raleigh Hits Sitdown Moves with Arrest of 41 Negroes: Students Charged with Trespassing," *Durham Morning Herald*, 13 February 1960, 1;
Charles Craven, "Police Arrest 41 in Raleigh Demonstrations: Trespassing Is Charged
in Village," *News and Observer*, 13 February 1960, 1, 2.

[5] "Village Official Orders Two More Students Arrested," *News and Observer*,
14 February 1960, 1, 2.

strategy of "filling the jails" was not generally employed in Raleigh in the 1960 demonstrations, in contrast to the larger demonstrations that emerged in greater strength throughout North Carolina and the South in 1963. Yet the arrests were significant to the movement even in 1960, as many students viewed an arrest as a "badge of honor" and a symbol of their commitment to the cause of freedom. Glenford E. Mitchell, a student protestor and editor of the *Shaw Journal* campus newspaper, wrote in 1962 that "when our few on the Shaw University campus got together and decided to add our bit to the history of the movement, we had no idea that our actions would transform the jails of the South from dungeons of shame to havens of honor."[6] Carrie Gaddy Brock recalls that for her Shaw classmates who participated in the movement, "jail was not a dirty word."[7]

The student participants had been taught by their parents most of their lives that they should never go to jail, but the sit-ins had brought a new perspective. As Saint Augustine's College graduate Pete Cunningham recollected, "That year was a break from the past." Challenging unjust laws and social practices was a key aspect of civil disobedience. Yet college students in Raleigh generally did their best to avoid jail in the 1960 demonstrations. Cunningham recalled that in the instances in which store managers called the police, demonstrators would leave when asked to do so by police. Even Shaw student protest leader David Forbes was only arrested once for his involvement in the demonstrations.[8]

The February 12 arrests were also important in strengthening an emerging group of student leaders from Shaw and Saint Augustine's. One of the most important student leaders in Raleigh was 1962 Shaw graduate David Forbes. Forbes attended the historic conference at Shaw in April 1960 that ultimately led to the creation of the Student Nonviolent Coordinating Committee (SNCC) and was one of the two initial North Carolina student representatives of SNCC, along with Charles Jones of

---

[6] Glenford E. Mitchell, "College Students Take Over," in Glenford E. Mitchell and William H. Peace, eds., *The Angry Black South* (New York: Corinth Books, 1962), 75.

[7] Carrie Gaddy Brock, interview by the author.

[8] Pete Cunningham, phone interview by the author, digital recording, 21 June 2016; David Forbes, interview by the author, digital recording, 13 April 2016, Raleigh, NC.

Johnson C. Smith University in Charlotte. But even before the conference at Shaw, Forbes had emerged as a dynamic leader in the student movement in Raleigh.[9]

While SNCC became a crucial organization in promoting sit-ins in the early 1960s, it did not even exist during the initial wave of sit-ins in North Carolina and was considered a temporary organization until October 1960. It is much more accurate to assert that the somewhat amorphous yet determined leadership that emerged among student protestors at HBCUs provided the initial foundation for SNCC rather than vice versa. Forbes attended three SNCC conferences in 1960, but his primary contribution to the movement remained as a leader in Raleigh. Historian Peter Ling has pointed out that the minor scholarly attention given to Forbes is not commensurate with his repeated presence at SNCC conferences because he forged a local career in Raleigh. Ling maintains that "the vast majority of individuals who attended SNCC events did not remain active within SNCC or emerge as nationally acknowledged protest figures more generally."[10] The lack of scholarly attention on Forbes is likely due to a tendency among some scholars (but certainly not all, as Ling's work demonstrates) to focus on studies of organizations and their impact on the movement. Any analysis of an individual such as Forbes should emphasize the significance he had in the local movement and the effect that a wide variety of individuals had on him, rather than simply attributing his significance to belonging to a famous organization.

Student athletes were often used as a defense against potential violence directed at protestors. Leslie Camm and Otis Tucker Jr. had been co-captains of the football team at Dunbar High School in Lynchburg, Virginia, and part of the reason they came to Shaw was to play football. Even though protestors were expected to remain nonviolent, the presence of football players could help deter angry Whites from inflicting physical violence on the demonstrators. Forbes recalled that "we got the football

---

[9] "Delegates to Youth Leadership Conference," 2 June 1960, Box 25, Folder 1, SNCC Papers, Martin Luther King Jr. Center for Nonviolent Social Change.

[10] Peter Ling, "SNCCs: Not One Committee, but Several," in Iwan Morgan and Philip Davies, eds., *From Sit-Ins to SNCC: The Student Civil Rights Movement in the 1960s* (Gainesville: University Press of Florida, 2012), 89.

team to be our buffer" at the protests.[11] Fellow 1962 Shaw graduate Louis Powell remembered that "it always made you feel a little bit better to be in the group when you had an offensive lineman from the football team there or the linebackers there, somebody at 310 or 290, that helped a whole lot. When I went to McLellan's to sit-in at the booth there, if I had somebody 290 pounds there with me, I'd feel pretty good."[12] Saint Augustine's students had a much longer walk to get downtown than those from Shaw. Students from "St. Aug" often walked in a pattern in which the women were in the middle of a row or on the inside (away from potential attackers) on their way to Shaw or to downtown stores.[13]

The strategic ways in which demonstrators marched downtown was not unique to Raleigh. On February 6 in Greensboro, the North Carolina A&T football team, with American flags in hand, "formed a flying wedge" that moved through groups of White hecklers to pave the way for activists to reach the lunch counters.[14] Evidently a White youth asked the demonstrators, "Who do you think you are?" One football player responded, "We the Union Army." Historian Iwan Morgan acknowledges that the army reference may not be a perfect metaphor for a nonviolent movement but contends that the response linked the past to the present. Morgan contends that "just as the Confederacy ultimately had to concede defeat to a militarily superior foe, the segregationist South's failure to suppress the sit-in protests ultimately ensured its own defeat by a morally superior foe."[15] Furthermore, the actions of the football teams from North Carolina A&T, Saint Augustine's, and Shaw revealed that African American men were displaying a manhood that was often stripped from them throughout American history.

Otis Tucker Jr. was among the football players arrested on February

---

[11] Vivian (McKay) Camm, interview by the author, digital recording, 27 April 2016, Lynchburg, VA; David Forbes, interview by the author.

[12] Louis Powell, interview by the author, digital recording, 13 April 2016, New Hill, NC.

[13] *Let Us March On: Raleigh's Journey Toward Civil Rights* (Raleigh: Raleigh City Museum, 2000), 32.

[14] Simon Hall, "The Sit-Ins, SNCC, and Cold War Patriotism," in Morgan and Davies, eds., *From Sit-Ins to SNCC*, 137.

[15] Morgan, "The New Movement: The Student Sit-Ins in 1960," in Morgan and Davies, eds., 18.

12 and he continued with the protests in the weeks following his arrest. He was at the scene when Otis Clark was struck with a chain on February 17 and witnessed Clark respond with a devastating punch to the White offender. Tucker recalls that the White man got the worst of the altercation and was the one who was arrested.[16] The twenty-five-year-old White man, who had a previous arrest for an altercation with his mother-in-law, was sentenced to sixty days for the incident with Clark. Tom Ellis, the judge who sentenced the man, stated that "the time has not come yet when the white citizens of this town must act as vigilantes and take the law into their own hands."[17] The judge's statement is notable in two regards: in one sense, he seems to imply that there *may* come a point when White vigilantes should take the law into their own hands. On the other hand, it is quite remarkable that Clark was not charged and the White man was. It is difficult to imagine such an outcome in any state in the Deep South. Regardless of the court verdict, Clark continued in the protest movement. His reaction to the chain incident was not consistent with the nonviolent approach of the student movement in Raleigh, which otherwise maintained its nonviolent discipline. Indeed, the previous day, a female protestor was slapped by a White man. One of the student leaders evidently had to talk some football players out of retaliating.[18] For student leaders, the lack of retaliation did not reveal a lack of courage but rather a strong show of discipline.

While some male protestors demonstrated their manhood, female protestors proved that they were capable of social activism in a public setting. More than a third of those arrested on February 12 in Raleigh were women. Many women took leadership roles in planning, and women were heavily involved in the demonstrations. 1961 Shaw graduate Vivian McKay (who later married 1962 graduate Leslie Camm) served as a demonstrator and organizer. She participated in two sit-ins, including one at Kress in which an egg was tossed and landed near her. She recalls that when the student protestors arrived, store employees would have a look on

---

[16] Otis Tucker, Jr., mail interview by the author, received 5 May 2016.

[17] "Student's Attacker Gets 60-Day Term," *News and Observer*, 19 February 1960, 1, 22.

[18] "Students Carrying Signs Picket at Raleigh Stores," *News and Observer*, 17 February 1960, 1; Mitchell, *Angry Black South*, 77.

their faces as if to suggest, "Here they come again." After the egg incident, she chose not to participate in more sit-ins, out of concern she would fight back if provoked. She was invigorated that the students took action, and her decision to stay away from the sit-ins did not mean she was completely removed from the movement, as she continued to help organize and make protest placards. While most of the participants agree that there was no coercion for students to become involved, there was some social pressure. Vivian remembered social pressure to become involved because Shaw was such a small, close-knit campus and the students were "buzzing" about the movement. "If you were not involved, you were not a part of the conversation" at dances and other social events.[19] Civil rights demonstrations unified the student body at Shaw and Saint Augustine's like no other force.

A system of "reciprocity" existed between Shaw University and Saint Augustine's College both in academic cooperation between the colleges and also among civil rights activists. The institutions had a "reciprocal arrangement" in which certain classes at either institution were open to students from the other.[20] And a type of reciprocity existed between civil rights activists at the two schools as well. On the night prior to her February 12 arrest, freshman Barbara Woodhouse and a group of other Saint Augustine's students met at Shaw to plan the following day's events. They agreed on how to dress and behave, a common practice throughout the era of the sit-ins in Raleigh and elsewhere. Saint Augustine's students often went to Shaw prior to the demonstrations to review strategy. Students commonly referred to their movement as the "Shaw-Saint Augustine's Student Movement." Several different committees existed, including the aptly named "Intelligence Committee," an idea advanced by Shaw student Cornell Adams. The group included five students from Shaw and four from Saint Augustine's. Shaw Student Council president Albert Hockaday took on a significant leadership role in the first few weeks of the sit-ins. He distributed blank forms to students on which they indicated when they had free time. The early leadership in the Raleigh movement was not elected but rather came into being after the second day of demonstrations

---

[19] Vivian Camm, interview by the author.
[20] *Saint Augustine's College Ninety-Third Catalogue, 1959–1960* 65, no. 3, 38.

in Raleigh (February 11).[21] Despite several important figures in the student movement in Raleigh, there was no clear, undisputed leader on either of the historically Black campuses in early 1960.

The sit-in movement in Durham was like Raleigh in the sense that the backbone of the movement came from African American students. The bulk of the protestors were from NCC, but students from Durham Business College, Hillside High School, and DeShazor Beauty School (which apparently gave extra credit to students who participated) also took part in the demonstrations.[22] Among the most essential protest leaders from NCC were Lacy Streeter, Robert Kornegay, and Callis Brown. Kornegay was the Student Government President for 1959–1960, a position that Streeter would hold the following year. These three students were instrumental in organizing the initial 1960 sit-ins in Durham on February 8. The plan for the sit-ins was advanced at a meeting at the "Freshman Bowl" on the NCC campus. At the meeting, the detailed plans for the demonstrations were revealed, stating that the protestors would adhere to nonviolence and accept any abuse from opponents. Streeter assured the students that the protests would get results. He claimed that the sit-ins would be "hurting the cash register, and when you hurt the cash register, you are bound to get results."[23]

On February 8, seventeen NCC students and three White Duke University students conducted a sit-in at Woolworth's until the counter was "closed in the interest of public safety." From there they went to Kress, which closed minutes after their arrival. When the students went to Walgreen's, they found the seats filled by Whites, and the group returned to NCC.[24] After the demonstrations, Kornegay stated that "this thing has been planned for some time and these groups have just come into the picture recently."[25] Kornegay was referring to the National Association for

---

[21] Mitchell, *Angry Black South*, 75–79.

[22] Christina Greene, *Our Separate Ways: Women and the Black Freedom Movement in Durham, North Carolina* (Chapel Hill: The University of North Carolina Press, 2005), 78.

[23] Willie G. Hall, "Students Stage Sit-Down Protest: Results Unknown on Negotiations," *Campus Echo* (North Carolina College at Durham) 19, no. 6 (26 February 1960): 1, 4.

[24] Hall, "Students Stage Sit-Down Protest," 4.

[25] Bill Frue and George Lugee, "Woolworth and Kress Close Lunch Counters

the Advancement of Colored People (NAACP), the Congress of Racial
Equality (CORE), and the Durham Committee on Negro Affairs
(DCNA). Whereas the February sit-ins in Greensboro were not organized
by established civil rights organizations, there had been discussion of the
tactic at statewide NAACP meetings prior to the emergence of protests in
1960. In the fall of 1959, participants at a statewide NAACP youth conference urged adult leadership to take a more aggressive approach to integration and even discussed "sit-down strikes in eating places such as bus
and train stations and dime stores." But at a late January 1960 NAACP
meeting, the adult leadership decided voter registration would be their focus for the year.[26] Thus, even though the sit-ins were seemingly sponta-
neous student demonstrations sprouting from Greensboro, there is evidence to suggest that had the "Greensboro Four" not initiated the new
phase in the movement, students from other Black colleges might have
pushed ahead with the sit-ins.

After the initial 1960 sit-ins in Durham on February 8, there was not
another in the city for nearly three weeks. Protestors gave a chance for an
agreement to be worked out between an NCC committee and the Durham
Human Relations Committee. Lacy Streeter said that the demonstrations
continued in late February because students did not expect much to come
of the negotiations and decided that they would "chart their own course of
action in the protest."[27] The failure of city leadership and Black adult leadership to negotiate a settlement with business leaders and a resumption of
sit-ins was a common pattern in many cities in 1960, a pattern that would
reemerge in the following four years. Student leaders were rarely represented at these meetings, and when they were, it was not in proportion to
their influence in the movement for integrated public accommodations.
As in most other cities in which sit-ins occurred, the primary student leadership did not just give instructions but participated in the demonstrations
themselves, inviting the same dangers and insults faced by other participants. On February 29, Callis Brown was spit on by a White girl, who was

---

Temporarily: Two Stores Open for Other Sales," *Durham Morning Herald*, 9 February 1960, 1.

[26] Greene, *Our Separate Ways*, 76.

[27] "Student Demonstrations Continue in Durham: Picket Stores: Negotiators Get
Statement Ready," *Carolina Times*, 5 March 1960, 1.

summarily arrested for assault and battery, another indicator that police in the Triangle were fairer than those in the Deep South.[28]

The movements in Raleigh and Durham shared many similarities, and in some cases there was interaction between activists in the two cities. Both cities had active NAACP branches, and the HBCUs had college chapters. Lacy Streeter was the president of the NCC chapter of the NAACP. This put him in contact with NAACP executive secretary Roy Wilkins and afforded Streeter many opportunities to extend his influence beyond Durham. In mid-March, he attended a conference with leaders of the organization in New York City. On the same trip, he spoke to students in Syracuse, New York, and was one of those to speak in front of over two thousand people at a mass rally in Detroit, Michigan.[29] Two weeks prior to the trip, Streeter appeared on NBC's *Today Show* on March 1 to show support for the demonstrations. Streeter stood in stark contrast to another member of the panel, Raleigh lawyer and staunch segregationist I. Beverly Lake. The show aired on the same day that Lake launched his bid for governor of North Carolina.[30] It was a rare moment, one in which perhaps the most outspoken voice for segregation in North Carolina in 1960 was in the room with an influential student leader who represented the student demonstrators.

Both Raleigh and Durham had eloquent and effective student protest leaders. But the movement in Durham was distinct from Raleigh in 1960 in some ways. For one, the students in Durham received a higher degree of support in the form of participation of White students, especially those from Duke University and even from the University of North Carolina at Chapel Hill (UNC). Four White Duke students participated in the first 1960 sit-ins in Durham on February 8. When sit-ins hit the Howard Johnson's restaurant on the Chapel Hill Boulevard on March 2, ten of the approximately thirty protestors were White students from Duke and

---

[28] Bill Frue, "Two White Teenagers Are Arrested in Sitdown Here: Negroes Picket Stores," *Durham Morning Herald*, 1 March 1960, 1.

[29] "Streeter Makes Northern Tour," *Campus Echo* 19, no. 7 (31 March 1960): 7.

[30] New York (UPI), "On Television Program: Lake Sees Chaos and Confusion if Restaurants Are Integrated," *News and Observer*, 2 March 1960, 10; Charles Clay, "Lake to Run: Sounds Segregationist Theme," *News and Observer*, 2 March 1960, 1.

UNC.[31] When forty-six protestors were arrested for trespassing after refusing to leave S. H. Kress in Durham on May 6, thirty-two were NCC students, four were sympathetic African American citizens, and ten were Duke students. Trespassing arrests due to sit-ins on May 11 at the same Kress store included three Duke students as well.[32] The importance of participation by White students was not limited to the increase in the actual numbers of protestors. Just as Black students challenged the myth that African Americans were content with segregation, White student involvement shattered the myth of a monolithic Southern White population that favored segregation.

Durham was also distinct from Raleigh in the sense that it had sit-ins prior to the emergence of sit-in demonstrations as a regional movement in 1960. While the 1957 sit-ins at the Royal Ice Cream Parlor in Durham have already been discussed, it is important to reiterate that many prominent African Americans in the city did not fully support those demonstrations. The DCNA did not support these initial sit-ins. As historian Christina Greene points out, the NCC chapter of the NAACP was unhappy with the DCNA's refusal to support a publicity campaign against segregated theaters in 1958.[33] While the DCNA was an important organization in promoting the rights of African American citizens, there were reasons for students to be critical of its lack of urgency in some instances. The ideological and moral force of the sit-ins in Durham in 1960 was too clear for the committee to ignore.

An important factor in pushing the DCNA toward supporting the activities of the sit-ins was the visit to Durham by the Reverends Martin Luther King Jr. and Ralph Abernathy. The Reverend Douglass Moore of Asbury Temple Methodist Church in Durham was instrumental in getting the two men to come to the city. A crowd of twelve hundred to fifteen hundred crowded into the White Rock Baptist Church for a rally on February 16. Reverend Moore addressed the crowd and asked them to be part

---

[31] John Langston, "30 White and Negro Students Join in Demonstration—Invade Howard Johnson's," *Durham Sun*, 2 March 1960, 1A.

[32] George Lugee, "46 Arrested Here at Kress' Lunch Counter," *Durham Morning Herald*, 7 May 1960, 1, 12; "Cops Arrest 57 Here in Food Service Case," *Durham Morning Herald*, 12 May 1960, 1.

[33] Greene, *Our Separate Ways*, 75.

of a "mass and mammoth attack on segregation."[34] Moore also asked how many of the people at the rally would be willing to forego new Easter outfits to help finance the work of challenging segregation. Moore asked people to stand up if they were willing to support a boycott of the stores that maintained segregated lunch counters. Nearly all stood up.[35] In addition to the call for a boycott, the most important part of the day's activities was the support given for the student sit-ins in North Carolina and throughout the South. King began his speech by saying, "Victor Hugo once said that there is nothing in all the world more powerful than an idea whose time has come." King continued, stating that "you students of North Carolina have captured this dynamic idea in a marvelous manner. You have taken the undying and passionate yearning for freedom and filtered it into your own soul and fashioned it into a creative protest that is destined to be one of the glowing epics of our time." Thus, even in the early stages of the sit-ins, King recognized the historic nature of the protests and their importance to the broader struggle for Black freedom. He also urged the demonstrators to "not fear going to jail. We must say we are willing and prepared to fill up the jails of the South."[36] Thus, from an early point in the new phase of the movement, King demonstrated his willingness to support an aggressive strategy that the young activists had put into practice.

Yet the demographics of the crowd at White Rock Baptist Church on February 16 were somewhat revealing. According to the *News and Observer* of Raleigh, most of the crowd was thirty years old or older.[37] These may indeed have been the people who needed direction from King to support the student sit-ins. The student demonstrators had already

---

[34] "King Leads Rally, Urges Nonviolent Crusade: Negroes Hint of Boycott Here," *Durham Sun*, 17 March 1960, 1, 2.

[35] "King Leads Rally, Urges Nonviolent Crusade," 1, 2; "King Stresses Non-Violence in Lunch Counter Sitdowns," *Durham Morning Herald*, 17 February 1960, 1, 2.

[36] Martin Luther King Jr., "A Creative Protest: American Students in the Struggle for Freedom," speech given in Durham, NC, 16 February 1960, Series 3, Box 1, Folder: "A Creative Protest," King Papers, King Library of the Martin Luther King Jr. Center for Nonviolent Social Change, Atlanta, GA.

[37] Gene Roberts Jr., "Negro Leader Urges Students to Continue Segregation Protest," *News and Observer*, 17 February 1960, 1, 2.

committed to the new strategy, and the forty-three protestors in Raleigh had already been arrested. While King's support for the sit-ins was significant, one should not overemphasize his role in sustaining the direct-action tactics of the 1960 sit-ins. It was a student-led movement that gained support and encouragement from important and well-known civil rights leaders such as King and Abernathy, not vice versa.

King's visit to Durham was significant in revealing the ways in which segregated businesses were attempting to limit media coverage of demonstrations. On February 16, King and Abernathy toured dime stores in downtown Durham where sit-ins occurred and had their pictures taken. A manager at one of the stores demanded that they leave. A store employee made a rush at one of the cameramen, and he ran away from his pursuer. Sensing the volatile situation, King and Abernathy left the scene. A cameraman was on his way out the door when a policeman attempted to confiscate his camera. An African American cameraman was initially detained by police and store officials until an African American lawyer advised them that his film could not be confiscated without a warrant. A *Durham Morning Herald* photographer was chased for nearly a block by a store official until he reached the safety of the *Herald* office.[38]

King's visit to Durham brought further attention to the sit-ins in the Triangle and North Carolina. The store employees realized King's influence in increasing media coverage of the movement. On February 16, some of the news media covering King's visit were literally on the run. In a figurative sense, the new aggressiveness of challenging segregation sparked by the 1960 sit-ins revealed that proponents of segregation would be on the run in the coming years. The die-hard proponents of segregation would dig in their heels, but many previous supporters of segregation began to increasingly question its ethical and practical implications.[39]

The pressure to reconcile the ostensible American ideals of equality and freedom with Southern traditions that rejected these values was mounting in early 1960. That pressure grew due to an increasingly

---

[38] Roberts, "Negro Leader Urges Students to Continue Segregation Protest," 1, 2.

[39] Roberts, "Negro Leader Urges Students to Continue Segregation Protest," 1, 2; David Forbes, interview by the author.

aggressive generation of activists who were nascent yet inspired, youthful but wise, idealistic but logical. These young activists would begin to solidify their goals and strategies when Dr. King returned to the Triangle in the middle of April for the historic conference at Shaw University.

Reverend Douglas Moore had been instrumental in getting King to come to Durham in February 1960. The primary organizer of the 1957 sit-ins in Durham, Moore also played a prominent role in the development of leadership that resulted from the new wave of sit-ins in North Carolina and throughout the South. On February 21, 1960, Moore hosted at his home approximately thirty students from historically Black colleges in Raleigh, Durham, Fayetteville, and Greensboro. Moore reported a bomb threat to his Asbury Temple Methodist Church by a woman claiming to be a member of the Ku Klux Klan, a threat that was likely the result of the meeting at Moore's home. While the students agreed at the meeting to continue the protests until they were successful, Moore said the strategy would be left up to the local leaders in each city. The participants agreed that they would "adopt the technique of nonviolent resistance as our primary method of protest and persuasion to win converts to the causes of equality and opportunity, freedom of assembly and freedom of speech on a nondiscriminatory basis in every avenue of life in our native land."[40] In many ways, the meeting at Moore's home was a precursor to the larger meeting of students at Shaw University from April 15–17.

The primary organizer of the April 15–17 meeting at Shaw was Ella Baker. By 1960, she had decades of activism and organizing experience. In 1931, Baker was elected to serve as the national director of the Young Negroes' Cooperative League (YNCL), a coalition of cooperatives and buying clubs that were part of a loose network of councils throughout the country. In her excellent biography on Baker, Barbara Ransby points out that the YNCL, whose founding statement included an emphasis on gender equality and the principle that young people should be in the forefront of the struggle for social change, represented the type of grassroots democracy and group-centered leadership that Ella Baker advocated throughout

---

[40] "Negro Leaders to Continue Café Segregation Protests," *Durham Morning Herald*, 23 February 1960, 2.

her career.[41] In 1936, Baker began a stint with the Workers Education Project of the Works Progress Administration, where she sought to make consumer education available to African Americans. Her approach to consumer education in the 1930s might well have applied equally to the students at the historically Black colleges who participated in the sit-ins: "the aim is not education for its own sake, but education that leads to self-directed action."[42] In the 1940s, Baker worked for the NAACP. Ransby contends that the organization's lack of mass mobilizations and grassroots organizing led her to resign her position.[43]

At the time that Baker was organizing the meeting of student leaders to be held at Shaw, she was the executive director of the Southern Christian Leadership Conference. In this position, she was arguably the third-ranking official in the organization behind King and Abernathy. But by early 1960, Baker had already planned to leave the organization, largely based on her differences of opinion with King and her concern that SCLC failed to operate as a "group-centered leadership, rather than a leadership-centered group."[44] Perhaps Baker's words from 1968 best exemplify her approach: "I never worked for an organization but for a cause."[45]

In early 1960, Baker knew that student activists had greatly contributed to the cause of Black freedom and that they should play the prominent role in determining the direction of the movement. Thus, when she came to Raleigh and Durham on March 16, 1960, to work on agreements for the student conference, she had a conviction that students retain their autonomy. This conviction was shared by a young NCC and Boston University graduate, Douglas Moore. At a meeting of Baker, Moore, and a White member of the Fellowship of Reconciliation, the three decided that adults would serve mostly in an advisory capacity at the Shaw meeting and "speak only when asked to do so."[46] Thus, as the planning for the meeting

---

[41] Barbara Ransby, *Ella Baker and the Black Freedom Movement: A Radical Democratic Vision* (Chapel Hill: University of North Carolina Press, 2003), 83.

[42] Ransby, *Ella Baker and the Black Freedom Movement*, 91, 93, 95.

[43] Ransby, *Ella Baker and the Black Freedom Movement*, 142.

[44] Joanne Grant, *Ella Baker: Freedom Bound* (New York: John Wiley and Sons, Inc., 1998), 123.

[45] Ransby, *Ella Baker and the Black Freedom* Movement, 209.

[46] Ella Baker memorandum to Dr. Martin Luther King Jr. and Rev. Ralph Abernathy, 23 March 1960, Box 32, Folder 10, SCLC Papers, Martin Luther King Jr.

at Shaw was taking place, Baker demonstrated her commitment to allowing students to take the leadership role in the conference.

While Baker's goal for a youth-centered conference formed the foundation for her strategy, she began the important task of working out practical details. She secured $800 from SCLC, no small amount for a relatively new organization that had been established in 1957. She also secured Raleigh's Memorial Auditorium, a literal stone's throw from the edge of the Shaw campus, for the public mass meeting on April 16. The mass meeting was co-sponsored by the Raleigh Citizens Association (RCA), a group that was revitalized in the wake of the student sit-ins. The executive secretary of the RCA was the dynamic dean of the Shaw school of religion, Dr. Grady Davis. Baker spoke with Davis and Shaw President William Strassner regarding the details of the conference. Baker also noted in her March 23, 1960, memorandum to King and Abernathy that the Dean of Saint Augustine's College (Prezell Robinson) and the student leadership pledged to cooperate on housing for the conference. Ultimately, several of the participants also lodged at the Bloodworth Street YMCA.[47]

Just as Saint Augustine's had been a wise choice for the 1959 conference that ultimately produced the Episcopal Society for Cultural and Racial Unity, Shaw was a logical choice for the April 1960 conference due to the relatively lower concern over violence that might come if it were held in the Deep South. Shaw was the oldest historically Black campus in the South and played a prominent role in the student sit-ins in Raleigh. Additionally, Raleigh was centrally located to pull students from Southern and Northern schools. But perhaps the biggest consideration for Baker was that she was a Shaw alumna. She graduated in 1927 as class valedictorian and was one of two students who spoke at the commencement.[48] Baker had connections with citizens in Raleigh, and she ultimately lodged with fellow Shaw alumna Effie Yeargan, one of the founders of the RCA.[49]

Center for Nonviolent Social Change, Atlanta, GA.

[47] Baker memorandum to King and Abernathy. In the SCLC document cited here, Ella Baker references "Mr. Alexander, Business Manager." This was a minor error on her part, as the Business Manager at Shaw University was John V. Anderson. See *The Bear*, Shaw University Yearbook, 1961, p. 15.

[48] Ransby, *Ella Baker and the Black Freedom Movement*, 63.

[49] Grant, *Ella Baker*, 127.

One of the most important aspects of planning the conference centered on whom to invite, and Baker invited several student government presidents from HBCUs. She also scanned newspaper accounts and wrote to student leaders. Among many others, the list included all of the "Greensboro Four" group, as well as NCC students Lacy Streeter and Callis Brown.[50] Baker sent a letter to potential student participants asking that they send a brief account of eight to ten pages describing the protest activities that had occurred at their college and in their communities.[51] As always, Baker took into account the various personal and community stories that were shaping the movement for Black freedom. Throughout her work as a civil rights organizer, she demonstrated a concern for the activists who carried the movement. These qualities would serve her well at the Youth Leadership Conference on Nonviolent Resistance held at Shaw University.

For nearly a century, the Shaw campus had been the site of an institution that improved the opportunities of African Americans through education. For three days in April 1960, Shaw became the center of the civil rights world, as both established leaders and burgeoning leaders met on the campus. Just as many of the student protest leaders from HBCUs were honored by *Who's Who Among American Colleges and Universities*, the April conference was a sort of "Who's Who" of the civil rights movement. Among those in attendance were Martin Luther King Jr., Ralph Abernathy, Ella Baker, Wyatt Tee Walker, Fred Shuttlesworth, James Lawson, Diane Nash, James Bevel, Julian Bond, Charles Sherrod, Marion S. Barry, Charles McDew, and Ezell Blair Jr.[52]

Accompanying North Carolina A&T student and "Greensboro Four" participant Ezell Blair Jr. to the conference was the lone delegate from UNC, David Dansby, who was one of the few Black students at

---

[50] "Persons Written to Regarding Youth Meeting," 5 April 1960, Box 25, Folder 1, SNCC Papers, Martin Luther King Jr. Center for Nonviolent Social Change, Atlanta, GA.

[51] Ella Baker, "We Need Your Story" (letter to several protest leaders), Box 25, Folder 1, SNCC Papers, Martin Luther King Jr. Center for Nonviolent Social Change.

[52] "Delegates to Youth Leadership Conference," 2 June 1960, Box 25, Folder 1, SNCC Papers, Martin Luther King Jr. Center for Nonviolent Social Change; "Students Set Up: Southwide Group to Direct Battle," *News and Observer*, 18 April 1960, 1.

UNC in 1960. In a sense he benefitted from the groundbreaking entrance to the UNC School of Law by four students in 1951, including Floyd B. McKissick Sr., the lawyer who would represent Dansby a few years later when he was arrested for his involvement in demonstrations. When Dansby came to Chapel Hill as a freshman in 1957, Black undergraduates had only been attending the university for two years. He recalled his experience at UNC, stating that "I was pretty much a pariah, since I was outspoken."[53] During his time at UNC, he would often go to NCC to hang out with Black students in order to "maintain my sanity.... I was over there all the time. Some people thought I was a student there."[54] Although he finished his undergraduate work in 1961, Dansby continued as a graduate student until 1964. He became increasingly involved in civil rights demonstrations in Durham. As a student at UNC, as a protestor in Durham, and as a delegate at the Shaw conference, Dansby represented a direct link between a "Research Triangle" school and those of the "Protest Triangle."

Dansby and Blair Jr. shared a commitment to improving social and economic conditions for African Americans. They had also attended the same high school, Greensboro's Dudley High. Historian William Chafe makes clear the contributions that teachers at Dudley High School made in breaking racial barriers. Ezell Blair Sr., a teacher at Dudley, had led an effort in 1959 to pressure merchants at a shopping center to employ African American salespersons in "nontraditional" jobs. Chafe's work repeatedly reveals the contributions of teachers like Nell Coley, who "instilled a sense of pride and provided a model of strength."[55] Thus Blair Jr. and Dansby took their various experiences in high school and their respective colleges with them to the Shaw conference, as did the other student participants. Like many other male participants, Dansby stayed at the Bloodworth Street YMCA.[56]

Dansby did not realize going into the meetings that there would essentially be a choice between the students becoming a sort of youth arm of the SCLC or creating a new student-led organization. He did not sense

---

[53] David Dansby, phone interview by the author, 14 June 2016.
[54] Dansby, phone interview by the author.
[55] William H. Chafe, *Civilities and Civil Rights: Greensboro, North Carolina and the Black Struggle for Freedom* (Oxford: Oxford University Press, 1981), 80.
[56] Dansby, phone interview by the author.

any tension at the meeting but also felt that Baker's inclination toward leadership was different than King's. Dansby believed at that time that the students should follow Dr. King but later came to believe that Baker's ideas about leadership were more beneficial. "I think they were right, and I was wrong," he recalled.[57] Dansby was cognizant of the tremendous leadership potential that existed among the students at the conference. Among these was Charles Jones, a protest leader at Johnson C. Smith University in Charlotte, and Shaw University's David Forbes, a student whom Dansby characterized as outspoken and articulate.[58]

Forbes was instrumental in the initial phase of demonstrations in Raleigh. He had helped organize a meeting at Greenleaf Auditorium on the Shaw campus to prepare for the first sit-ins in Raleigh in February 1960. He was on a committee assigned by President William Strassner to work out details for accommodations and hospitality for the conference. Forbes was one of eight Shaw students who were delegates for the April conference.[59] He points out that many more Shaw students participated in some capacity in the conference or attended the mass meeting at the Memorial Auditorium on April 16. Several Shaw faculty members were also encouraging of the students at the conference, including Elizabeth Coffield, Wilmoth Carter, Charles Robson, and perhaps the most supportive member of the faculty, Grady Davis.[60]

Like other participants, Forbes attended the session meetings at the conference, which were held on the Shaw campus and local churches. The workshops had a moderator, and many of the sessions were practical rather than theoretical, with some involving practice in picketing and enduring abuse.[61] The sessions had a student chairperson and an adult counselor. Among the more notable adult counselors of the workshops were James Lawson, Ella Baker, Wyatt Tee Walker, Ralph Abernathy, and Fred

---

[57] Dansby, phone interview by the author.

[58] Dansby, phone interview by the author.

[59] "Delegates to Youth Leadership Conference," 2 June 1960, Box 25, Folder 1, SNCC Papers, Martin Luther King Jr. Center for Nonviolent Social Change. The other Shaw students in attendance were Charles Sparks, David Walker, Fred Marshall, Albert Hockaday, Eleanor Nunn, Glenford E. Mitchell, and Howard Edward Anderson.

[60] David Forbes, interview by the author.

[61] Forbes, interview by the author.

Shuttlesworth. Among the notable student chairpersons of the sessions
were Johnson C. Smith protest leader Charles Jones, and a critically important student leader from Fisk University, Diane Nash.[62] The workshop
chaired by Charles Jones was titled "Inter-racial Thrust of Movement: Encouraging White Persons to Join Movement." This session discussed what
type of help students desired from White supporters and concluded with
a recommendation that the "movement should not be considered one for
negroes but one for people who consider this a movement against injus-
tice." Participants at this session also articulated that the movement "will
affect other areas beyond 'service,' such as politics and economics."[63]

The issue of including Whites was also brought up in Group 3, titled
"Techniques of Nonviolence." One of the notes said that sit-ins in which
the demonstrators only filled every other seat at a lunch counter were more
effective as this would "allow the white public to demonstrate their willingness to eat or demonstrate with the Negroes."[64] Other notes in this
session revealed the frustrations that protestors had already encountered in
many cities, as one pointed out that "Bi-racial committees appointed by
the mayor are usually not useful because they do not represent person involved," and the ensuing note stated that "cooling of [sic] periods should
only be used when the movement gets out of hand and takes on violent
aspects."[65] It is quite clear that students brought their experiences with
them to the conference. In many ways, the sessions were merely refining
the methods that student protestors had already adopted in their respective
cities.

Many of the students had already been arrested as a result of the protests, but the topic of going to jail was nonetheless a difficult one to navi-
gate. A key question addressed in Group 7 pondered whether students
would be bailed out of jail or if fines would be paid. The participants made
their position quite clear, stating that "the members of this group

---

[62] "Workshops," Box 1, Folder 1, SNCC Papers, Martin Luther King Jr. Center
for Nonviolent Social Change.

[63] "Group 4," Box 1, Folder 1, SNCC Papers, Martin Luther King Jr, Center for
Nonviolent Social Change.

[64] "Group 3," SNCC Papers, Box 1, Folder 1, Martin Luther King, Jr, Center for
Nonviolent Social Change.

[65] "Group 3," SNCC Papers, Box 1, Folder 1.

recommended that no bail be posted nor fines paid" in order to "1) Solidify the Negro Community 2) Mobilize public opinion 3) Weaken the opposition by showing that a threat of arrest cannot deter us."[66] Students were understandably concerned about the impact that going to jail could have on their future. They were emboldened by Martin Luther King Jr.'s support. In his February 16 speech in Durham, he had stated that "maybe it will take this willingness to stay in jail to arouse the dozing consciousness of our nation."[67]

King's presence at the conference was notable for several reasons. By 1960, he was already well known and was a hero to many African Americans. His presence made the conference a newsworthy event, and television cameras were set up to capture some of the scenes. He had given his support to the sit-in tactics at an early stage, and he reiterated his encouragement in his statement to the press that opened the conference. He stated that the opponents of justice were well organized and that the students must become organized as well. And he suggested that "the students must seriously consider training a group of volunteers who will willingly go to jail rather than pay bail or fines." King also pointed out the importance of reconciliation, ending his press statement by noting, "Our ultimate end must be the creation of the beloved community. The tactics of nonviolence without the spirit of nonviolence may indeed become a new kind of violence."[68] King was providing guidance to the students and demonstrating his talent for expressing his support for an aggressive tactic while simultaneously soothing the concerns of some potentially sympathetic Whites and conservative African Americans.

The interaction between King and Ella Baker and the seeming contrast in their leadership styles has received extensive analysis from several scholars and civil rights activists. In her biography of Baker, former SNCC

---

[66] "Group 7," SNCC Papers, Box 1, Folder 1.

[67] "King Leads Rally, Urges Nonviolent Crusade: Negroes Hint of Boycott Here," *Durham Sun*, 17 February 1960, 1, 2.

[68] Martin Luther King Jr., "Statement to the Press by Dr. Martin Luther King Jr. at the Beginning of the Youth Leaderships Conference," 15 April 1960, Series III, Box 1, Folder: "Statement to the Press at the Beginning of the Youth Conference, Raleigh, North Carolina," King Papers, Martin Luther King Jr. Center for Nonviolent Social Change.

member Joanne Grant argues that "King saw the need to mobilize the masses, but he did not understand the need to organize them. Baker did her best to try to nudge him into an organizer."[69] Barbara Ransby makes clear the differences in approaches between Baker and King and the reasons for Baker's frustrations with King. She emphasizes Baker's focus on group-centered leadership that conflicted with King's approach. Additionally, she maintains that King was focused on how the movement was perceived externally and the impact of those perceptions on SCLC, while Baker was more concerned with developing potential leaders than worrying about the organization's eminence.[70] But perhaps Baker's own words indicate the source of tension as she suggests that she believed King did not view her as an equally important contributor: "After all, who was I? I was female, I was old. I didn't have no Ph.D."[71]

King and the SCLC leadership respected Baker, but in addition to some of their strategic differences, there was also a significant difference in age. Andrew Young, who was working with the National Council of Churches in 1960 but eventually became one of King's most trusted allies, called Ella Baker the "Momma Superior" due to her many years of experience in the movement but also because she took a sort of "mother role." He maintains that "she tried to do it with Martin and Wyatt Walker and SCLC, it really didn't work. And it was an age problem." Young makes it clear that despite their respect for each other in certain ways, "Martin and Ella Baker didn't get along. And Wyatt Walker and Ella Baker didn't get along, because it was like having your mother in your dorm room."[72] The irony that presented itself at the April 1960 Shaw conference was that the elder Baker was the one who seemed to be most in tune with the aspirations of the younger generation. Young points out that Baker got along with the students because they were younger, and "they needed her wisdom. The thirty-year-olds didn't want anybody's wisdom."[73]

The underlying strategic and generational tensions manifested

---

[69] Grant, *Ella Baker*, 4.

[70] Ransby, *Ella Baker and the Black Freedom Movement*, 178, 250.

[71] Ransby, *Ella Baker and the Black Freedom Movement*, 173.

[72] Andrew J. Young, interview by the author, digital recording, 18 May 2016, Atlanta, GA.

[73] Young, interview by the author.

themselves among the adult leadership at the Shaw conference. On the second day of the conference, Baker, King, Abernathy, and Walker met at the home of Shaw president William R. Strassner. In *The Making of Black Revolutionaries*, former SNCC member James Forman points out that the SCLC leaders tried to convince Baker that the students should become an arm of SCLC. They believed they could procure the votes for such a move, with King delivering student votes from Georgia, led by Lonnie King; Abernathy delivering the vote from the Alabama group, led by Bernard Lee; and Walker securing support from the Virginia delegation.[74] According to Baker's version of the story, she criticized the ministers for trying to "capture" the student leadership and walked out of the meeting.[75] Historian J. Todd Moye maintains that the SCLC leadership should not have been surprised by Baker's commitment to allowing the students to determine their own course, especially because of her previous statement that the adults should only act in an advisory capacity. Moye argues, "If they honestly expected her to prioritize the organization's interests ahead of those of the long-term movement as she understood them, they had not been paying much attention to her over the years."[76] But Moye also points out that the reports of SCLC's attempt to "capture" the student movement may have been overblown, noting King's press statement at the beginning of the conference that emphasized "the need for some type of continuing organization."[77] The extent to which King desired such a "continuing organization" to fall under SCLC leadership remains a matter of interpretation. It was initially a goal of King, Abernathy, and Walker, but the fact that they did not fully use their influence to push for such a course may indicate that they appreciated the students' right to chart their own course.

Whereas a good amount of scholarship has focused on the leadership of the Shaw conference, the primary gap in the historiography of the conference remains in how the students themselves viewed the conference. The disagreements among the adult leaders at the conference were not

---

[74] James Forman, *The Making of Black Revolutionaries* (New York: The Macmillan Company, 1972), 216–17.

[75] Ransby, *Ella Baker and the Black Freedom Movement*, 243.

[76] J. Todd Moye, *Ella Baker: Community Organizer of the Civil Rights Movement* (Lanham, MD: Rowman and Littlefield Publishers, Inc., 2013), 112, 113.

[77] Moye, *Ella Baker*, 113.

made evident to the students. As previously mentioned, David Dansby does not recall any sense of tension at the meetings and remembers that the students were "just so enthusiastic to be there."[78] Regardless of how students viewed the goals and leadership approaches, they were excited to have the chance to meet some of the most important civil rights leaders, such as Dr. King. David Forbes recalls that King "was so calm and self-confident and warm that you were not intimidated by him. You were inspired by his rhetoric, but you were not intimidated."[79] Forbes did not personally know any of the students who came from outside of North Carolina prior to the conference, and he was not aware of who Ella Baker was. But at the conference he found her to be nurturing, almost like a mother. He recalls that she got to know all the students and warned them not to allow adults to undermine the student-led movement. In the following summers while working in New York City, Forbes would visit Baker at her apartment on Lennox Terrace. It was during their conversations that Forbes learned of her disagreements with King. But at the Shaw conference, the tensions between Baker and King were not evident to Forbes.[80]

Many of the Shaw students did not have a true sense of the historic nature of the conference. Surprisingly, some of the students from Shaw and Saint Augustine's do not recall a major "buzz" on campus prior to the conference, whereas others do. The conference was held on Easter weekend, and many of the students traveled home or visited friends or relatives. Those who had participated heavily in the movement were aware of the conference, but few recognized its historical significance. 1960 Shaw graduate McLouis Clayton did not attend the conference and acknowledged that "the event was much bigger than I thought at the time."[81]

It may have been difficult for many student protestors to fully comprehend the historic nature of the conference, but most realized that they were struggling for more than just the ability to sit at lunch counters. In an article from the May 1960 edition of the *Southern Patriot*, Ella Baker reiterated some of the themes that she addressed in her speech at the

---

[78] David Dansby, interview by the author.
[79] David Forbes, interview by the author.
[80] Forbes, interview by the author.
[81] McLouis Clayton, interview by the author, digital recording, 2 March 2016, Raleigh, NC.

conference. Baker started the article by claiming that the "Student Leadership Conference made it crystal clear that current sit-ins and other demonstrations are concerned with something much bigger than a hamburger or even a giant-sized Coke." She declared that Black and White students in the North and the South were seeking to end racial discrimination not merely at lunch counters but in all aspects of society. Baker further pointed out that many communities in the South "have not provided adequate experience for young Negroes to assume initiative and think and act independently" and that this "accentuated the need for guarding the student movement against well-meaning, but nevertheless unhealthy, over-protectiveness."[82] Herein lies one of the primary reasons students were drawn to Baker. She recognized that students had a desire to take leadership and that the sit-ins had provided them a chance to exhibit leadership and seek changes in society to improve their future opportunities. Baker realized that students had already demonstrated their ability to lead the movement in the right direction and wanted to make sure they would not cower to adult leaders who, in her estimation, had failed to produce significant changes in the past.

The legacy of the Shaw conference was multifaceted. It helped foster the development of a youth leadership that was already emerging on various campuses. On the final day of the conference, the participants decided to form a temporary Student Nonviolent Coordinating Committee. The "Recommendations" of the "Findings and Recommendations Committee" were not very detailed, but in addition to creating the temporary committee, it proposed that "nonviolence is our creed" and that the conference endorsed the movement and the "practice of going to jail rather than accepting bail."[83] The conference participants also produced a statement of purpose, which emphasized the commitment to nonviolence. Perhaps the most telling portion of the statement read, "The redemptive community supersedes systems of gross social immorality."[84] This brief sentence

---

[82] Ella Baker, "Bigger Than a Hamburger," *Southern Patriot* 18 (1960): 4; Forman, *The Making of Black Revolutionaries*, 217–18.

[83] "Recommendations of the Findings and Recommendations Committee Are as Follows," Box 1, Folder 2, SNCC Papers, Martin Luther King Jr. Center for Nonviolent Social Change. Underline in the original.

[84] "Statement of Purpose," 17 April 1960, Box 1 Folder 1, SNCC Papers, Martin

reveals a commitment to noncooperation with unjust laws and a devotion to civil disobedience.

The creation of the temporary Student Nonviolent Coordinating Committee at the Shaw conference was reinforced at the October 14–16 meeting in Atlanta, at which SNCC took on the form of a permanent organization. SNCC went on to become one of the most vital organizations in the black freedom movement and was perhaps the most effective group in conducting community organizing efforts in the South in the early and mid-1960s. But the legacy of the April 1960 Shaw conference was not simply the creation of a new organization. Rather, it was the reinforcement of a student leadership that was already coming into prominence before the conference began, as well as the establishment of connections among activists in different cities. Sit-ins had already occurred, and local leadership had already emerged well before the conference took place. According to Forbes, the conference impacted strategies in Raleigh "mostly by the reinforcement and learning that we were on the right road because basically most of the cities and states were having the same experience."[85]

Aside from Baker and King, perhaps the most influential adult leader at the conference was James Lawson. Lawson was born in Pennsylvania and attended Baldwin-Wallace College in Ohio. During the Korean War, Lawson was a conscientious objector, and his refusal to serve in the military landed him in prison. But one of the most significant experiences for Lawson in his eventual role as a leader in the civil rights movement was the three years he spent as a missionary in India, where he studied Gandhian nonviolence. Historian Clayborne Carson argues that of all the participants at the Raleigh conference, Lawson was the most versed in the doctrines of nonviolent direct action. In the late 1950s, Lawson put his knowledge into practice by conducting workshops on nonviolence for the Nashville Christian Leadership Council. After enrolling as a theology student at Vanderbilt University, Lawson conducted a workshop in 1959 that drew student participants who would go on to become seminal figures in the movement, including Diane Nash, Marion Barry, John Lewis, and

---

Luther King Jr. Center for Nonviolent Social Change.

[85] David Forbes, interview by the author.

James Bevel. Later that year, the group staged test sit-ins. Although their attempt to achieve voluntary integration by the business owners failed, their efforts continued the following year.[86]

The connection between the sit-in movement in Nashville and that in the Triangle, however, did not begin at the Shaw conference. According to Lawson, the spark that set off the February 1960 sit-ins in Nashville was a telephone call on February 10 from the Reverend Douglass Moore of Durham, in which Moore asked him "if there was anything the students over here [in Nashville] could do to show their sympathy for the North Carolina sit-ins."[87] The following night, approximately fifty students met at Fisk University to discuss the possibility of sit-ins, and the Nashville sit-in movement began two days later with heavy participation from Fisk University and Tennessee Agricultural and Industrial State University (now Tennessee State University) students.[88] It is quite likely that the Nashville sit-ins would have eventually occurred regardless of whether Moore had called Lawson or not, but the impact of the call further demonstrates the important role that Moore played in the sit-in movement in North Carolina and beyond.

In conjunction with his knowledge of the philosophy of nonviolence and in his practical application of its tactics, Lawson brought to the conference an approach to leadership similar to Baker's. In mid-March, approximately halfway between the beginning of the sit-in movement in Nashville and the Shaw conference, Lawson reflected, "What was my role? I was not the leader. My understanding of the Christian non-violence concept is that you don't have a single leader but group leadership."[89] Like Baker, he recognized the importance of allowing local leadership to develop.

Of course, some students played a more important role than others.

[86] Clayborne Carson, *In Struggle: SNCC and the Black Awakening of the 1960s* (Cambridge: Harvard University Press, 1981), 22.
[87] "Call Sparked Sit-ins: Lawson: Carolina Friend Asked Sympathy Show, Report Quotes Minister," *Tennessean*, 21 March 1960, unknown page, Series 4, Box 7, Folder: "Banner Clippings," Nashville Public Library Civil Rights Collection, Nashville, TN.
[88] "Call Sparked Sit-ins."
[89] "Call Sparked Sit-ins."

One of the most significant student protestors in Nashville was Diane
Nash, who also participated in the Shaw conference. By the time of the
Shaw conference, Nash had already challenged the mayor of Nashville at
a press event, delivered speeches to large crowds, and given interviews to
the national press.[90] In the week following the Shaw conference, Nash
delivered perhaps her most shining moment (among many) in the movement. Following the bombing of Black attorney and integration advocate
Z. Alexander Looby's home, Nash was at the forefront of a silent march
that culminated in her asking Mayor Ben West whether he believed it was
wrong to discriminate against a person based solely on their race or skin
color. West had undoubtedly grappled internally with such a question previously, and in this crucial moment he responded by saying he did not
believe it was right. It was quite simply one of the most beautiful moments
in the civil rights movement. Nash's leadership in this historic moment
presaged her later civil rights activism, including in the Freedom Rides.
According to Ransby, Nash arrived at the Shaw conference looking for
reassurance and affirmation, and Ella Baker provided both.[91] The ques-
tioning of Mayor West in the week following the conference revealed that
Nash had fully emerged as a leader in her own right, a role buoyed by her
experiences at the Shaw conference and by the guiding influence, but certainly not the directing influence, of Ella Baker and James Lawson.

In addition to fostering student activism, Reverend Lawson brought
to the Shaw conference an experience that demonstrated the connections
between civil rights activism and academic freedom. Lawson had been an
ordained minister since 1952 and was one of 5 African Americans among
130 divinity students at Vanderbilt University in 1960. He was a senior
when he was expelled on March 3 for his leadership in the sit-ins in Nashville.[92] The reaction at the predominantly White school was mixed. The
student senate passed a resolution supporting the university's action in ex-
pelling Lawson, stating that the university "could not stand aside in the
face of Lawson's strong commitment to civil disobedience." But the

---

[90] Ransby, *Ella Baker and the Black Freedom Movement*, 247.

[91] Ransby, *Ella Baker and the Black Freedom Movement*, 246.

[92] Little Rock AP, "Ousted Lawson Urges More Demonstrations," *Tennessean*,
10 April 1960, 1, 6, Series 4, Box 7, Folder: "Banner Clippings," Nashville Public
Library Civil Rights Collection.

president of the student body of the divinity school, Gene Davenport, declared that the university's action was "legally right but morally wrong."[93] In those few words, Davenport seemed to capture the whole essence of segregation.

Lawson received early support from part of the faculty, when 111 faculty members, including 12 department heads, released a statement that was sent to Mayor Ben West's biracial peace committee and to the heads of all of Nashville's colleges and universities. The declaration stated that "we are distressed that recent actions by Vanderbilt University may be interpreted as condoning the denial of rights of Nashville Negroes to speak and act lawfully in their cause, or of sympathetic individuals at Vanderbilt or elsewhere to support and defend them by word or deed."[94] The statement ultimately expressed sympathy and support for the demonstrations and their efforts to secure equal rights. Among the Vanderbilt professors who signed the statement was a White professor, Charles E. Roos, whose mother was an important figure in the Fellowship of Reconciliation, as was Lawson. Roos recalls that the Vanderbilt faculty was split on the issue, with about half in favor of the university's action and half opposed.[95] Support for Lawson was strong in the divinity school, and fourteen of the sixteen faculty members had resigned in protest by the end of the spring semester. Ultimately, Lawson chose to enter Boston University Divinity School.[96] But at the time of the Shaw conference, Lawson shared a similar story with many of the student participants. He had a deep commitment to nonviolent direct action and had been directly involved in sit-ins. Like the expelled students from Alabama State, he also experienced the reality that involvement in civil rights activities pushed the limits of how certain colleges would draw the line on the civic and academic freedom of their students.

The thirty-one-year-old Lawson was the same age as King at the time

---

[93] "VU Group Urges Race Tolerance," *Tennessean*, 9 March 1960, 1, Series 4, Box 7, Folder: "Banner Clippings," Nashville Public Library Civil Rights Collection.
[94] "VU Group Urges Race Tolerance," 1.
[95] Charles E. Roos, interview by Kathy Bennett, 3, 14, Series 3, Folder: "Roos, Charles E," Nashville Public Library Civil Rights Collection.
[96] "Vanderbilt Univ. Faculty Quits Over Negro Student's Ouster: Two Graduates Return Degrees to Tenn. School," *The Carolina Times*, 1A, 6A.

of the Shaw conference. According to Adam Fairclough, Lawson's role in the Nashville sit-ins and his expulsion from Vanderbilt had made him a hero in the eyes of the students. Fairclough argues that it was not only his grasp of Gandhianism but also his blunt and radical language that made him so popular, including his appeals to a "nonviolent revolution" that could "transform the system." Lawson was instrumental in the adoption of the "Statement of Purpose" of what eventually became SNCC.[97] Perhaps his most enduring legacy was his impact on the Nashville group, including John Lewis, Diane Nash, and James Bevel, but also on the students present at the Shaw conference. But the most newsworthy aspect of Lawson's involvement in the Shaw conference and its aftermath was his criticism of the NAACP. Lawson insisted that the NAACP was too conservative and that its magazine, *The Crisis*, was the "magazine of the black bourgeoisie."[98]

Fairclough argues that the relationship between SNCC and the NAACP never really recovered from Lawson's critical remarks at the conference, in which he criticized the "overreliance on the courts" and the "futile middle-class technique of sending letters to the centers of power."[99] Of course, SNCC did not exist prior to the conference, and thus there was never really any inter-organizational relationship from which to recover. While criticism of the NAACP would be common in the following years among SNCC activists, it is important not to paint the NAACP in one monolithic stroke. Indeed, the NAACP was changing due to the increased emphasis on direct action that resulted from the sit-ins. The national NAACP fully encouraged the actions of the students, and on February 11, 1960, executive secretary Roy Wilkins sent a telegram to the national presidents of F. W. Woolworth and S. H. Kress indicating the organization's support of the student protests and calling for an end to stores' "outmoded"

---

[97] Adam Fairclough, *To Redeem the Soul of America: The Southern Christian Leadership Conference and Martin Luther King, Jr.* (Athens: The University of Georgia Press, 1987), 64–65.

[98] "Students Set Up: Southwide Group to Direct Battle," *News and Observer*, 18 April 1960, 1.

[99] Adam Fairclough, *Better Day Coming: Blacks and Equality, 1890–2000* (New York: Penguin Putnam, Inc., 2001), 246, 247.

policies.[100] After an initial meeting was canceled due to snowy conditions, National Youth Secretary Herbert L. Wright met with student leaders in Durham to plan strategy after the February 16 speech by King. The students met at St. Joseph A.M.E. Church and outlined plans to effectively coordinate the demonstrations. Kelly M. Alexander, the president of the North Carolina Conference of NAACP Branches, addressed the students and pledged the full support and resources of the state branch. At the meeting, NCC junior Lacy Streeter was elected chairman of the newly created State NAACP Special Coordinating Committee.[101] Streeter had already established himself as one of the primary leaders in the Durham movement. But many of the experiences mentioned previously in this chapter were at least partially afforded by his involvement in the NAACP.

Many members of the NAACP youth councils and college chapters were pushing for the organization to become more militant not only through direct appeals for such an approach but also through their own actions. In *NAACP Youth and the Black Fight for Freedom, 1936–1965*, Thomas L. Bynum asserts that many of the activists who ultimately joined SNCC had begun their activism in the youth councils. He points out that NAACP college chapters throughout North Carolina ultimately supported the sit-ins, including those at Shaw, Saint Augustine's, and NCC.[102] Durham was one of the most active cities in terms of NAACP youth council activity, which included the youth chapters at NCC, Durham Business College, Bull City Barber College, and DeShazor Beauty College, in addition to the Durham Youth Crusaders of the NAACP Council.[103] R. Arline Young, the head of the biology department at Shaw University, had been a key figure in the Durham NAACP. In the late 1940s, Young helped establish a college chapter of the NAACP on the NCC campus. According to Christina Greene, Young was

---

[100] Roy Wilkins, telegram to George Cobb, 11 February 1960, NAACP Papers, microfilm 22:00106.

[101] "North Carolina NAACP Establishes Coordinating Unit for Sit-Down Protests," press release, 18 February 1960, NAACP Papers, microfilm 22:00125.

[102] Thomas Bynum, *NAACP Youth and the Fight for Black Freedom, 1936–1965* (Knoxville: The University of Tennessee Press, 2013), xiv, 101.

[103] "Callis Brown," 16 May 1960, NAACP Papers, Microfilm 22:00163, University of North Carolina at Greensboro; original at Library of Congress, Washington, DC.

instrumental in establishing a statewide NAACP youth council as well.[104]
Young's efforts in Durham while a professor at Shaw University in Raleigh
provide an example of the connections between two of the "Protest Triangle" schools.

In addition to providing encouragement and organizational support,
the NAACP also provided practical and financial support for students who
became involved in sit-ins and protest demonstrations. One example occurred when Glenford Mitchell required financial assistance to remain at
Shaw. Mitchell was an important figure in the student movement in Raleigh and the editor of the school newspaper, *The Shaw Journal.* He was
also a Shaw delegate in the North Carolina Student Legislature in 1960.
Dr. Marguerite Adams, who was the State Director of the Youth Program
and also a professor at Shaw, had appealed to NAACP Field Secretary
Charles A. McLean for financial help, and after some fundraising, more
than three hundred dollars was given to Mitchell for educational expenses.
Yet McLean's report about the funding given to Mitchell is also revealing
in the way it ostensibly views the student leadership. The report states that
had Mitchell not been able to remain in college, "it would have seriously
affected, if not brought to an end, the local demonstrations."[105] Perhaps
this claim was merely a way of making the donation to Mitchell appear
more critical. But it also may give a window into an important NAACP
official not fully recognizing the group-centered leadership that existed in
the Shaw-Saint Augustine's student movement. Mitchell was undoubtedly
an important individual on campus and in the movement, but so were
many others.[106] The point here is that the student leadership in Raleigh
was diffuse and talented enough that it did not hinge on the fortunes of
one individual.

At Shaw, an important member of the College Chapter of the
NAACP was Albert Sampson, who became both the chapter president

---

[104] Greene, *Our Separate Ways*, 21–25.

[105] Charles A. McLean, "Report on Sit-in Lunch Counter Strikes in North Carolina," 23, NAACP Papers, microfilm 22:00092.

[106] David Forbes, interview by the author; Albert Sampson, interview by the author; Carrie Gaddy Brock, interview by the author; Louis Powell, interview by the
author; McLouis Clayton, interview by the author; Otis Tucker Jr., mail interview by
the author.

and the Student Council president for the 1960–1961 academic year.[107] Sampson had attended high school in Everett, Massachusetts, the same city in which Grady Davis pastored the Zion Baptist Church.[108] In 1956, Davis convinced Sampson to attend Shaw, and he entered as a freshman in the following year. Sampson was a junior when the sit-in movement broke out in February 1960. He recognized that students had an important role to play and could augment the work of the local, state, and national NAACP. He recalled that "my position was: Roy Wilkins you go into the courts; we're going into the streets."[109] In one instance, the twenty-one-year-old Sampson conducted a sit-in with nineteen-year-old James Fox, six-foot-four power forward who averaged double-digit rebounds as a freshman for the Shaw basketball team.[110] Sampson and Fox were arrested for trespassing after refusing to leave the McLellan's Store on Fayetteville Street in downtown Raleigh on March 22, 1960.[111] Sampson was another of the leaders who demonstrated that leadership in the direct-action campaigns in Raleigh literally went from campus to counter.

But student leadership in pushing for better social and economic opportunities for African Americans was not limited to involvement in sit-ins and picketing stores with segregated lunch counters. At the North Carolina Student Legislative Assembly in March 17–19, 1960, Shaw was represented by seven delegates: James Ballard, Mae Helen Covington, David Forbes, Albert Hockaday, Glenfield Knight, Glenford Mitchell, and William H. Peace. The Shaw delegation, along with students from the Woman's College of Duke University, introduced a resolution calling for

---

[107] *The Bear*, 1961, 26.

[108] Albert Sampson, interview by the author; Earl Thomas Wooten, "An Analysis of the Community Organization Process Employed by the Urban League of Greater Boston, Incorporated, In the Initial Stages of a Community Survey" (1951), *ETD Collection for AUC Robert W. Woodruff Library, Atlanta University Center*, Paper 726, http://digitalcommons.auctr.edu/cgi/viewcontent.cgi?article=2302&context=dissertations.

[109] Albert Sampson, interview by the author.

[110] "Reece, Fox Big 'Bounders,'" *Shaw Journal*, March–April 1960, 7, NAACP Papers, Microfilm 22:00160, University of North Carolina at Greensboro; original at Library of Congress, Washington, DC.

[111] "Two Negroes Are Arrested for Trespass," *News and Observer*, 22 March 1960, 22.

the abolishment of capital punishment in North Carolina. Senator William H. Peace introduced the bill that passed both houses with "dignity and masterly eloquence" and was ultimately given an award for best speaker in the senate of the student assembly. And the Shaw delegation was also awarded a plaque for the best senate bill at the meeting. The Shaw delegation also supported a bill introduced by North Carolina A&T that called for desegregation of eating facilities in public establishments, which also passed. The assembly failed to act on a bill sponsored by Johnson C. Smith University that called for the end of state aid to school boards that practiced racial discrimination. A bill introduced by Saint Augustine's to lower the voting age from twenty-one to eighteen also failed to pass.[112]

Nonetheless, the March 1960 North Carolina Student Legislative Assembly was a major success in revealing that among students there was general support for the end of discriminatory practices at eating establishments in the state. In this sense, the assembly gave a formal political voice to the student-led protests in North Carolina. It also demonstrated that student leaders throughout the state, especially at historically Black campuses, were acting as a counter to the adult political leadership that often defended segregation. Just as the sit-ins and picketing of segregated businesses were spreading throughout the state and the Student Legislative Assembly gave support to desegregation, a civil rights bill (albeit limited) was being debated in the US Congress with opposition coming from North Carolina representatives. North Carolina Senators Sam Ervin Jr. and B. Everett Jordan were among only eighteen senators who voted against the civil rights bill that passed in the Senate less than a month after the meeting of the North Carolina Student Legislative Assembly.[113] Just as the student protestors from Shaw and Saint Augustine's literally proceeded from campus to the lunch counters in Raleigh, they also acted as a counter to city and state political leaders such as Mayor W. G. Enloe, Governor Luther Hodges, and Senators Ervin and Jordan.

The success of the Shaw delegation at the March meeting of the

---

[112] "Shaw Captures NCSLA Awards," *The Shaw Journal*, March–April 1960, 1, 2, NAACP Papers, Microfilm 22:00148, 22:00150; "Resolution on Protests is Debated," *News and Observer*, 19 March 1960, 16.

[113] Washington UPI, "Assures Negro of Vote: Civil Rights Measure Passes Senate, 71-18," *News and Observer*, 9 April 1960, 1, 2.

Student Legislative Assembly was bolstered by further success at the December 1960 meeting. Albert Sampson nearly did not attend, as students from African American colleges considered boycotting the legislative sessions due to the segregated housing situation. Ultimately, the legislature's president, Stephen R. Brasswell of Duke, urged the students to reject the boycott and encouraged them to attend and air their grievances. Due to segregated practices, White student legislators lodged at local hotels, while Black student representatives stayed on the campuses of Shaw and Saint Augustine's.[114]

Just as Shaw was the epicenter of the civil rights movement in the South for three days in mid-April, so was Shaw at the heart of the movement in North Carolina in early December. Aside from providing housing for the African American representatives, delegates from Shaw also introduced a resolution stipulating that "all housing assignments for delegates to this Assembly be made on a totally racially non-segregated basis." Ultimately, a compromise resolution was passed based on a proposal by Duke's delegation that mostly promoted the new commitment to desegregated housing: "More specifically in the future, whenever humanly possible, that the housing for this body while it is in session shall be arranged on a racially non-segregated basis."[115]

Sampson and the Shaw delegation also supported a bill introduced by the delegation from Livingstone College, a historically Black college in Salisbury, which sought to abolish all forms of racial segregation in North Carolina. Specifically, part of the bill called for "full and equal privileges in places of public accommodation, resort, entertainment and amusement, and equal rights in employment." The bill passed in the Student Legislative Assembly House of Representatives 66–12 and 22–18 in the Senate.[116] Students from HBCUs had shown that the momentum of the sit-in movement helped reinforce a will to use political influence to help bring about integration. They had received extensive, though not unanimous, support from White college students in the state. Yet securing support

---

[114] "Legislators Compromise on Housing," *News and Observer*, 9 December 1960, 40.

[115] "Legislators Compromise on Housing," 40.

[116] "Race Issue Is Debated by Students," *News and Observer*, 10 December 1960, 18.

from adult state political leaders in 1960 and the following years would prove a much more daunting task.

In a 2016 interview, Andrew J. Young likened the leadership of SCLC to that of a basketball team.[117] While Young was not involved in the April 1960 conference at Shaw, a basketball metaphor appears equally applicable to the events of the conference and to the emergence of student leadership that preceded and was enhanced by discussions during that Easter weekend. Different types of leaders contributed in unique ways, much as basketball players at different positions might contribute to a team. After his involvement in the Montgomery bus boycott and the 1957 Prayer Pilgrimage, Martin Luther King Jr. became the most nationally recognized civil rights leader.[118] He was at the center of the media attention during the conference. Regardless of criticism from both conservatives and more radical elements in the movement in the following years, King was very much at the center of the national movement. In her role as primary organizer of the conference and as an advocate for allowing student leadership to blossom, Ella Baker was perhaps the most important guiding voice at the conference. Ransby argues that Baker was not the "hands-off facilitator that some have made her out to be." She maintains that students needed guidance in some situations, and Baker's intention was to provide a mentorship enabling the sit-in movement to "develop in a direction that she could influence but would not determine."[119] While Baker may not have been a "hands-off" facilitator, she was a facilitator nonetheless, a sort of point guard. Thus, at the conference and in the civil rights movement more generally, a variety of individuals played key roles. Their various styles and approaches were effective in different ways, and each had their own specific contribution to the conference.

Much of the historiography of the Easter weekend conference at Shaw in 1960 has dealt with the ostensible tensions between Baker and King as well as James Lawson's criticism of the NAACP. Those are indeed important aspects of the conference and in some cases are symbolic of the

---

[117] Andrew Young, interview by the author.

[118] James L. Hicks, "King Emerges as Top Negro Leader," *New York Amsterdam News*, 1 June 1957, page number unknown, NAACP Papers, Microfilm 13:00008.

[119] Ransby, *Ella Baker and the Black Freedom Movement*, 243.

larger movement. But what can often be lost in focusing on the more prominent adult leaders is that the true significance of the Easter conference was the blooming of a student leadership that had already weathered many storms.

Student participants from the Protest Triangle schools had already braved winter storms, obstinate politicians and business leaders, verbal assaults, exploding yolks, eggshells, and ominous shotgun shells, and they brought these experiences with them to the conference. In many ways, they had already demonstrated that they could take leadership roles in the movement, and the events of April 15–17 reinforced that reality. Returning to the basketball analogy, one could argue that King was the center, while people like Baker played a sort of point guard role. The allegorical "basketball position" of any civil rights leader could be debated endlessly and is perhaps best left to the occupants of the bar stool or even the lunch counter stool. But what should always be remembered both in historical scholarship and American memory is that in 1960, it was truly the student leaders who most forcefully helped the movement power forward.

Chapter 5

Education vs. Segregation: The 1960 Gubernatorial Election and the Reaction to The Sit-Ins

From his pulpit at Pullen Memorial Baptist Church in Raleigh on June 12, 1960, the Reverend William Wallace Finlator took a clear stance on the impending Democratic primary runoff election between Terry Sanford and Dr. I. Beverly Lake. The White preacher told his congregation that "whether consciously or unconsciously, it is to [a] vote of prejudice that Dr. Lake's campaign is pitched. It's just that simple. The issue is race and the appeal is prejudice."[1] Ten days later, State Board of Education Chairman Dallas Herring stated that North Carolina had "dedicated itself to the unalterable truth that education is the open door to freedom and prosperity. That door must not be closed in this critical hour—not for fear or prejudice or any other reason or excuse."[2] Whereas Finlator's words expressed a clear disapproval of I. Beverly Lake's appeal for maintaining segregation, Herring's statements also appear to be a shot at Lake's candidacy and his plans to block further school integration in North Carolina. Both Herring and Finlator were representative of two population segments that provided strong (albeit not always unified) resistance to Lake's approach

---

[1] "Pastor Hits Lake Candidacy," *News and Observer*, 13 June 1960, 22.
[2] Chapel Hill AP, "Herring Says: Forces of Reaction Threaten Education," *News and Observer*, 23 June 1960, 34.

to maintaining segregation in North Carolina: religious leaders and advocates of maintaining and improving public education.

This chapter addresses the response of White political and religious leaders and that of important social figures to the sit-ins and other civil rights protests in North Carolina. It will also analyze how the increased focus on civil rights and the corresponding reaction among North Carolinians shaped the gubernatorial election in 1960. I will demonstrate the ways in which student activists, especially those from historically Black colleges, had an influence on the election, including Lake's decision to enter the race.[3] My primary argument is that in the 1960 Democratic primary election, a forward-looking view that emphasized improvements in public education trumped a reactionary view focused on halting integration in schools and in society. Ultimately, the sit-ins and civil rights activism played a role in shaping some of the central debates in the election, and in the ensuing months and years, the results of the election would play a role in the reaction to civil rights activism in the state.

In the dime stores and lunch counters in Raleigh and Durham, Southern hospitality was indeed complicated hospitality. In response to the sit-ins in early February 1960 in North Carolina, state Attorney General Malcolm Seawell publicly reminded the people that no North Carolina law existed requiring segregation at eating places. But he also declared that business owners could order customers to leave and request to have them arrested if they refused to comply.[4] But what really made the segregated lunch counters at chain stores like F. W. Woolworth, S. H. Kress, and Walgreen's complicated was that they accepted African American customers everywhere in the store except the lunch counters. An unsigned editorial in Raleigh's *News and Observer* provided an apt metaphor, stating that Black patrons were "cordially invited to the house but definitely not the table. And to say the least this was complicated hospitality."[5] In some establishments, Black customers were allowed to order at the lunch counter and take the food outside to eat. In the wake of the sit-ins, the

---

[3] Gene Roberts Jr., "Court Order His Springboard: Lake Stirring Passions on Desegregation Issue," *News and Observer*, 19 May 1960, 1, 2.

[4] Graham Jones, "Seawell Says Proprietors Can Select Their Customers," *News and Observer*, 11 February 1960, 1.

[5] "Complicated Custom" (editorial), *News and Observer*, 11 February 1960, 4.

downtown Raleigh S. H. Kress store took away the stools from an upstairs lunch counter, and Blacks and Whites were served standing up.[6]

The awkward practices of segregation seemed to validate *Carolina Israelite* editor Harry Golden's tongue-in-cheek suggestion that he initially made in reference to school integration. In 1956 Golden had sardonically proposed a "Vertical Negro Plan" in which all of the seats at schools could be removed since "it is only when the Negro 'sets' that the furs begin to fly."[7] Golden's biographer Kimberly Marlowe Hartnett asserts that Golden undoubtedly knew about Durham merchant and the city's first Jewish mayor, E. J. "Mutt" Evans, who had removed the stools from his department store's snack bar and allowed Whites and Blacks to eat standing up.[8]

Golden's support of civil rights for African Americans went beyond his clever wit in his book *Only in America* and in his Charlotte-based newspaper, *Carolina Israelite*. Golden was a strong supporter of the student-led sit-ins. He was a guest speaker at the aforementioned Student Legislative Assembly session in which Shaw University delegates won awards for the best bill and best speaker in the Senate. Golden encouraged the students to "watch and be alive" to the sit-in protests in the South.[9] He was also a featured speaker at North Carolina College's Golden Anniversary in November 1960, celebrating fifty years since the founding of the college. Golden, who was Jewish, emphasized how non-Whites had been mistreated in the United States, especially in the South. Furthermore, Golden discussed the relation between accelerated social action and desegregation. He acknowledged that desegregation was not the answer to all racial problems but that it was first on the list. Perhaps most importantly, Golden argued that because education was so important in the United States, it was the best place to start in improving conditions for African

---

[6] "At Local Store: Stand-Up Service Satisfies Pickets," *News and Observer*, 21 February 1960, 1, 2.

[7] Kimberly Marlowe Hartnett, *Carolina Israelite: How Harry Golden Made Us Care about Jews, the South, and Civil Rights* (Chapel Hill: The University of North Carolina Press, 2015), 166.

[8] Hartnett, *Carolina Israelite*, 166.

[9] "Shaw Captures NCSLA Awards," *Shaw Journal*, March–April 1960, 1, 2, NAACP Papers, microfilm 22:00147, 22:00150, Manuscript Division, Library of Congress, Washington, DC.

Americans.[10] Thus, Golden was one among a small minority of Whites in North Carolina who used his fame to advance the rights and opportunities of African Americans, and he would continue to do so in the following years. And like many of the students at historically Black colleges, he also seemed to appreciate the connection between education and civil rights in a region that often fell short of most of the rest of the nation in both regards.

The type of clear, strong support and encouragement Golden gave to student civil rights activists was rare among prominent Whites in North Carolina in 1960. Religious leaders, however, were one population segment that demonstrated leadership in promoting the goals of the sit-ins. Among the White pastors in Raleigh who supported the student activists, no one was more important than the Reverend W. W. Finlator. The minister took a principled stand in support of the sit-ins from a very early stage when it was quite risky and uncommon for Whites to do so. In the same week in which the Raleigh sit-ins began, Finlator praised the local students for protesting against segregation at the lunch counters. He issued a statement asserting that the students "are doing in our day what we honored our forefathers for doing in their day. And that is struggling for liberty."[11]

Finlator also understood the reality that the sit-ins were part of a broader struggle for the rights of African Americans. In March 1960, he was the opening speaker at the annual state convention of the AFL-CIO. The reverend called for "a ban henceforth and forever against discrimination" and also asked the more than 245 delegates, "Will you not understand that the fortunes of the Southern white laborer and the Southern Negro rise or fall together?"[12] Finlator was not the only White person in Raleigh who favored integration or supported the efforts of the student demonstrators and Black community members to achieve integration. But his support was unabashed, and unlike some Whites, he did not value preserving unfair social and economic practices merely because they were a tradition in Raleigh and North Carolina. In a year in which many White

---

[10] "Golden Featured in Symposium," *Campus Echo*, 28 November 1960, 5.

[11] Raleigh AP, "Raleigh Hits Sitdown Moves with Arrest of 41 Negroes: Students Charged with Trespassing," *Durham Morning Herald*, 13 February 1960, 1.

[12] David Cooper, "Minister Urges Labor to Abolish Racial Discrimination in Unions," *News and Observer*, 17 March 1960, 30.

political leaders in the state either wholeheartedly supported segregation or at the least tempered their personal support for civil rights for the sake of political expediency, Finlator was a beacon of moral leadership.

Finlator's support for the civil rights activists was echoed by a large number of Raleigh ministers representing all of the Protestant denominations in the city. On March 2, 1960, forty-six White ministers and thirteen Black ministers signed a public statement that gave support to the civil rights demonstrators. They commended "students and other persons who use orderly and non-violent means in a forgiving spirit to express their views on the practices of discrimination."[13] Thus, the ministers were recognizing not merely that they favored integration but also that they supported the direct-action tactics to achieve that end. Among the significant African American signers of the statement were John W. Fleming, who helped resuscitate the Raleigh Citizens Association, and, not surprisingly, the Dean of the Shaw University School of Religion, Dr. Grady Davis. Among the notable White ministers were Finlator and Oscar B. Woolridge, who was the spokesperson for the group and the religious coordinator at North Carolina State College. The group also sent letters to the New York headquarters of F. W. Woolworth and S. H. Kress urging them to adopt nondiscriminatory practices at their stores in which segregation still existed. They also sent a similar letter to Raleigh Mayor W. G. Enloe, who did not demonstrate the same type of commitment to civil rights that the group of fifty-nine ministers showed.[14]

Support for integration from religious leaders in Raleigh and Durham was certainly not unanimous. Woolridge qualified his group's statement by making clear that the fifty-nine ministers were speaking as individuals and did not intend to speak for all of their members. More specifically, he emphasized that the action of producing the statement was done independently of the Raleigh Ministers Association.[15] Later that month, the Durham Ministers Association pledged their support for the goals and tactics of the demonstrators: "We recognize and honor the desire and the

---

[13] Gene Roberts Jr., "Racial Troubles Prompt Statement by Preachers," *News and Observer*, 3 March 1960, 1, 3.

[14] Roberts, "Racial Troubles Prompt Statement by Preachers," 1, 3.

[15] Roberts, "Racial Troubles Prompt Statement by Preachers," 1, 3.

right of all citizens, whether Negro or white, to seek by all appropriate, just, peaceful, and legal means, equal public treatment as citizens." The statement also promised support to any stores that would initiate a policy of integration.[16] Thus, in Durham, the actual Ministers Association demonstrated unified support for integration.

However, not every minister in the city supported desegregation. The Conservative Ministers Association held a meeting the following day and issued a statement that made it clear that "we feel the public should be informed that the recently expressed views of the Durham Ministers Association as reported in the March 15 Herald ARE NOT the views of the Conservative Ministers Association."[17] Hence the opposition to segregation among religious leaders was not monolithic. Yet the extensive support for integration given by White ministers demonstrated that White support for segregation in North Carolina was not monolithic either. Sympathetic ministers used their social position to take a principled stand that few political leaders cared or dared to take.

An analysis of North Carolina's most famous preacher, Billy Graham, sheds light on many of the central conflicts in the South regarding segregation. Graham had personally supported integration and held integrated revivals.[18] He admired Martin Luther King Jr. and developed a personal relationship with him. The evangelist and Charlotte native also provided moral support to Dorothy Counts, who attempted to integrate Harding High School in Charlotte in 1957. After reading about her courageous efforts, Graham wrote a letter to the fifteen-year-old: "Democracy demands that *you* hold fast and carry on…. Those cowardly whites against you will never prosper because they are un-American and unfit to lead."[19] After an early 1960 trip to South Africa, Graham declared that segregation was doomed in that nation. He argued that "in no period of history had

---

[16] "Ministers Take Stand on Food Service: Individual Rights Are Supported," *Durham Morning Herald*, 15 March 1960, 1B.

[17] "Ministers Group Issues Statement," *Durham Morning Herald*, 16 March 1960, 1B. Emphasis in the original.

[18] Steven Patrick Miller, *Billy Graham and the Rise of the Republican South* (Philadelphia: University of Pennsylvania Press, 2009), 28.

[19] Frye Gaillard, *The Dream Long Deferred* (Chapel Hill: University of North Carolina Press, 1988), 10.

apartheid worked," and he also described race relations in the United States as an embarrassment to Americans in Africa.[20] In this sense, Graham seemed to demonstrate his aversion to segregation. His statements also can be viewed in light of the Cold War-era concern for winning the hearts and minds of South Africans and the people of other nations in Africa, which was undoubtedly negatively affected by the reality of segregation in the American South.

Yet when Graham was asked about segregation in the American South, he said he would prefer to wait to get back home to discuss that and said, "I don't think Southerners appreciate people sitting in New York and pointing the finger at them."[21] In essence, Graham tried to walk a fine line between supporting integration and not alienating his White supporters in the South. But his stance was also emblematic of the tendency of many White Southerners to view civil rights agitation as emanating from New York or the North more broadly. References to "outside agitators" were a common strategy among Southern politicians to attempt to portray civil rights demonstrations as being inspired by outsiders when in fact the majority of student activists were Southerners, even if they were not always members of the local communities in which they demonstrated.

It is important to reiterate that general support for gradual integration was not the same as supporting the direct-action tactics. Graham essentially favored the former and was wary of the latter. Like many other Southerners who were open to integration, he did not support direct-action tactics like sit-ins in 1960. Historian Clive Webb points out that Graham had raised the ire of many Southern Whites by suggesting that there was no biblical basis for segregation. But Webb also maintains that the sit-ins ran counter to Graham's gradualist approach to improving race relations. In November 1960, Graham told a reporter, "No matter what the law may be—it may be an unjust law—I believe we have a Christian responsibility to obey it."[22] Graham's stance ultimately decried segregation

---

[20] New York AP, "'Segregation Doomed,' Billy Graham Declares," *News and Observer*, 30 March 1960, 3.

[21] New York AP, "'Segregation Doomed,' Billy Graham Declares," 3.

[22] Clive Webb, "Breaching the Wall of Resistance: White Southern Reactions to the Sit-Ins," in *From Sit-Ins to SNCC: The Student Civil Rights Movement in the 1960s*, ed. Iwan Morgan and Philip Davies (Gainesville: University Press of Florida,

but also did not support the tactics that sought to hasten its demise. In the final analysis, he was wary of civil disobedience even when it carried a moral imperative.

The Episcopal Church provided leadership on a national level in supporting the sit-ins. In late March 1960, the church's National Council issued a statement to its approximately three million members that declared, "The Church in its basic teachings insists upon the dignity of all men before God. It is therefore not surprising that Christians are in the forefront of the demonstrations and that this 'passive resistance' movement has definite relationship to the churches both in teaching and leadership." The statement also made the point that Christianity has taught that civil disobedience is justified in certain cases involving moral issues.[23] At the forefront of support among Episcopalians was the Episcopal Society for Cultural and Racial Unity (ESCRU). Members of ESCRU challenged Episcopalian leaders in the South who opposed integration. Thomas Pettigrew, who was a member of the ESCRU board of directors, claimed that every so-called moderate in the segregated South was really "a paternalistic segregationist of nineteenth century vintage" and was clinging to archaic ideas in regards to race relations.[24]

The leadership of ESCRU was steadfast in their support for integration and the sit-ins, but they also recognized the need not to alienate the more conservative elements in the church organization. For example, Carl and Anne Braden were excited when they heard about the founding of ESCRU and asked one of the organization's founders, John B. Morris, about starting a chapter in Louisville. But Morris was wary of associating the nascent group with the Bradens since Carl had been imprisoned for his refusal to answer questions before the House Un-American Activities Committee (HUAC). Gardiner Shattuck argues that Morris's Cold War mentality in this instance revealed the essentially centrist political leanings of the ESCRU leadership.[25]

2012), 66–67.

[23] George W. Cornell (New York AP), "Episcopal Church Backs Sitdown Movement," *News and Observer*, 31 March 1960, 13.

[24] Gardiner H. Shattuck, *Episcopalians and Race: Civil War to Civil Rights* (Lexington: University Press of Kentucky, 2000), 104.

[25] Shattuck, *Episcopalians and Race*, 105.

Yet even if the organization was centrist in its political leanings, it by no means took a "moderate" stance on race relations, at least by Southern standards. Supporting the sit-ins as a tactic was much more aggressive than simply stating that the group favored integration. The ESCRU leadership ultimately supported efforts by activists to integrate churches in the South through the use of "kneel-ins." In perhaps its most progressive stance, a resolution was adopted at the ESCRU annual meeting in 1961 that recognized "neither theological nor biological barriers to marriage between persons of different color."[26] As Shattuck points out, this position caused some moderately liberal bishops and church leaders in the South to cancel their membership in ESCRU, as the clear stance on interracial marriage may have alienated their support in their local churches.[27] Ultimately, taking a strong stand on integration was a risky move for some church leaders, but many believed it was consistent with the teachings of the church and Christianity more broadly. ESCRU took a forward-looking stance that rejected archaic social traditions. In supporting the sit-ins and ultimately the kneel-ins, the organization gave moral and spiritual support to integration leaders, including student leaders who attended the school that was the site of the organization's founding, Saint Augustine's College.

In addition to receiving support from certain church leaders and church organizations both within and beyond the Triangle, student protestors in Raleigh and Durham received official support from some religious groups at the primarily (or exclusively) White schools in the region. On March 2, 1960, Baptist student leaders at North Carolina State College in Raleigh called for a boycott of stores that practiced segregation. The resolution was announced by the Baptist Student Union Executive Council, which represented over four hundred of the approximately six thousand students at the college. The resolution indirectly endorsed the sit-in tactics, giving support to "the moral goal of the Negroes for social equality under the law of our land and to uphold the right of Negro students and leaders to use the instrument of active but non-violent public demonstration to advance their cause."[28]

---

[26] Shattuck, *Episcopalians and Race*, 106.

[27] Shattuck, *Episcopalians and Race*, 106.

[28] Raleigh UPI, "Baptist Students Ask Boycott in Raleigh," *Durham Morning*

Similar support came from Duke University Divinity School students in a resolution in which they endorsed the nonviolent student movement and even acknowledged guilt for their own past participation in the "broken community among men." The statement even targeted segregated practices directly: "We believe that the policy of segregated lunch counters, followed by certain local merchants and chain stores is not in harmony with Christian principles."[29] The resolution also expressed the students' willingness to eat at integrated lunch counters.[30] The resolutions from Duke University and North Carolina State College were important in revealing that support for the sit-ins was more widespread than just the few students from these two colleges who actually participated in the sit-ins. They also provide another example that sympathy for the cause of civil rights was generally strong (although far from universal) among religious leaders and students—even White students—in the region.

An editorial in the *News and Observer* on March 15, 1960, lucidly revealed the intersections between race relations and education that became more apparent as a result of the student-led civil rights demonstrations in 1960. Vance Barron, a White pastor at The Presbyterian Church in Chapel Hill, criticized Woman's College Chancellor Gordon Blackwell's speech that discouraged students at the college in Greensboro from participating in the sit-ins, and he also condemned Governor Luther Hodges's approval of the speech. Barron made the point that the duties and responsibilities of the student cannot be confined to the limits of the campus. He suggested that for a chancellor of a college to limit the activities of students outside the college would be a limit to their freedom to act and think as responsible individuals. He further asserted that efforts from the college administration or the state government to limit students from acting on their convictions would be an example of "thought control by the State...and the end of true education: for true education depends upon freedom, just as freedom depends upon education."[31] Hence Barron

---

Herald, 13 March 1960, 10.

[29] "Sitdown Move Commended y Duke Divinity Students," *Durham Morning Herald*, 16 April 1960, 1B.

[30] "Sitdown Move Commended," 1B.

[31] Vance Barron, "Chancellor Blackwell's Speech" (editorial), *News and Observer*, 15 March 1960, 5.

made the connection between academic freedom and civil rights protests that so many Black and White college students in the Triangle made in 1960. And like the student protestors, Barron recognized the interrelation between freedom and education that would become quite apparent in the 1960 gubernatorial Democratic primary runoff election between Fayetteville lawyer and racial moderate Terry Sanford and Raleigh lawyer and staunch segregationist I. Beverly Lake.

Sanford and Lake ultimately squared off in a Democratic Party primary runoff election that had tremendous implications for the future of segregation in the state. For all intents and purposes, in the nine decades after Reconstruction, winning the Democratic primary for governor was tantamount to winning the general election. By 1960, only one Republican had won the governor's office since 1877. For much of that period, African Americans had been largely disenfranchised in the state through various tactics, including poll taxes and literacy tests. North Carolina had eliminated the use of the poll tax by 1920, and by 1944 only certain counties utilized the all-White primary. Michael J. Klarman maintains that North Carolina never conducted statewide all-White primaries.[32] Thus, the 1944 Supreme Court decision in *Smith v. Allwright* deeming the all-White primary unconstitutional had a lesser impact in North Carolina than in other states in the South. Nonetheless, in a state in which Republicans were often not competitive in major elections, the Democratic primary was the crucial election. The 1960 Democratic primary election for governor of North Carolina was initially a four-man race among former North Carolina Democratic Party Chairman John D. Larkins Jr., Attorney General Malcolm Seawell, Terry Sanford, and I. Beverly Lake. My analysis will focus primarily on the runoff election between Sanford and Lake. Focusing on these two candidates will make clearer the contrast between two competing ideologies that the candidates represented, one that emphasized improvements in education and the other that emphasized doubling down on preserving segregation in the state.

Students at historically Black colleges and universities played a

---

[32] Michael J. Klarman, "The White Primary Rulings: A Case Study in the Consequences of Supreme Court Decision-making," *Florida State University Law Review* 29 (2014): 65, http://ir.law.fsu.edu/lr/vol29/iss1/2.

significant role in influencing the 1960 North Carolina gubernatorial election. The sit-in movement in various locations throughout the state pushed the issue of race relations to the forefront of the election, and the ways in which the candidates navigated the contentious issue played a significant role in determining the eventual winner of the Democratic Party primary elections. In many ways, Black (and some White) college students galvanized support for civil rights through an expanded concept of academic freedom that connected civil rights protest activity with opening societal opportunities. Many sit-in participants viewed their actions as part of their education, as dismantling segregation would potentially open more societal and economic opportunities.[33]

Thus, for Black college students, education and civil rights protests were mutually reinforcing. Although the sit-ins primarily targeted segregated public accommodations, they were part of a broader assault on segregation that included segregated schools. Before the sit-in movement began in North Carolina, the race issue had not registered as a serious concern among potential voters, according to a poll that Sanford had commissioned prior to the outbreak of sit-ins in the state.[34] This result does not imply that race relations was not an issue at all but suggests it was not a top priority to address in the upcoming election. But the sit-in movement heightened the concern over race relations in the state and helped to set the stage for the Democratic primary election in which concerns over segregation, including school segregation, would play a crucial role.

The most direct, yet unintended, consequence of the sit-ins in shaping the 1960 Democratic primary gubernatorial election was their influence in pushing Lake to decide to run for governor. Lake had considered a run for the state's highest position, but by mid-February 1960, he had withdrawn himself from the race due to a lack of potential campaign funds. But as the sit-ins continued to spread throughout the state, letters and financial contributions came in from supporters asking him to reenter the race.[35] On March 1, the same day that Lake appeared on NBC's *Today*

---

[33] See survey results in appendix.

[34] Howard E. Covington Jr. and Marion A. Ellis, *Terry Sanford: Politics, Progress, and Outrageous Ambitions* (Durham: Duke University Press, 1999), 205.

[35] Gene Roberts Jr., "Court Order His Springboard: Lake Stirring Passions on Desegregation Issue," *News and Observer*, 19 May 1960, 2.

Show with a panel that included NCC student protest leader Lacy Streeter, Lake announced in a separate press conference that he was entering the governor's race. In his announcement, he stated that he would support "the right of the owner of any store, restaurant or café to decide for himself what customers he will serve and what prices he will charge."[36] Lake characterized the segregation issue as the "most far-reaching problem North Carolina has faced in this century," and vowed to preserve the social order that maintained segregation.[37] Lake himself made it clear from an early point in his candidacy that he would be the strongest supporter of segregation among the four candidates vying to be the Democratic nominee.

Lake's entrance into the gubernatorial race came approximately a month after Terry Sanford officially announced his candidacy. Sanford had graduated from the University of North Carolina at Chapel Hill in 1939 and was a World War II veteran. He served one term as a state senator from 1953–1955. From 1948–1960, he practiced law in Fayetteville, where his office overlooked the historic Market House in the heart of downtown, a structure both historically revered and reviled due to it having been a primary site of the slave market in the city prior to the Civil War. It was from this historic site that Sanford announced his candidacy for governor on February 4, 1960, a day known in Fayetteville as "Terry Sanford Day."[38]

From an early point in his campaign, Sanford made clear his commitment to improving education in North Carolina. In a speech to the Young Democratic Club in Chapel Hill on March 16, he called education the "dominant issue in this campaign and...the dominant purpose of our administration."[39] Later in the campaign Sanford declared that "I am for, above all, lifting our school system from the bottom 10 to the top 10."[40] Like the other three candidates, Sanford also addressed other issues in the

---

[36] Charles Clay, "Lake to Run: Sounds Segregationist Theme," *News and Observer*, 2 March 1960, 1.

[37] Clay, "Lake to Run," 1.

[38] Covington and Ellis, *Terry Sanford*, 92–93, 201–202.

[39] "School Issue: Terry Sanford Takes 'Moderate Approach,'" *News and Observer*, 17 March 1960, 1.

[40] Charles Craven, "Sanford Lead Tops 82,000," *News and Observer*, 31 May 1960, 1.

campaign such as improvements in roads, industrial expansion, and agricultural policies. But it was clear throughout the campaign that his emphasis was on improving public education, and ultimately his actions as governor would validate that this emphasis was not merely campaign posturing.

It would be inaccurate to suggest that I. Beverly Lake did not emphasize education in the 1960 election. However, the way in which he emphasized education was nearly always in relation to preserving segregated schools at all costs. Lake was adamantly opposed to even the token integration taking place in the state. His acknowledgment that the spread of the sit-in movement caused him to reenter the race seems to indicate that he recognized that the student-led movement could potentially lead to more aggressive efforts at integrating the public elementary and secondary schools in the state. In mid-March, Lake declared that he would not support the 1954 Supreme Court decision in *Brown v. Board of Education* and that he would use every gubernatorial power "to the fullest extent practicable" to prevent integration of the schools.[41] Although the other three candidates were clearly not integrationists themselves, they favored a so-called "moderate" approach, which allowed for minimal integration or at least permitted integration to occur at schools in which local school boards chose to accept African Americans. But Lake drew the line in the sand between himself and the other three candidates, explicitly acknowledging that he was different. On April 19, he asserted that the primary difference between himself and the other candidates was in the "attitude and awareness" of the integration issue. He claimed that "integration of the schools would be a tragic development for both whites and Negroes," and that "if elected I will do all I can to avoid that situation. I would also take my election to mean that's what the people want."[42] Thus, Lake recognized that his election prospects were closely tied to his strategy of emphasizing resistance to integration.

At the heart of Lake's candidacy and his plan if he were elected was

---

[41] Gene Roberts Jr., "Lake Attacks State's Approach to School Integration Problem," *News and Observer*, 18 March 1960, 1.

[42] Wilmington UPI, "On Integration: Lake Says He's Different," *News and Observer*, 20 April 1960, 5.

to create a "climate of public opinion" against integration of the schools. One of his most consistent tactics was not to criticize African Americans in general but to attack the NAACP. Even during Lake's time as the Assistant Attorney General of North Carolina in the mid-1950s, he had declared that "the NAACP is our enemy, not the Negro people."[43] Opposition to the NAACP among White politicians in the South was hardly novel in 1960, but he made the attacks on the NAACP a central part of his campaign. Lake also attacked the Hodges administration for "appeasing" the NAACP with token integration. He blamed the administration for making North Carolina the "soft spot in the South" in regards to integration.[44]

Attacking Hodges on his positions on race relations demonstrates Lake's reactionary views about race relations. Hodges portrayed himself as a moderate on race relations. But he had made his opposition to the *Brown* decision abundantly clear early in his first term as governor when he assumed the position after the death of William Umstead in November 1954.[45] He also supported the "Southern Manifesto," a declaration signed by 101 Southern Congressman expressing formal protest against what they deemed as the US Supreme Court's usurpation of power. As demonstrated in chapter 2, Hodges opposed the tactics of the sit-in demonstrators. He also ostensibly played the subliminally racist game of blurring his pronunciation of the widely accepted word "Negro" and the much more offensive and phonetically similar word, resulting in "Nigra."[46] According to Saint Augustine's College student LaMonte Wyche, Hodges spoke at the campus, and in a somewhat playful protest, the students dropped their books

---

[43] Asheboro, NC, AP, "Assistant Attorney General Sees Need—Private Schools Asked to Avoid Integration," *Durham Sun*, 15 July 1955, 1.

[44] Raeford AP, "Lake Raps Governor's Programs," *News and Observer*, 1 April 1960, 7; Greenville AP, "Campaign Trail: Lake Says NC 'Soft Spot,'" *News and Observer*, 6 May 1960, 6.

[45] Luther H. Hodges, "The Segregation Problem in the Public Schools of North Carolina," Box 131, untitled folder, Special File: Governor's Committee for Public School Amendment, Governor's Papers, Luther Hodges, North Carolina State Archives, Raleigh.

[46] LaMonte Wyche, phone interview by the author, digital recording, 29 June 2016; Walter Riley, phone interview by the author, digital recording, 14 June 2016.

each time he said "Nigra."[47] Hodges was far from an integrationist or a liberal when it came to race relations, but Lake's campaign was making it clear that he would be a more reactionary governor than Hodges in terms of race relations.

It was in this context that the four-man race for the Democratic nomination for governor of North Carolina would take place at the end of May 1960. A last-minute full-page ad in the *News and Observer* sponsored by the Wake County "Lake for Governor Committee" revealed the focus of Lake's campaign, as it headlined:

"A BALANCED BUDGET...SCHOOL SEGREGATION...
STATE'S RIGHTS...and PROPERTY RIGHTS."

The ad also emphasized that "the mixing of our two great races in the classroom and then in the home is not inevitable and is not to be tolerated," in addition to bluntly stating that "THE NAACP IS OUR ENEMY."[48] Aside from the reference to school integration opposition, the ad's eight bullet points do not make clear reference to improving education, a striking omission in any governor's race. Of course, Lake did not avoid discussing education in his campaign, but it was clear where his focus lay: maintaining segregation.

On May 28, 1960, the voters of North Carolina turned out in record numbers with over 653,000 casting votes in the four-way Democratic primary. Sanford won a clear plurality with about 41 percent of the vote, while Lake got 28 percent, and Seawell and Larkins roughly split the remaining difference.[49] State law stipulated that if one candidate did not secure a majority, then the second-place finisher was entitled to call for a runoff. According to Sanford biographers Howard E. Covington Jr. and Marion Ellis, Lake was encouraged by the results, claiming that the "thrill of victory was strong at Lake's headquarters."[50] It was indeed impressive

---

[47] LaMonte Wyche, interview by the author.

[48] "If You Really Know Dr. Beverly Lake: You'll Vote For Him on May 28," political advertisement, *News and Observer*, 26 May 1960, 31. Emphasis in the original.

[49] Covington and Ellis, *Terry Sanford*, 223.

[50] Covington and Ellis, *Terry Sanford*, 223.

that Lake had garnered such support with somewhat limited resources and had defeated the ultimate Democratic Party insider and former state chairman of the party, John Larkins Jr., as well as state Attorney General and Hodges favorite, Malcolm Seawell. Larkins and Seawell were much more closely aligned with Sanford in terms of their position as "moderates" on segregation. Thus, the runoff election would ultimately make much clearer the choice between two approaches to race relations and segregation.

In 1960, Terry Sanford was not a clear supporter of integration. The simple reality is that taking a strong stand in support of integration in North Carolina during the election of 1960 would likely have been political suicide. The previously mentioned survey that Lou Harris conducted showed that Whites favored segregation overall by a margin of 2 to 1. Additionally, over half of those polled believed that Blacks had no right to be served where they were not wanted.[51] Even though Sanford did not promote integration, he represented a clear alternative to the staunchly segregationist Lake. Sanford advocated continuing community-based decision-making and thus very gradual integration of the schools, a strategy that he and others believed would prevent the Supreme Court or the federal government from intervening and forcing integration. By the end of the 1959–1960 school year, a mere thirty-four Black children were in the previously all-White schools.[52] But Lake sought to promote a "climate of public opinion" against school integration, and his approach to race relations ran contrary to the moderate approach to race relations, which could be a winning strategy when promoted by a candidate like Sanford who was popular in other aspects, especially in regards to his approach to education (aside from the integration issue).

Perhaps Sanford's approach to racial issues in the election of 1960 can be most simply demonstrated when he said, "Let's don't highlight it."[53] In addition to a commitment to improving state roads, Sanford continued to focus on improvements in public education during the four weeks between the initial primary and the runoff and stressed that Lake's approach to

---

[51] Covington and Ellis, *Terry Sanford*, 215.
[52] Covington and Ellis, *Terry Sanford*, 222
[53] Charles Craven, "Sanford Lead Tops 82,000," *News and Observer*, 31 May 1960, 1.

resisting the *Brown* decision would lead to the closing of public schools in order to resist integration. And thus we return to the statements made by the Chairman of the State Board of Education, Dallas Herring, on June 22 that opened this chapter in which he ostensibly took a shot at Lake's appeal to fear and prejudice. Herring said that "reaction was never characteristic of the people of North Carolina" and that education "will always be the basic ingredient of our progress."[54]

The runoff election tested whether the forces of reaction (in terms of race relations) would characterize the position of North Carolinians. Any election has several variables, including the amount of funding the candidate can secure, popularity in certain geographical areas due to the candidate living there, personal charm and charisma, and a variety of issues that might lead certain voters to vote for the candidate. But ultimately, the choice came down to a reactionary approach to race relations coupled with a "hold the line" view on educational funding on one hand and, on the other hand, a moderate view on race relations that left hope for future gains coupled with a forward-looking vision that emphasized the importance of public education.

On June 25, 1960, Sanford defeated Lake with a total of 352,133 to 275,288 votes.[55] In a state in which Democrats had a stranglehold on gubernatorial elections, this result all but assured Sanford to be the next governor, a reality made clear in the *News and Observer*'s slightly presumptuous but not exactly controversial statement on June 26 that Sanford "will succeed Luther Hodges as Governor of North Carolina."[56] The African American vote was heavily in favor of Sanford. In the initial primary, Sanford had fared very well among Black voters. In three mostly Black precincts in Raleigh, Sanford had won 95 percent of the vote, with a similar pattern in Winston-Salem and Greensboro. An interesting anomaly occurred in Durham in the initial primary, in which Seawell won 89 percent of the vote in the five mostly Black precincts to Sanford's 7 percent. Years later, Sanford admitted that he purposely conceded the Black vote in

---

[54] "Herring Says: Forces of Reaction Threaten Education," *News and Observer*, 23 June 1960, 34.
[55] "Sanford Win Margin Is 76,288 Votes," *News and Observer*, 2 July 1960, 20.
[56] "Sanford Nominated for Governor," *News and Observer*, 26 June 1960, 1.

Durham and even took steps for Seawell to win in the Black neighborhoods so as not to appear to racial conservatives as having gotten the "bloc vote" among Blacks.[57] Sanford's willingness to essentially concede Black votes in the initial primary revealed that he believed it likely that the race would proceed to a runoff and that he would be one of the two to move on. It may also indicate that Sanford had predicted that Lake would be his opponent in the runoff and that securing the votes in Durham's primarily Black precincts would not be a problem against Lake.

Not surprisingly, the African American vote for Sanford was nearly unanimous among those who chose to vote in the runoff election. In Durham County, Lake narrowly defeated Sanford. But in the Black precinct of Hillside High School, Sanford defeated Lake 812 to 2.[58] Sanford beat Lake in Wake County, with the bulk of his support coming in the city of Raleigh in which he held a nearly 2 to 1 advantage. Sanford dominated in the primarily Black districts, such as the twentieth district, in which he won by a total of 1,055 to 12.[59] For the election as a whole, it is quite possible that Black voters provided the difference in determining the victor. Sanford won by approximately 76,000 votes. Durham's Black newspaper, *The Carolina Times*, credited the African American vote with providing the winning votes for Sanford. The newspaper estimated that 70,000 to 90,000 Blacks had voted. If about 90 percent of African Americans who voted chose Sanford, then it is possible that Black votes did sway the election in Sanford's favor. The newspaper stated that "it is also encouraging to know that a majority of white voters in North Carolina are no longer duped by a candidate for public office whose major platform plank is the race issue.[60] If indeed Blacks had delivered the difference in the election, then Lake had received a very slight majority of White voters. In his analysis of the race, John Drescher argues that "Lake's pride in winning a majority of white voters assumes that the votes of black citizens

---

[57] John Drescher, *Triumph of Good Will: How Terry Sanford Beat a Champion of Segregation and Reshaped the South* (Jackson: University Press of Mississippi, 2000), 162.

[58] "Tabulation of Durham Voting," *Durham Morning Herald*, 26 June 1960, 6.

[59] "Total Vote in County is 28,519," *News and Observer*, 26 June 1960, 3.

[60] Drescher, *Triumph of Good Will*, 218; "Negro Vote Sanford's Win Margin: Estimated 75 Thousand Held Power Balance," *Carolina Times*, 2 July 1960, 1.

somehow are worth less than the votes of white citizens. To him, they were."[61]

Among the Black voters who had helped deliver Sanford's victory were students from historically Black colleges. Pete Cunningham, who graduated from Saint Augustine's College only a month before the runoff primary, recalled that the 1960 election was the first time that he had voted. He supported Sanford and believed that Lake "was a redneck from his heart."[62] 1960 Shaw University graduate Carrie Gaddy Brock remembers that she "was pro-Sanford all the way." When asked about her thoughts on Lake, she believed that "he would have the place [North Carolina] go from bad to worse."[63]

The number of students at the "Protest Triangle" schools who voted for Sanford remains unclear. Based on student interviews I conducted, it seems that far less than a majority voted in the election. First, some of the students were residents of other states. Second, many of the students were not old enough to vote in an era when the voting age was twenty-one. But for those who did follow the race, they were ostensibly unanimous in their dislike for Lake. Joseph Holt Jr.'s family had gone through death threats and bomb threats during their attempt to desegregate Josephus Daniels Junior High and Needham Broughton High School in Raleigh, and the family was already keenly aware of who Lake was prior to 1960, largely due to his adamant opposition to school integration. Holt Jr., who became a freshman at Saint Augustine's College in the fall of 1960, believed that Lake was a "demagogue that spewed the venom of racial hatred."[64]

The relatively low numbers of students at historically Black colleges who voted in the 1960 gubernatorial election do not tell the entire story of their impact on the election. First and foremost, the students had helped mobilize the Black community to take a stronger stand for civil rights. Many African Americans in their respective communities appreciated the

---

[61] Drescher, *Triumph of Good Will*, 218.

[62] Pete Cunningham, phone interview by the author, digital recording, 21 June 2016.

[63] Carrie Gaddy Brock, interview by the author, digital recording, 2 March 2016, Raleigh.

[64] Joseph Holt Jr., interview by the author, digital recording, 7 July 2016, Raleigh.

principled stand that the students took in pushing for integration and responded by becoming more involved in efforts to dismantle segregation and improve the quality of life for people of their race. One obvious way to express their opposition to segregation was to vote against Lake. The student-led sit-in movement also served to mobilize African American organizations. In Raleigh, the advent of the sit-in movement in that city led to the resuscitation of the Raleigh Citizens Association (RCA).[65] One of the primary functions of the RCA was the promotion of political candidates, and in the 1960 Democratic primary runoff, Sanford was the clear choice over Lake. The peaceful protest movement also inspired new allies in the fight for racial justice. Whereas many religious leaders had supported better conditions for African Americans prior to 1960, the advent of the sit-in movement also helped raise the consciousness of both White and Black religious leaders to take a clearer moral stand against segregation. The aforementioned statement from the pulpit by W. W. Finlator is but one example of a well-respected religious figure taking a moral stand against segregation and its most outspoken proponent in North Carolina, I. Beverly Lake.[66]

Sanford's victory portended changes in segregated practices and in opportunities for African Americans in the following years. But some major changes took place before Sanford was even inaugurated as governor in January 1961. One of the most significant changes in Raleigh came when William Campbell became the first African American accepted into a previously all-White public school in the city. Just as with the Holt family four years prior, it took tremendous courage for the Campbell family to push for their children to attend previously all-White schools. Ralph Campbell Sr. had served in World War II and the Korean War before becoming an employee of the United States Postal Service; he also served as the president of the Raleigh chapter of the NAACP in the early 1960s. As a federal employee, he was less concerned about losing his job in retaliation for his attempts to get his children into formerly all-White schools

---

[65] "Citizens' Committee Reactivated in City," *Carolinian*, 20 February 1960, 1; "Citizens Association Plans Session to Organize Here," *Carolinian*, 18 June 1960, 1.
[66] "Pastor Hits Lake Candidacy," *News and Observer*, 13 June 1960, 22.

than if he had been employed by a White-owned business.[67]

Ralph Campbell Sr. and his wife June made the courageous decision to seek entrance for Ralph Jr. and Mildred to Morson Junior High School and for William Campbell to enter Murphey Elementary School for the 1960–1961 school year. Small-scale school integration had already taken place in several cities in North Carolina, including Durham the previous year. The city board of education in Durham had approved 7 of 205 five applications for African American students to attend formerly all-White schools for 1960–1961, an indicator of the slow approach in many school districts throughout North Carolina at the time. In Durham, five students had been accepted the previous year, bringing the total to twelve before Raleigh had accepted the first Black student into a previously all-White school.[68] The other community in the Triangle, Chapel Hill, accepted its first three Black students at the previously all-White Estes Hills Elementary School for the 1960–1961 school year.[69]

In early September 1960, the city school board of Raleigh voted unanimously to accept William Campbell into Murphey Elementary School. However, Mildred and Ralph Jr. were denied acceptance to Morson Junior High on the grounds that the school was already overcrowded. Ralph Campbell Sr. told the school board, "I feel discriminated against as a citizen and as a taxpayer…. To assign a child at any time to a segregated school is in violation of the Constitution and the Supreme Court Decision of 1954."[70] Despite Campbell Sr.'s expression of frustration, Mildred Campbell (Mildred Christmas) recalls that her parents were focused on William, who had been accepted, and viewed it as a baby step in the right direction. For Mildred, she shared in the ramifications of being part of the family that first integrated the Raleigh city schools. She recalls the

---

[67] Ron Cornwall, "Throng at Campbell Rites: Gov.'s Tribute Is One of Hundreds," *Carolinian*, 19 May 1983, 1, 2.

[68] Durham AP, "Seven More Negroes Transferred at Durham," *News and Observer*, 26 August 1960, 8. In 1955, Durham's Catholic School had accepted three African American students, making it the first desegregated school in the city. See Jerry Gershenhorn, *Louis Austin and the Carolina Times: A Life in the Long Black Freedom Struggle* (Chapel Hill: University of North Carolina Press, 2018), 132.

[69] Chapel Hill AP, "At Chapel Hill," *News and Observer*, 7 September 1960, 2.

[70] Jane Hall, "Reassignment Asked for Two Pupils," *News and Observer*, 28 September 1960, 1, 2.

consistent threatening phone calls and even bomb threats made toward her family. The Campbell children briefly stayed with relatives when the threats appeared realistic.[71] In this sense, they faced some of the same experiences as the Holt family over the previous four years.

June Campbell played a critical role in the effort at integrating Murphey Elementary and also in the broader struggle for improved conditions for African Americans in Raleigh. Her strength in taking William to school amid verbal threats was part of the reason that her son later claimed that "she was an absolute warrior" and that "leadership knows no gender bounds."[72] She also played an important informal role in the struggle for African American freedom in Raleigh. She was a tremendous cook, and she provided meals for civil rights leaders who met at the Campbells' home. In the wake of the enhanced consciousness among African Americans that largely stemmed from the student-led sit-ins, and the Campbell family's challenge to segregated schools, 1960 was a crucial year in establishing the Campbell household as a hive of civil rights activity. That year provided the roots of what would become known as the Oval Table Gang, an informal and changing group of activists who discussed civil rights issues at an oval table in the house in the 1960s. Among June Campbell's delicious signature dishes were shrimp gumbo and macaroni and cheese. Yet she was not only providing comfort food in the traditional sense. The activists who sat at the legendary oval table found comfort in the camaraderie and friendship that eased the tension of an activism that could be exhausting and even downright dangerous in a segregated society.[73]

William Campbell's experiences on the way to school and in the school revealed many of the contradictions and hostilities of the segregated society in Raleigh. It exposed the ugliest face of a culture deeply rooted in unfair and even inhumane treatment of African Americans. But it also revealed some of the consistencies and connections among the various advocates of integration and improved opportunities for African Americans

---

[71] Mildred (Campbell) Christmas, phone interview by the author, digital recording, 10 September 2016.

[72] William Campbell, phone interview by the author, digital recording, 12 September 2016.

[73] William Campbell, phone interview by the author; Ron Cornwall, "Throng at Campbell Rites," 1, 2.

in the city and beyond. Some of the ugliest moments in William's experiences were balanced by examples of some of Raleigh's citizens, both Black and White, demonstrating their most altruistic and beautiful essence.

William Campbell's road to Murphey Elementary School included what he termed a "caravan of civil rights leaders."[74] Dedicated African American citizens provided support for Campbell on his way to school to help protect the seven-year-old boy from facing violence. Among the most consistent supporters were two Shaw University professors who had previously provided encouragement to sit-in demonstrators, Marguerite Adams and Grady Davis. According to William's sister Mildred, school officials would only allow his mother to escort William from the car to the school door. But Davis and Adams were among those who would sit and wait in their car to ensure that William was not harassed. Ralph Campbell Sr. was not able to walk William into the school due to having to be at his job with the post office. Thus, June Campbell courageously walked William up to the school door each day and often told William to keep his head down and count the steps up to the school.[75] For both June and Ralph Campbell, the decision to put their child in harm's way and face the potential psychological trauma of threats and abuse demonstrated a major commitment to improving African American opportunities. As William later pointed out, "Nothing could show the courage and commitment more than sacrificing your children."[76]

The excruciating reality for June and Ralph Campbell was that once William was inside Murphey Elementary School, there was little they could do to protect him. And the impact of children growing up in a segregated society reared its ugly head inside the walls of the school. William recalls that many of the students despised him. While he did not suffer from any physical violence that resulted in serious injuries, certain students tripped and pushed him. After his first year at Murphey, he continued on in grades 3 through 6 and had some teachers who were not very supportive. He described his five years at the school as a "long, hard slog."[77]

---

[74] William Campbell, phone interview by the author.
[75] Mildred (Campbell) Christmas, phone interview by the author.
[76] William Campbell, phone interview by the author.
[77] William Campbell, phone interview by the author.

Despite the malice that came from certain students and even teachers during his time at Murphey, there were examples of affection and acceptance as well. He received support from the Black cafeteria workers who would always go out of their way to ask him how he was doing and to encourage him. But it was a White woman who likely had the most positive impact on his transition to the new school in 1960. In his first year at the school, William was assigned to Nell Abbott's class. He later characterized her as warm, loving, and caring. She went out of her way to treat him the same as everyone else, but she also kept a close watch on him to ensure that other students were not harassing him. Her support was encouraging and provided William with an environment that helped him succeed in the classroom. In William's first year, his fellow classmates did not know what to expect, and many had been conditioned to believe that Blacks were intellectually inferior. His academic success in his first year "crushed the notion that they (White students) were superior."[78]

On November 8, 1960, the same day that Terry Sanford was elected as governor over Republican candidate Robert Gavin, more than four hundred parents of Murphey Elementary School students asked the Raleigh Board of Education to reassign William Campbell to another school. Several parents had already made separate complaints and about fifty had asked for reassignment for their children. Parents had complained to the school board about the children playing "circle games" in which they had to hold hands with each other, and thus White children were holding hands with William Campbell. Present at the meeting in which the request was made for Campbell's reassignment was none other than Dr. I. Beverly Lake. The group claimed that they were not asking for reassignment of Campbell on the grounds of race but for the good of the community. Part of the petition submitted to the school board stated, "We residents of the attendance area of Murphey School in the city of Raleigh believe the integration of the school will not be for the best interests of the children in its attendance area and will decrease the values of the residential and business properties in the area."[79] Ultimately, the request for Campbell's transfer was denied.

---

[78] William Campbell, phone interview by the author.
[79] "Negro Student Transfer Sought," *News and Observer*, 9 November 1960, 30.

The results of the gubernatorial election and the integration of schools were interrelated in a political as well as personal way. The campaign of Lake made it clear that he would have opposed integration vehemently if he were elected. But there was a personal aspect to Sanford's election as governor that had an impact on school integration. In a fateful coincidence, Murphey Elementary School was only about a block away from the governor's mansion. Thus, Sanford had to make the important decision whether to allow his children to attend a school that had recently accepted a Black student or to have his children attend a private school. He ultimately decided to allow his two children to attend Murphey, stressing that his children should have no more privileges than other students.[80] Just as Sanford had made the political decision to emphasize improving public education over stressing segregation in the schools, after being elected Sanford made the personal decision to allow his children to attend a school that included the only Black student in the city attending a formerly all-White public school. Whether he viewed it in such terms or not, the implication was clear: in both political and personal ways, Terry Sanford emphasized education over segregation.

By the end of 1960, the impact of the sit-in movement in North Carolina was evident in both tangible and immeasurable ways. In Raleigh and Durham, student activists from the "Protest Triangle" increased the consciousness of African Americans in the two cities by enhancing support for challenging segregation. They provided a spark for resuscitating organizations like the Raleigh Citizens Association in Raleigh and pushing the Durham Committee on Negro Affairs to take a more aggressive approach to integration. In Raleigh, the response to the sit-in movement impacted school integration and influenced the Campbell family in their efforts. As William Campbell later noted, the sit-ins "set a standard" and "paved the way for more thoughtful integration."[81] In a general sense, the sit-in movement in North Carolina had galvanized support from some White religious leaders and members of the academic community in the form of White and Black college students and professors. In the most direct

---

[80] Washington AP, "Sanford Talks on Integration in TV Forum," *News and Observer*, 23 January 1961, 1.

[81] William Campbell, phone interview by the author.

impact, the sit-in movement was primarily responsible for the integration of several lunch counters throughout the state by the end of 1960. By early August, integration in some eating places had taken place in Winston-Salem, Charlotte, Greensboro, High Point, and Durham. On August 1, 1960, African Americans in Durham were served at S. H. Kress, F. W. Woolworth, and Walgreen's Drug Store. By mid-August, several lunch counters in Raleigh began offering service on an integrated basis. According to the Southern Regional Council, integrated lunch counter service had taken place in at least twenty-seven Southern cities by mid-August, including ten cities in North Carolina.[82]

The sit-in movement in 1960 also had an impact on the 1960 gubernatorial election. By inadvertently influencing Lake's decision to run for governor, student activists helped set the scene for a Democratic primary runoff that largely boiled down to education versus segregation. Terry Sanford, while far from publicly condemning segregation, emphasized improving public education in the state, while Lake focused on vehemently defending segregated schools. Sanford's election ultimately led to the governor's children attending an integrated school, a reality that was difficult to imagine in many Southern states in 1960. Just as the sit-in movement impacted the 1960 gubernatorial election, so would Sanford's victory impact the reaction to the sit-in movement when it reached another widespread wave in 1963.

In the speech referenced at the beginning of this chapter, State Board of Education Chairman Dallas Herring stated in the days before the runoff election between Sanford and Lake that "reaction was never characteristic of the people of North Carolina" in the struggle for liberty. This statement also seemed to be a shot at Lake, and Herring's contention that education "will always be the basic ingredient of our progress" was a pretty clear endorsement for Sanford, who emphasized improvements in education above all other matters.[83] Sanford's victory was an important indicator that a campaign focused primarily around maintaining racial segregation was

---

[82] "Integrated Lunch Counters: Durham Fifth N.C. City," *News and Observer*, 2 August 1960, 3; *Let Us March On: Raleigh's Journey Toward Civil Rights* (Raleigh: Raleigh City Museum, 2000), 14; Atlanta AP, "27 Southern Cities Now Serve Negroes," *News and Observer*, 7 August 1960, 2-II.

[83] "Herring Says: Forces of Reaction Threaten Education," 34.

not a winning strategy in North Carolina in 1960. It demonstrated that many North Carolinians (yet certainly not all) were willing to support a candidate who would likely have lost in states like Mississippi, Georgia, or even Arkansas. From his pulpit at Pullen Memorial Baptist Church less than two weeks before the runoff election, Reverend W. W. Finlator warned that if Lake were elected, "The Faubuses and Talmadges and the Eastlands will rejoice that at long last they have one of their own kind at the helm of North Carolina."[84] Finlator recognized the power that men like Arkansas Governor Orval Faubus and US Senators Herman Talmadge (Georgia) and James Eastland (Mississippi) had in leading opposition to desegregation and to calls for expanded civil rights for African Americans. There was a clear difference between these staunch defenders of segregation and Sanford. While Sanford was far from being an integration advocate in 1960, his lack of emphasis on the issue in the 1960 election left the door open for a more progressive stance on civil rights than that of his predecessors and nearly all of his contemporaries in Southern politics.

"There is a new day in North Carolina! I am not here to proclaim it, but rather to acknowledge its arrival," Sanford pronounced at the beginning of his inaugural address on January 5, 1961.[85] The event was held at Raleigh's Memorial Auditorium, the same site in which Martin Luther King Jr. spoke in the midst of the Youth Leadership Conference at Shaw University less than ninth months prior. Sanford's address took a forward-looking approach to the possibilities in the state. "I believe that the people of this state will rise in boldness and will go forward in determination that we have chosen wisely when we base our future hopes on quality education."[86] He envisioned North Carolina taking a leadership role in the nation and did not present a parochial regional view that vilified the national government like many Southern politicians did at the time. "Today we stand at the head of the South, but that is not enough. I want North Carolina to move into the mainstream of America and to strive to become the

---

[84] "Pastor Hits Lake Candidacy," 22.

[85] Memory F. Mitchell, ed., *Messages, Addresses and Public Papers of Terry Sanford, Governor of North Carolina, 1961–1965* (Raleigh: Council of State, State of North Carolina, 1966), 3.

[86] Mitchell, ed., *Messages, Addresses and Public Papers of Terry Sanford*, 6.

leading state of the nation."[87]

Sanford's inaugural address stands in stark contrast to Alabama Governor George Wallace's inaugural address two years later. Wallace harkened to the past, invoking the memory of Jefferson Davis and Robert E. Lee, and claimed that he spoke from the "very Heart of the Great Anglo-Saxon Southland." He portrayed the South as being in a battle with federal power and asserted that "we give the word of a race of honor that we will tolerate their boot in our face no longer." Wallace spoke very little of actual plans to improve education in the state. And, of course, he uttered the words that would become the rallying cry of many pro-segregation forces when he declared, "In the name of the greatest people that have ever trod this earth, I draw the line in the dust and toss the gauntlet before the feet of tyranny...and I say...segregation today...segregation tomorrow...segregation forever."[88] In contrast to Wallace, Sanford's address had neither segregationist rhetoric nor appeals to a past that valorized the resistance to federal power, especially when it came to defending the rights of African Americans. Perhaps the clearest indication that Sanford would be a forward-looking governor who would not take a reactionary approach on the issue of race came when he proclaimed that "no group of our citizens can be denied the right to participate in the opportunities of first-class citizenship."[89]

Upon exiting Memorial Auditorium after his inaugural address, Sanford could look to his right and see the historic campus of Shaw University. Whether he realized it or not, the actions of the students on the campus and those at the other historically Black colleges had had an impact on the election. In early 1961, it remained unclear what impact the students at Shaw and the other historically Black campuses would have during his term as governor. Many African Americans in Raleigh and throughout the state were encouraged that Sanford had triumphed over a strong advocate of segregation. Sanford said that his election showed that "an appeal to

---

[87] Mitchell, ed., *Messages, Addresses and Public Papers of Terry Sanford*, 7.

[88] George C. Wallace, "The Inaugural Address of Governor George C. Wallace," Montgomery, AL, 14 January 1963, Alabama Department of Archives and History, available at http://digital.archives.alabama.gov/cdm/ref/collection/voices/id/2952.

[89] Mitchell, ed., *Messages, Addresses and Public Papers of Terry Sanford*, 8.

fear, hate and social prejudice will not win an election" in the state.[90] His decision to have his children attend an integrated school provided hope that African Americans might be able to count him as an ally, or at a minimum not a foe, in the struggle for integration and improved opportunities for members of their race. But like other African Americans and sympathetic Whites throughout the state, the students at Shaw University recognized that Terry Sanford, or any other prominent figure for that matter, would not "bestow" freedom upon them.[91] If Sanford or any other political leaders in the state were going to take a strong stand on the side of civil rights for African Americans, student activists would have to pressure them to do so.

---

[90] Charles Craven, "Sanford Hopes Race Question Laid to Rest," *News and Observer*, 28 June 1960, 1.

[91] See appendix for survey responses.

Martin Luther King, Jr. at rally in Durham, 1958.

Courtesy General Negative Collection, State Archives of North Carolina

"Negro Students Refused Food Service,
Study at Counter Here," February 1960.

Unidentified boy looks on as (left to right) Rev. Douglas Moore,
Rev. Martin Luther King, Jr., Rev. Ralph Abernathy, and North
Carolina College student Lacy Streeter walk on Main Street in
Durham toward a closed Woolworth lunch counter, February 1960.
Photo by Jim Thornton.

Pamphlet for mass meeting featuring Dr. Martin Luther King, Jr. at Raleigh Auditorium, April 16, 1960.

Courtesy State Archives of North Carolina

Line of "round-robin" demonstrators stretches from the
Carolina Theatre box office west along Manning Place
in Durham, March 15, 1962. Photo by Jim Sparks.

Courtesy Durham Herald Co. Newspaper *Photograph Collection,*
Wilson Special Collections Library, UNC-Chapel Hill

National Student Association activists (including Jane Phillips and Ray Raphael on left) present Mrs. Hinton with flowers, Summer 1962. The Hinton family opened their home to accommodate voter registration volunteers.

Courtesy Susan Jhirad (Schwartz)

A group of protestors (in lowest row shown) challenge segregated
seating at a baseball game in Raleigh, Summer 1962.

Courtesy Susan Jhirad (Schwartz)

"A 'Swim-in' Demonstration at Raleigh's Pullen Park,"
August 1962.

A crowd estimated at 500 people demonstrates against
segregation at Howard Johnson's Restaurant on
Durham-Chapel Hill Boulevard, August 12, 1962.
Photo by Harold Moore.

Courtesy Durham Herald Co. Newspaper *Photograph Collection,
Wilson Special Collections Library, UNC-Chapel Hill*

"Jailed Girls Sing in Crowded Cellblock
after Wednesday Night Arrests," May 1963.

Chapter 6

Campus to Counter

More than five hundred protestors marched from Shaw University to the governor's mansion in Raleigh on May 10, 1963. They clapped their hands and sang freedom songs outside the mansion, which was heard by Governor Terry Sanford while the North Carolina Symphony ball was in progress inside. In addition to the festive singing, the protestors chanted, "We want the governor" for nearly twenty minutes. Sanford walked out onto the porch and told the protestors, "I have enjoyed the singing." One of the protestors then shouted, "We are not here to entertain you, Governor." Sanford responded, "You are not here at my request, either, friend.... If you want to talk to me at any time about your plans and your problems, let my office know." A protestor then shouted that Sanford "should have known our troubles." Boos followed the governor as he walked back into the mansion, and Shaw student body president Charles Earle told the crowd, "He said we did not come here at his request. Since we are not here at his request, we are going to stay anyway." Earle's statement was more figurative than literal. Shortly after making the comment, the group marched back to Shaw University. But there was little doubt that the protestors would continue to challenge Sanford's tentative dance around the issue of integration.[1]

---

[1] Bob Lynch and Roy Parker Jr., "Negroes Boo Gov. at Mansion," *News and*

The incident at the governor's mansion was in many ways emblematic of the movement in Raleigh and helps to illuminate the arguments in this chapter. Many of the protestors at the governor's mansion were part of a new wave of demonstrations in 1963, which put increasing pressure on political and business leaders in the city and the state to support integration. Students from Shaw University and Saint Augustine's College in Raleigh and North Carolina College (NCC) in Durham who participated in sit-ins literally went from campus to counter (or table) at segregated eating establishments, in addition to segregated theaters. But my primary argument is that these students also were the principal force that countered the established political and business leaders who had preserved segregated practices in the state for so long. The student activists clearly sought to oppose the die-hard supporters of segregation. They also sought to counteract the tentative "moderate" leaders, who could be considered anything but leaders on the issue of race relations.[2] They used protests to challenge White political and business leaders who appealed to tradition to preserve archaic social and economic practices at the expense of African American civil rights. They challenged the complicated hospitality throughout the state that denied fellow American citizens full access to public accommodations and quality job opportunities on the basis of race. In short, the activists challenged a segregationist vision of Tar Heel hospitality.

The protest at the governor's mansion further demonstrates that Shaw University was the epicenter of civil rights activism in Raleigh. It is also an indicator that civil rights activists no longer accepted Sanford's tentative dance around civil rights issues. Their involvement in protests in the spring and summer of 1963 presented a direct challenge to city political leaders and businessmen who sought to preserve segregated practices. Since Raleigh is the capital of North Carolina, the local movement for integration also had statewide implications. Sanford could not ignore the local movement, nor could state legislators who witnessed the demonstrations firsthand. Several business leaders were opposed to integration based

---

Observer, 11 May 1963, 1. A UPI article in the *Durham Sun* reported the crowd at 1,000: Raleigh UPI, "1000 March on Mansion: Negroes Finally Leave After Interrupting Ball," *Durham Sun*, 11 May 1963, 1.

[2] See survey (students) in appendix.

on simple prejudice, but many were skeptical of integration due to economic concerns. Many business leaders were willing to integrate only if all of their competitors did so as well. Student civil rights activists and their allies recognized that they needed to keep the pressure on the businesses to integrate, and sit-ins were among the most aggressive and effective practices for doing so.[3]

This chapter focuses primarily on civil rights activism in Raleigh and Durham in 1963, which was a crucial year for civil rights protests in the two cities and throughout the nation. Before analyzing that important year, I will address some of the activism and changes in conditions for African Americans that took place in 1961 and 1962 and illuminate some of the changes that occurred between 1960 and 1963.

In May 1961, John Winters became the first African American to be elected to the Raleigh City Council. Throughout the state, Black voter registration was much lower than that of Whites. In 1960, only 31 percent of African Americans in the state were registered to vote, compared with 90 percent of Whites.[4] But Winters's election represented a major victory for the mobilization of African American voting in the city. Black voters had played a crucial role in defeating the staunch segregationist I. Beverly Lake in his gubernatorial bid in 1960, and now they had another tangible victory on the local level.

Perhaps the most significant examples of civil rights activism in 1961 occurred during the Freedom Rides, in which Black and White "riders" challenged segregated bus terminals and facilities. The riders tested the enforcement (or lack thereof) of US Supreme Court decisions in *Sarah Keys v. Carolina Coach Company* (1955) and *Boynton v. Virginia* (1960), which had ostensibly banned segregation in interstate buses and in bus terminals and restaurants. Two of the groups of riders stopped in Raleigh in mid-June and were welcomed by Dr. Grady Davis, the Dean of Religion at Shaw. One group, which was composed of eight White and six Black Protestant ministers along with four rabbis, spent the night at Shaw

---

[3] Mack Junior Sowell, interview by the author, digital recording, 20 April 2016, Raleigh, NC; Richmond, VA, AP, "Negotiating Integration at Durham," *News and Observer*, 3 June 1963, 1.

[4] Roy Parker Jr., "Registered Electorate of N.C. Said Disproportionately White," *News and Observer*, 11 June 1961, 1.

University before continuing on to Tallahassee, Florida.[5] Some of the most influential riders who became nationally known figures in the civil rights movement had also attended the Youth Leadership Conference in April 1960, including John Lewis, Diane Nash, and Bernard LaFayette. Another one of the riders, Candida Lall, was an eighteen-year-old White student from Long Beach State College in California, who in January 1963 married Durham civil rights activist Walter Riley.[6]

Riley was among the activists who sought to bring about the end to segregation at the Raleigh-Durham airport. In 1961, the airport still had signs pointing people to the segregated bathrooms, although this separation was not strictly enforced by that time. The Durham Youth and College Chapters of the NAACP led the push. NCC student John Edwards, who had taken a leadership role in the sit-ins in 1960, telephoned airport commission chairman James Patton in early October, urging the end to segregated facilities at the airport. Patton stated that there was little he could do since the state required segregated toilet facilities. Edward (Ned) Opton, a White PhD student from Duke University active in the NAACP state youth chapter, called another member of the airport authority and told him of their plans to wire President Kennedy if the signs were not removed. Evidently, the official responded by saying, "You can wire the President or any damn body you please."[7] The decision to contact Kennedy was strategic and timely, as Kennedy had plans to land at the airport to open the North Carolina International Trade Fair. The warning by the young NAACP activists was not an empty threat. They wired Kennedy the following message:

> Racial segregation is practiced at the Raleigh-Durham airport, at which you are scheduled to open the North Carolina International Trade Fair on Oct. 12, 1961. The Chairman of the Airport Board of Control, Mr. Patton, has refused to remove the offensive racial signs from the airport rest rooms. We urge you, as the leader of our

---

[5] "Pass Through, No Incidents: Two 'Freedom' Groups Here," *News and Observer*, 14 June 1961, 24.

[6] "Delegates to Youth Leadership Conference," 2 June 1960, Box 25, Folder 1, SNCC Papers, Martin Luther King Jr. Center for Nonviolent Social Change, Atlanta, GA; Walter Riley, phone interview by the author, digital recording, 4 June 2016.

[7] "Kennedy Erases Jim Crow Signs," *Carolina Times*, 14 October 1961, 1, 2.

democracy, to decline to open an international trade fair within the wall of a state facility where African delegates, as well as members of your staff, would be subject to embarrassment and possible arrest.

In response, US Assistant Attorney General Burke Marshall sent a telegram to the airport manager that stated, "We would accordingly appreciate prompt action to remove these signs in compliance with federal law." Members of the airport authority met and voted to comply with the request. Ultimately, the signs were removed, and State Attorney General Wade Bruton gave the opinion that the state law requiring segregated toilet facilities could no longer be enforced.[8]

The irony and symbolism of the controversy over the segregation signs in preparation for the international trade fair could not have been more striking. Like other Cold War-era presidents, Kennedy mostly viewed civil rights issues in an international sense, and it was often the fear of international embarrassment and concerns over losing the Cold War propaganda battle that pushed Kennedy into action. But in a more direct sense, it was the actions of local Black and White student activists like Edwards and Opton that led to the Kennedy administration requesting the removal of the segregation signs. The situation made it clear that the young civil rights leaders in the Triangle recognized that Kennedy could be an ally, but only when pushed. They already had experience with a liberal who was cautious on the issue of civil rights from their indirect dealings with Terry Sanford. Young Black activists like Edwards and Riley, and sympathetic White activists like Opton, were keenly aware that they had to counter the defenders of segregation, such as the airport authorities who either supported segregation outright or claimed impotence to make changes. But the most insightful student leaders in the movement also realized that they had to counter the excuses, delay tactics, and tentative leadership that often characterized their intermittent allies like Kennedy and Sanford.[9]

---

[8] "Kennedy Erases Jim Crow Signs," 1, 2; "Pardon, Your Signs Are Showing," *The Campus Echo*, 27 October 1961, 2.

[9] Edward Opton, phone interview by the author, digital recording, 11 April 2016; Walter Riley, phone interview by the author, digital recording, 14 June 2016. Also see Thomas Borstelmann, *The Cold War and the Color Line: American Race Relations in the Global Arena* (Cambridge: Harvard University Press, 2001).

In the wake of the airport situation, Opton was elected president of the state youth chapter of the NAACP. Opton's leadership in pushing for desegregating the airport was far from his first action toward desegregation in the Triangle. After graduating from Yale in 1957, Opton chose Duke over another prestigious school, Syracuse University in Syracuse, New York. One of the factors for why he chose Duke was that there were opportunities to challenge segregation. According to Opton, in 1958 he drew up a petition to the Duke trustees to allow African Americans to enroll in the school, and he circulated the document among the students and faculty. The administration told him that many of the trustees were Methodist ministers and that a vote to desegregate would mean the end of their careers. Opton recalls that a few faculty members signed his petition, but a larger number refused. Blatant prejudice certainly accounted for some of those who refused, but others were fearful of losing their jobs. Hence, the looming threat of termination represented a restriction on the faculty's academic freedom. Many faculty members from Duke were reluctant to take a principled stand for desegregation in the late 1950s. But in the wake of the sit-ins and other demonstrations in the early 1960s, the moral imperative to take a stronger stand grew.[10]

Opton participated in sit-ins and efforts aimed at desegregating theaters. He recalled one instance in which he was chased down by the owner of a cafeteria on Main Street in Durham, not far from the law of office of Floyd McKissick. McKissick had played a major role in Opton's ascension to becoming the state NAACP youth leader. Opton developed connections with African American protest leaders in Durham and those from NCC. Walter Riley, the Hillside High School student who had become one of the most significant leaders by 1961, characterized the White student from Duke as one of the most important leaders in the Durham movement. For Riley, Opton was symbolic of the increasing White support for direct challenges to segregation, which ultimately became even stronger by 1963.[11] Opton also represented a critical connection between the private "Research Triangle" school (Duke) and the "Protest Triangle"

---

[10] Edward Opton, phone interview by the author.
[11] Edward Opton, phone interview by the author; Walter Riley, phone interview by the author.

public school (NCC).

Duke University was still one of the bastions of segregation in the early 1960s. Despite the actions of Opton and other Duke students who pushed for desegregation in public accommodations and at the university, the school remained closed to African Americans until 1961. In March 1961, the Board of Trustees resolved that qualified candidates of all races would be allowed into graduate and professional programs.[12] This action was a step toward integrating the undergraduate program, but the push for broader integration of the school continued. Zoology professor Peter Klopfer was one of the members of the faculty who most forcefully advocated for Duke to change its policies. A UNC student and writer for the *Durham Morning Herald* in the early 1960s, maintained that "there was no gutsier or grittier contender in either the external struggle or internal struggle than Peter Klopfer."[13] In January 1962, Klopfer proposed to the Undergraduate Faculty Council a strong pro-integration resolution addressed to the trustees. The trustees ultimately responded favorably to the resolution later that year. The first five Black undergraduate students entered Duke University in the fall of 1963.[14]

While the process of securing support for integration at Durham's most prestigious college played out, a small group of students from colleges around the country came to Raleigh in the summer of 1962 for a National Student Association (NSA) program focused on voter registration. Consideration was initially given for conducting the program in Mississippi, but the NSA Southern Project Board believed it to be too dangerous there. The project in Raleigh was coordinated by twenty-four-year-old Texan Dorothy Dawson and included a balance of female and male, Black and White activists. The group included students from prestigious universities in the North and West and from underfunded Black colleges in the South.

---

[12] Len Pardue and Galen Griffin, "Grad Schools Desegregated," *The Chronicle* (Duke University student newspaper), 8 March 1961, 1, Box 1, Folder 2, Black History at Duke Reference Collection, 1948–2001, David M. Rubenstein Rare Book and Manuscript Library, Duke University, Durham, NC.

[13] Jake Phelps, "Integration in North Carolina: An Outside Agitator Looks Back," *Ruby* (Duke University's Fiftieth Anniversary Issue), 12 April 1975, 1B, Box 1, "Desegregation" Folder, Black History at Duke Reference Collection, 1948–2001.

[14] "First Black Undergraduate Students," Box 1, Folder 3, Black History at Duke Reference Collection, 1948–2001.

To plan for the program, Dawson consulted with many activists, including Ella Baker, who suggested Dawson contact the Raleigh Citizens Association (RCA), which became one of the sponsors of the program, along with the NAACP. Dawson spent many hours planning and charting out maps showing registration target areas with members of the RCA, including Grady Davis from Shaw University. Dawson acknowledged that "Working closely with the RCA and with students from Saint Augustine's and Shaw University helped us avoid being rendered ineffective as outsiders, do-gooders, or naïve young people, though we were all of the above."[15]

One White activist from Radcliffe College, Susan Schwartz, was inspired to join the movement after hearing SNCC leader Chuck McDew speak on campus. She went against her parents' wishes, came to Raleigh, and lodged with an African American high school student from Kentucky. Like other participants in the project, she stayed in the dorm rooms of Saint Augustine's College and lamented the poor conditions on the campus. "You could see it [the campus] was really impoverished," she recalls.[16]

The NSA activists went door to door in Raleigh attempting to get African Americans registered to vote. They also attended African American churches in which many of the preachers were encouraging voter registration to their congregation. The efforts of NSA activists and of community members were effective in getting more than sixteen hundred African Americans registered to vote. Another primary focus of the NSA project was to tutor African American students who would be attending desegregated schools in the fall of 1962. Ray Raphael, a White New York native attending Reed College in Portland, Oregon, when he heard of the NSA project, recalls that he spent about as much time tutoring the students in math as he did in working on voter registration. The successful efforts of the NSA voter registration workers were a launching point for further activism that summer. Raphael quipped that the events later that summer were like an after-party where all the real action happened.[17]

---

[15] Constance Curry et al., *Deep in Our Hearts: Nine White Women in the Freedom Movement* (Athens: The University of Georgia Press), 107, 108.

[16] Susan Schwartz, phone interview by the author, digital recording, 30 October 2021.

[17] Ray Raphael, Phone interview by the author, digital recording, 8 November 2021.

For some local and national activists in Raleigh, the direct-action and integration efforts of the late summer of 1962 were a whirlwind of jack-knife evasions, highly publicized splashes, spitball-absorbing clashes, tense jailhouse encounters, and real-life civil rights education. Raphael described one integration effort at a wrestling match at the Municipal Auditorium as "absolutely harrowing." He purchased tickets for a few Black and White activists, and they proceeded to sit a few rows from the ring, well away from the section reserved for African Americans. Other attendees hurled beer cans and launched spitballs at the activists.

Then came an ominous silence.

When the hecklers went silent, the group began to fear the worst. When they exited the auditorium, a group of Whites brandished knives. As the potentially violent scene unfolded, a group of African American men that had been sitting in the Black section came to their defense. The group walked off to a nearby Black neighborhood, where the White students from outside the South and their Black friends could find safety. For Susan Schwartz, it legitimized a belief she had for much of the summer, that "we had the feeling that the white people around us would just as soon see us dead."[18]

Some of the students previously involved in the NSA voter registration project joined with four African Americans in Raleigh in August to integrate the for-Whites-only Pullen Park swimming pool in Raleigh. This was a less harrowing but much more publicized endeavor than their stance at the wrestling match. Raphael purchased tickets for the group. Then they rushed past the unsuspecting teenager working at the gate, went through the locker room, and immediately jumped in the refreshing water. Raphael cleverly describes the scene as similar to an old-time movie with the reel played in reverse. "A person who has just dived into the water seems propelled back upward, the splash of water becoming still once again. That's exactly what happens. We dive in and twenty or thirty swimmers dive out, leaving us alone for a refreshing dip."[19]

---

[18] Ray Raphael, phone interview by the author; Susan Schwartz, phone interview by the author.

[19] Ray Raphael, *A Life in History*, portion of unpublished work shared with the author; Ray Raphael, interview by the author.

The men were joined in the pool by Jane (J. J.) Phillips, a light-skinned African American who could often "pass" as White, and Susan Schwartz, a dark-skinned Caucasian who had separately gone through the women's locker room. Schwartz and Phillips had previously visited the African American pool at Chavis Park, which Schwartz described as a "horrible little swimming hole" and Phillips characterized as "more akin to a swamp." As the shock of the onlookers played out, a loudspeaker message announced, "will the colored boys and their white friends please leave the pool," followed by increasingly aggressive messages.[20]

As was the case with much of the civil rights activism in Raleigh in the early 1960s, Shaw University students were at the heart of the action. One of the leaders of the group was Shaw ministerial student Percy High, whom Raphael characterized as accessible, knowledgeable, and "kind of like our star [in the pool integration efforts and other activism]."[21] When questioned about the group's motivation, High stated simply, "It was a hot day and we decided to go swimming."[22] Eleanor Nunn, a student representative at the 1960 Youth Leadership Conference at Shaw and the president of the Shaw chapter of the NAACP by 1963, echoed High's straightforward reasoning: "They had all the reason they needed to go in the pool. It was a hot day." The group of swimmers included students from the Deep South and from the North. High rejected the idea that they were outside agitators: "Why shouldn't they be entitled to swim at a public pool in Raleigh? They are Americans."[23]

After the group of swimmers refused to leave, City Recreation Director Jimmy Chambers ordered the pool to be closed. He also ordered the city's pool for African Americans at Chavis Park to be closed. The Raleigh City Council voted 5–2 in favor of closing the pools, with the only dissenting votes coming from John Coffey and the council's lone Black

---

[20] Susan Schwartz, phone interview by the author; Jane Phillips, "Night Train to Raleigh: Summer 1962 Voter Registration, Chased by the Klan, and Going Incognegro Below the Mason-Dixon Line," 2016, https://www.crmvet.org/nars/phillips.htm; Ray Raphael, phone interview by the author.

[21] Ray Raphael, phone interview by the author.

[22] Raleigh AP, "City Pools in Raleigh Are Closed," *Durham Sun*, 7 August 1962, 3A.

[23] Gene Roberts Jr., "A Look at the Negro Student: Thunder on the Campus: Protest on Mainstreet," *News and Observer*, 3 March 1963, section 3, 1.

member, John Winters. Mayor William Enloe said that he felt integration of the public pools would be unacceptable to the public. He reasoned that it was not up to the city council to decide whether it was right or wrong, but whether it would be acceptable.[24] Enloe's logic was classic Tar Heel hospitality—feigning concern for African Americans but ultimately hiding behind archaic social customs that made municipal government an accomplice to preserving traditions that were untenable in an effective democracy.

Shaw University students sought to counter the mentality that preserved segregation, and Percy High was among those at the forefront of this effort. He was involved in the mass demonstration at the Howard Johnson restaurant on August 21, 1962, in which approximately three hundred protestors arriving in about sixty cars converged on the segregated restaurant on Highway One North. The RCA, the Raleigh Women's Voters Council, the NAACP, and the Congress of Racial Equality (CORE) had sponsored the demonstrations. Prior to the picketing outside of the restaurant, the protestors had met at the Black First Baptist Church in Raleigh. High provided remarks, and one of the speakers described High as "another Martin Luther." The mass meeting was symbolic of the movement, as it revealed an amalgamation of various local and national civil rights groups and enjoyed support from local Black religious leaders. It was also emblematic of the crucial role of Shaw students in the movement that was about to reach its zenith in the following year. The slogan of one of the protestors at the mass meeting seemed to portend the apex of the movement against segregation in Raleigh and throughout the South: "Free by 63."[25]

The actions of civil rights protestors in Raleigh and Durham in 1961 and 1962 were in many ways a continuation of increased activism sparked by the sit-in movement. But in many respects, 1963 represented a new "wave" of mass protests in the two cities and throughout the South that was even more dynamic than the one in 1960. In 1960, much of the focus of the protests had been chain stores that operated lunch counters within

---

[24] "City's Pools in Raleigh Are Closed," *Durham Sun*, 7 August 1962, 3A.
[25] "300 March on Raleigh Howard Johnson: Vigorous Protest Begun By RCA, RWVC, NAACP, CORE," *Carolinian*, 25 August 1962, 1, 2.

the broader store that permitted Black customers to shop but denied them from sitting down there to eat a meal. Thus, the contradictions of segregation were right in the store itself. By 1963, activists targeted a wider range of establishments and focused even more on opening economic opportunities for African Americans. By the end of 1960, some desegregation of lunch counters had occurred in the two cities, and further desegregation had occurred by the end of 1962.[26] But even greater changes came by the end of 1963, largely a result of mass protests and individual acts of courage. 1960 was a watershed moment in the history of nonviolent civil rights activism in the US, but 1963 represented its zenith.

Student protestors attending Shaw and Saint Augustine's in 1963 recognized that White political leaders would not "bestow" freedom upon them. The African American students understood that business and political leaders would have to be pressured to make changes to segregated practices.[27] One strategy utilized by protestors to pressure movie theaters into desegregating was to approach the ticket windows in pairs and ask for tickets for seating in the sections reserved for Whites. When they were refused, they returned to the end of the line and repeated the process. Hence, the protestors not only made a stand that segregation was morally wrong but, by creating a long line, they also in effect discouraged White patrons from attending the theaters. This practice, often referred to as "rotation" or "round robin," was not unique to Raleigh. But the targeting of one of the theaters in Raleigh demonstrated the strategic aspect of certain demonstrations. Protestors especially targeted the Ambassador Theater, not only due to its segregated policies but also because Mayor Enloe was the manager of the theater and district manager of North Carolina Theater, Inc., a group that owned the Ambassador Theater.[28]

Demonstrations at the Ambassador Theater put Enloe in a precarious position. Police estimated that four hundred protested outside of the

---

[26] Charles Craven, "Mayor Enloe Will Resign Today," *News and Observer*, 9 April 1963, 1; "Integrated Lunch Counters: Durham Fifth City," *News and Observer*, 2 August 1960, 3.

[27] See survey (students) in appendix.

[28] Charles Craven, "Mayor Enloe Will Resign Today," *News and Observer*, 9 April 1963, 1; Jonathan Friendly, "76 Business Firms Here Integrating," *News and Observer*, 6 June 1963, 1, 3.

theater, mostly from Shaw and Saint Augustine's, on April 8, 1963. The protests nearly caused Enloe to resign his position as mayor, and he claimed, "Bill Enloe could do things concerning his business that would be of local interest only, but Mayor Bill Enloe would make front page headlines statewide, if not nationwide."[29] Last-minute negotiations with adult African American leaders caused Enloe to change his mind and remain as mayor. Davie Street Presbyterian Church pastor Oscar McCloud told him that it was likely that the students would eventually stop. Nonetheless, the protests continued. Enloe stated that he was not opposed to picketing but was opposed to students blocking White patrons' access to the box office, calling such tactics "vicious." Shaw student protest leader Charles Earle denied that the demonstrations were vicious, claiming that only the young White men who heckled the protestors were vicious.[30]

As mayor and as an important business official in the capital city, Enloe was in a position to exhibit leadership and help set a new vision for Tar Heel hospitality that accepted integration, but he mostly failed to do so. Raleigh did not have a city ordinance requiring segregation in establishments that served both races. In 1963, Raleigh only had one local ordinance mandating segregation, and it required segregated cemeteries.[31] Thus, Enloe could have advocated for integration at the Ambassador Theater and encouraged other establishments to follow suit. On the same day that protestors marched to the governor's mansion, Shaw graduate and North Carolina Teachers Association (a Black teacher organization) Executive Secretary Dr. Charles Lyons met with Enloe and White business leaders. Lyons stated, "We came from that meeting not greatly encouraged as to where we were." Later that day, Lyons spoke to a crowd of some five hundred at Shaw University auditorium, claiming that "the students are prepared to go back on the streets."[32] By not taking a strong stand in favor

---

[29] "Mayor Keeps Post: Picketing Continues," *News and Observer*, 10 April 1963, 1.

[30] "Enloe's Statement to Council," *News and Observer*, 11 April 1963, 31; "Enloe 'Symbol,' Not Target of Protests," *News and Observer*, 11 April 1963, 31.

[31] David Cooper, "Sit-In Laws Struck Down: No Court Answer on Trespass Arrests," *News and Observer*, 21 May 1963, 1.

[32] Jonathan Friendly, "Truce Efforts Too Slow, Leaders of Negroes Say," *News and Observer*, 11 May 1963, 1.

of integration as mayor, Enloe was similar to many political leaders throughout the state who ultimately put the ball in the court of individual businesses to voluntarily integrate. As a businessman, he made little effort to set a precedent for others to follow.

In the face of the tentative city leadership, students from Shaw and Saint Augustine's also targeted businesses in the city that catered to state political leaders such as the Sir Walter Hotel and Coffee House. The Sir Walter was one of the sites in which ninety-two protestors were arrested for trespassing in Raleigh on May 8, 1963, the first mass arrests since the new wave of protests began in April.[33] A major reason that demonstrators targeted the Sir Walter, in addition to its segregated practices, was due to the hotel serving as the primary lodging site for members of the state legislature. Thus, it was an ideal target for challenging segregation and the lawmakers who upheld the practices or at least were tentative in challenging segregation.

June 10, 1963, was one of the most significant evenings of the direct-action movement in Raleigh. Six young African Americans entered the lobby of the Sir Walter Hotel and applied for rooms. The manager told them that the hotel did not accommodate "Negroes" and asked them to leave. The group of six refused to leave and sat down in the lobby. The manager called the police and they were arrested for trespassing.[34] The hotel's refusal to accommodate African Americans represented the ugly side of Southern hospitality.

The arrests on June 10 did not deter the protestors. In fact, after they were taken to the police station and fingerprinted and cited to appear in court, the six arrested protestors returned to the hotel, where they joined an increasing number of protestors who sat on their suitcases just outside. Shaw student leaders Charles Earle and Mack Junior Sowell claimed that the protestors planned to stay there "from now on." Around midnight, the demonstrators sang out, "Tell Mayor Enloe we will not be moved," a refrain that they repeated and replaced with the same message to Governor

---

[33] Bob Lynch, "92 Negroes Arrested Here: County Jail Filled with Demonstrators," *News and Observer,* 9 May 1963, 1.

[34] Bob Lynch, "Negroes 'Sit-In' at Sir Walter," *News and Observer,* 11 June 1963, 1.

Sanford and the legislature. Sowell recollects that the protestors' goal throughout the demonstrations was to pressure those in power to make changes, and he recognized that "we had to have pressure on them to make the changes."[35] The young protestors confronted the business leaders in the city who upheld segregation. And just as they had done a month prior at the governor's mansion, they directly challenged the political leadership that often served the interests of segregated businesses at the expense of African American civil rights.

Perhaps the most egregious act on June 10 at the Sir Walter was when a hotel patron threw a bag of water on the demonstrators from an upper floor. There is no indication that the perpetrator was a state legislator, but an equally appalling moment occurred that day and did involve a legislator. After a verbal exchange with one of the protestors, the unidentified legislator claimed he would do something about the African American protestors, stating, "I'd cut off their school appropriations." The legislator's comment was consistent with segregationist politicians who sought to restrict the freedom of students to become involved in protests. But his comments were also ironic since the majority of the protestors in Raleigh were students at Shaw and Saint Augustine's, which were private historically Black colleges. Perhaps demonstrating his frustration over an inability to thwart the protests, the legislator said to the protestor, "There is one thing in my power. I can slap hell out of you," as he drew a rolled-up newspaper to potentially hit the protestor but was discouraged by another legislator.[36]

African Americans comprised most of the protestors at the Sir Walter Hotel on June 10. But it is noteworthy that the protestor whom the legislator threatened to hit was a White UNC student. Whites became increasingly involved in civil rights activism in 1963, and in the Triangle much of the support came from students at the Research Triangle schools. UNC student Pat Cusick also participated in the demonstrations at the Sir Walter Hotel. Cusick became one of the most significant leaders of the push for integration in Chapel Hill in 1963 and 1964. Without a historically

---

[35] Bob Lynch, "Negroes 'Sit-In' at Sir Walter," *News and Observer,* 11 June 1963, 1; Mack Junior Sowell, phone interview by the author.

[36] Bob Lynch, "Negroes 'Sit-In' at Sir Walter," *News and Observer,* 11 June 1963, 1.

Black college and with the state's preeminent public institution, the movement in Chapel Hill was much different than in Raleigh or Durham. But Cusick's involvement in civil rights activism in Raleigh was just one example of the interconnections among movements in the Triangle. UNC assistant professor of psychology Albert Ammons was also at the protests on June 10 in Raleigh. Ammons consistently participated in the demonstrations in Chapel Hill in 1963, and on January 3, 1964, he was severely beaten by customers and employees at Watts Grill in Chapel Hill. He died from a brain aneurysm several months later, although it was not proven to be related to the beating.[37] In the ostensibly progressive college town, this attack was an ugly example of the lengths to which some Whites would go to preserve a segregationist vision of Tar Heel hospitality.

Some White faculty members at Research Triangle schools played a significant role in the push for integration and offered support for Black students. David Dansby, an African American student at UNC, recalls that his faculty advisor, Dr. Dan Pollitt, was essential in starting a campus NAACP chapter at UNC. Dansby served as president of the campus NAACP and ultimately graduated from the UNC graduate school in 1964. Dansby was the lone representative from UNC at the Youth Leadership Conference at Shaw in April 1960 and became the first African American to receive an undergraduate degree from UNC in 1961. He initially did not have many White allies but began to receive increasing support from White faculty and students in 1963. He also received support from Anne Queen, the campus YWCA-YMCA director, who made efforts to include African American students at the school in the organization's activities.[38]

UNC assistant basketball coach Dean Smith provided cautious support for integration in Chapel Hill. In 1959, Smith and the White Reverend Robert Seymour entered The Pines restaurant with a Black theology student and received service. But events in 1963 revealed that The Pines and most other eating establishments remained segregated. Even after

---

[37] Art Chansky, *Game Changers: Dean Smith, Charlie Scott, and the Era that Transformed a Southern College Town* (Chapel Hill: The University of North Carolina Press, 2016), 63.

[38] "First Negro Gets Degree at Carolina," *News and Observer,* 6 June 1961, 1; David Dansby, phone interview by the author, 14 June 2016.

becoming head coach in 1961, Smith took a cautious approach to integration, largely due to his tenuous coaching status early in his career. By 1962, UNC had fifty-four Black undergraduate students, and Smith attempted to recruit Dudley High School's (Greensboro) Lou Hudson, but UNC admissions denied him based on his SAT scores. Dansby was among those who talked to Smith to try to get him to recruit Black players. Ultimately, Smith landed Charlie Scott, the Harlem native and Laurinburg Institute (Laurinburg, North Carolina) alum who began his playing career at UNC in 1967 and became one of the all-time great Tar Heels. In *Game Changers: Dean Smith, Charlie Scott, and the Era that Transformed a Southern College Town*, Art Chansky asserts that "it's good that Charlie Scott wasn't born three years earlier. Chapel Hill was far less ready for him in the early 1960s."[39]

In Raleigh, certain North Carolina State College students and faculty supported civil rights activists. Allard Lowenstein was perhaps the most influential member of the faculty relating to contributions to the local movement. A 1949 graduate of UNC, Lowenstein served as the third president of the National Student Association (NSA) from 1950–1951. In a speech in Oklahoma in December 1960, he made it clear that the association supported the ending of racial barriers as part of America's responsibility. Lowenstein taught social science courses during his employment from 1962–1964. He made financial contributions to the campaign to reelect Raleigh's lone Black city councilman, John W. Winters. In the wake of the sit-ins at the Sir Walter, Lowenstein tried to encourage Eastern Air Lines to discourage their flight crews from lodging at the segregated hotel.[40]

Lowenstein had extensive contacts with students at NC State and those at Shaw and Saint Augustine's. He discussed issues in his classes and

---

[39] David Dansby, phone interview by the author; Art Chansky, *Game Changers,* 27, 34, 36, 54.

[40] Unsigned speech about Allard Lowenstein, Tulsa, OK, December 1960, Series 1, Box 28, Folder 985, Allard Lowenstein Papers, Southern Historical Collection, Louis Round Wilson Special Collections Library, University of North Carolina at Chapel Hill; Frank L. Turner to Allard Lowenstein, 20 May 1963, Series 1, Box 8, Folder 289, Lowenstein Papers; Malcolm A. McIntyre to Allard Lowenstein, 5 July 1963, Series 1, Box 8, Folder 294, Lowenstein Papers.

surveyed students on their perceptions of segregation and the potential impact of integration. Chancellor John Tyler Caldwell called him an "extraordinary teacher," and students chose him as one of three professors for the "Blue Key Award" for exceptional service. In *The Pied Piper: Allard Lowenstein and the Liberal Dream*, Richard Cummings maintains that "Lowenstein figured prominently in a number of anti-segregation demonstrations climaxing with a march of about a thousand people to the governor's mansion." According to Cummings, Lowenstein "was a regular Pied Piper. If he started saying anything to students, why they just followed him like the old Pied Piper."[41]

Shaw student Mack Sowell recalled that he and other students visited Lowenstein at his apartment. Lowenstein's interactions with Black and White students were symbolic of the occasional interactions between the Research Triangle Schools and those of the "Protest Triangle." But Lowenstein's and other White liberals' impact should not be overemphasized in the push for integration in Raleigh. The sit-ins and other demonstrations were the primary force that was putting the pressure on businesspeople and city leaders to desegregate. In most cases, less than 10 percent of the demonstrators were White. In the survey asking student respondents to rank the statement "White men and women played a significant role in the demonstrations in Raleigh" on a scale of 1–10, the average was only 2.33.[42]

The primary impetus for change came from the historically Black colleges in Raleigh, at which participation in the demonstrations was common. Eleanor Nunn, president of the Shaw NAACP chapter, estimated in the spring of 1963 that 60 to 70 percent of students at the college had participated in sit-ins, stand-ins, pray-ins, or other forms of protest at some point.[43] In my survey asking student respondents to rank certain groups and institutions in order of importance to their bringing about

---

[41] Richard Cummings, *The Pied Piper: Allard K. Lowenstein and the Liberal Dream* (New York: Grove Press, Inc., 1985), 226, 257.

[42] Mack Junior Sowell, interview by the author. The 2.33 average response was for students in Raleigh only. See appendix for survey results that include Raleigh and Durham.

[43] Gene Roberts Jr., "Thunder on the Campus: Protest on Mainstreet," 3 March 1963, section 3, 1.

integration and increased employment opportunities for African Americans, nearly every respondent ranked the Shaw University/Saint Augustine's College student groups first.[44]

Most demonstrations in Raleigh had a communal aspect, and protestors found comfort in the company of fellow protestors. But there were also acts of courage in which individuals took a stand against segregation on their own. Shaw student Charles Earle was a leader in the direct-action movement, but one of his most courageous actions was to apply to become a member at Raleigh's First Baptist Church on Salisbury Street. The church was established in 1812 with fourteen Black slave members and nine White members, and it remained integrated until 1868, when Black members of the church formed their own congregation. As church historian Glen Jonas asserts, "The First Baptist Church on Salisbury Street was keenly aware of its biracial history as civil rights events unfolded both nationally and locally in 1963."[45]

Earle maintained that his decision to apply "was a personal decision." He frequently attended the church, largely due to being inspired by the pastor, Dr. John Lewis, when he had spoken at Shaw two years prior. While Earle claimed it was a personal decision, he also stated that the church "should be a leader in civil rights."[46] There is little reason to doubt that Earle was indeed primarily making a personal decision to join. Shaw student and protest leader Mack Sowell recalls that he was "shocked" when Earle applied for membership at the church.[47] Thus, Earle's decision to apply was not officially related to his leadership in the student protest movement, but he likely recognized that his action would draw attention. On April 10, 1963, the same day that he stated that Mayor Enloe "is a symbol, not a target" of the protests at segregated theaters, Earle held that "I don't want them to accept me as a Negro, as the president of the student

---

[44] See appendix. The author acknowledges the capacity for bias in this instance, but the point remains clear: students at the historically Black colleges in Raleigh viewed their classmates as the crucial force in bringing about change in the city.

[45] Glen Jonas, "Two Roads Diverged: The Civil Rights Movement Comes to FBC Raleigh," *Baptist History and Heritage Society*, 22 June 2019.

[46] "First Baptist Receives Application of Negro," *News and Observer*, 8 April 1963, 1.

[47] Mack Junior Sowell, interview by the author.

body at Shaw, or anything else in particular...just accept me as Charles Earle."[48]

The decision on whether to integrate the church membership was symbolic of the underhanded ways in which certain institutions maintained segregated practices. Upon Earle's application, the deacon board chairman, R. N. Simms Jr., told the congregation that unless there were objections, the decision would be referred to the deacons. This strategy was different from the normal handling of membership applications—through an immediate vote by the congregation.[49] One church leader playing a role in the decision was Jesse Helms, a WRAL television broadcaster and executive vice president who was also a former Raleigh city council member. Helms's *Viewpoints* editorials on WRAL beginning in November 1960 often opposed civil rights activism. The eventual US Senator blamed White liberals for the civil rights movement and contrasted "responsible" Blacks who accepted segregation with "irresponsible" Blacks who had brought social disorder. According to historian William A. Link, in 1963 Helms opposed integration and offered a motion for the congregational vote that ultimately denied Charles Earle's application for membership.[50] Years later, Helms told reporters that he had merely stood up in front of the congregation to "move the previous question" to end the debate and hold a vote. But according to journalist Ernest B. Furgurson, Helms was strongly opposed to Earle's acceptance. While the deacons presented a façade of a democratic vote, it came only after they recommended that the congregation deny Earle's membership. Ultimately, the congregation voted 367–147 in a secret vote against Earle's admission.[51]

The denial of Earle's membership exposed many realities about Raleigh in 1963. First and foremost, support for segregation was still common among many White citizens. But it also revealed that many Whites

---

[48] "Church Application Not Protest, Student Says," *News and Observer*, 11 April 1963, 11.

[49] "First Baptist Recieves Application of Negro," *News and Observer*, 8 April 1963, 1.

[50] William A. Link, *Righteous Warrior: Jesse Helms and the Rise of Modern Conservatism* (New York: St. Martin's Press, 2008), 70, 74, 127.

[51] Ernest B. Furgurson, *Hard Right: The Rise of Jesse Helms* (New York: W.W. Norton and Company, 1986), 227; Jane Hall, "Church Rejects Negro Applicant," *News and Observer*, 16 May 1963, 36.

found ways to deemphasize the legitimate grievances of African Americans who sought integration. One of the primary objections to accepting Earle was due to his status as one of the protest leaders.[52] Of course, he and the hundreds of other protestors only conducted protests because so many White citizens had taken a passive approach to segregation. In many cases, supporters of segregation presented a circular logic for maintaining segregation. Reverend Elias Stephanopoulos from Holy Trinity Greek Church abstained from a vote by members of the Raleigh Ministerial Association endorsing hotel and café integration. He argued, "Our churches are still segregated. We are asking other people to do something we haven't been able to do ourselves."[53] Of course, as the leader of his congregation, he could have taken a moral stand against segregation in his own church, which would have allowed him to also take a principled stand against segregation elsewhere.

African Americans in Raleigh made concerted efforts to integrate churches in the city on May 12, 1963. They were allowed to enter at most of the churches, but at Calvary Baptist Church, White men stood at the doorway and denied their entrance. The Reverend Earl Crumpler claimed, "It was obvious to some of us that they did not come in the spirit of Christ." But Crumpler also stated that he sympathized with their goal and asserted, "The one place where there should be no prejudice is within the fellowship of the church…like the door of Heaven, the doors of every church should be open to all mankind."[54] Perhaps Crumpler truly believed the words he spoke, but it certainly seemed that he could have presented a more welcoming environment.

Despite the discouraging actions at First Baptist Church and Calvary Baptist Church, religious leaders were among the most sympathetic groups in supporting integration efforts. On May 14, the Raleigh Ministerial Association passed a resolution 42–1 calling for the immediate desegregation of restaurants, theaters, and hotels in the city. This action presented a more pointed attack on segregation than the resolution that thirty

---

[52] Furgurson, *Hard Right*, 227.

[53] "Cleric Group Backs Hotel, Café Mixing," *News and Observer*, 15 May 1963, 26.

[54] "Negroes Crowd Church Sunday: Turned Away from Calvary Baptist," *News and Observer*, 13 May 1963, 20.

ministers had signed three years prior in the wake of the 1960 sit-in movement, in which they agreed to support any establishments that desegregated. The 1960 resolution was also not presented as an official Raleigh Ministers Association resolution. One of the pastors who supported both resolutions was Reverend W. W. Finlator of Pullen Memorial Baptist, who had been supportive of civil rights activism for many years.[55]

Ironically, the president of the Raleigh Ministers Association in 1963 was Dr. John Lewis from First Baptist Church, whose church denied the membership of Charles Earle. Unlike many of the members of his congregation, Lewis had been in favor of accepting Earle as a member of the church. His support demonstrated the fissures in Raleigh over the issue of segregation that often existed within institutions, whether it was specific churches, business groups, or political organizations. Lewis laid out both sides of the argument to the congregation, but he clearly leaned toward admitting Earle. He pointed out that segregation was hurting foreign missions and that the New Testament said race should not be a qualification for membership. He then asked the question, "What would Jesus have me do?"[56] Perhaps the most poignant comment that Lewis made was also one that seemingly could have been stated to all opponents of integration and opponents of civil rights demonstrations. When some members of his church claimed about Earle, "He's just testing us," Lewis replied, "Right—let's pass the test."[57]

Lewis was not the only minister who took a principled stand against continued segregation in the city. Perhaps the boldest move by a White pastor came from Reverend Dr. Albert Edwards of First Presbyterian Church. He implored his congregation to write letters to restaurant owners encouraging them to support integration. On May 12, 1963, he asked his congregation to raise their hands if they had done so, but only three did. In a striking demonstration of moral leadership, the frustrated Edwards refused to preach and gave the benediction and left. He later posed the question, "If Christian people do not express themselves in a time like

---

[55] "Cleric Group Backs Hotel, Café Mixing," *News and Observer*, 15 May 1963, 26.

[56] "Church Integration: Minister Talks of Application," *News and Observer*, 22 April 1963, 22.

[57] Furgurson, *Hard Right*, 227.

this then who will?"[58]

Later that week, the congregation of First Presbyterian gave Edwards a vote of confidence to continue in his position. The confidence vote demonstrated that many members of the church were likely in favor of integration. But the fact that only three members had sent letters to segregated businesses was symbolic of the lack of leadership most White people in the city took in pushing for integration. However, Edwards's refusal to preach was an indicator of the impact that the student-led protest movement was having on some individuals. It is unlikely that Edwards would have taken such a principled stand if the sit-ins and protest marches were not gripping the city.[59] The student-led movement mobilized sympathetic figures to take a stronger stand for integration. Perhaps more importantly, the movement pressured tentative leaders to decide whether to support integration or defend segregation. By late spring 1963, the direct-action movement in the city made it clear that the tentative approach so many politicians and business leaders had taken was increasingly untenable.

A May 14, 1963, editorial in the *News and Observer* titled "No Bystanders Now" pointed out that "hardly any human being in Raleigh at this moment can be an uncommitted bystander in the situation which confronts the community."[60] By mid-May, more than 160 protestors had been arrested, nearly all of them students from Shaw and Saint Augustine's. On May 13, the Raleigh Merchants Bureau called for "the removal of all policies in both government and business which deny rights and services because of race," the most significant example of leadership to date demonstrated by a business group.[61] The following week, activists avoided demonstrations so the mayor's biracial committee could work out a solution. But demonstrations continued May 21, as activists remained dissatisfied with the pace of progress. As in other Southern cities, protests were often followed by a temporary cessation, only to resume after biracial

---

[58] "Negroes Crowd Churches Sunday: Turned Away from Calvary Baptist," *News and Observer*, 13 May 1963, 20; "Presbyterian Minister Explains His Actions," *News and Observer*, 13 May 1963, 20.

[59] "Confidence," *News and Observer*, 16 May 1963, 36.

[60] "No Bystanders Now," *News and Observer*, 14 May 1963, 4.

[61] Bob Lynch and Tom Inman, "Committee Named: Merchants Here Urge End to Segregation," *News and Observer*, 14 May 1963, 1, 2.

committees or businesses failed to offer a viable solution.[62]

Among the most important groups in pushing for integration in Raleigh was the Citizens Coordinating Committee, a group of African Americans who sought to "dispel any notion that we either recognize or accept the fiction that the Negro citizen has a place separate from or less than that of other American citizens." In a May meeting, the group asserted that demonstrations would continue in Raleigh until complete desegregation occurred in downtown theaters, hotels, motels, and restaurants and in businesses in Cameron Village. The group also called for an end to employment discrimination, for a plan for further desegregation of Raleigh's public schools, and for the city council to create an ordinance prohibiting licensed businesses from discriminating against any person based on race, creed, or color.[63]

The Citizens Coordinating Committee attempted to funnel the power of the student-led demonstrations, and the group did not trivialize the importance of the student leadership. In the opening line of its "Declaration of Principles and Intentions," the group declared itself as being constituted of "public minded citizens who represent the Negro Community of Raleigh, including the student bodies of Shaw University and Saint Augustine's College."[64] Mack Sowell was among the nine signatories, as was Saint Augustine's student and vice president of the college's NAACP Youth Chapter, Raymond Cauthorn. Charles Earle also became heavily involved in the committee's activities. Dr. Charles Lyons was the chairman of the group. The group included the well-respected Shaw Divinity School dean, Grady Davis, who was also president of the Raleigh Citizens Association. Another prominent member was the father of the first African American child in Raleigh to attend a previously all-White school, the president of the Raleigh NAACP, Ralph Campbell Sr.[65]

On June 5, 1963, Raleigh's biracial committee announced that

---

[62] "Negroes March Again in Downtown Raleigh," *News and Observer*, 21 May 1963, 21.

[63] "Declaration of Principles and Intentions of the Citizens Coordinating Committee," 11 May 1963, Series 2, Box 32, Folder 1130, Lowenstein Papers, Southern Historical Collection.

[64] "Declaration of Principles and Intentions."

[65] "Declaration of Principles and Intentions."

seventy-six business establishments either had or would adopt nondiscriminatory policies, but the group did not specify which establishments were doing so. Perhaps most tellingly, Mayor Enloe did not say if the Ambassador Theater would be among those that were integrating, which was typical of his tentative leadership on the integration issue. Student leaders from Shaw and Saint Augustine's recognized that, with the help of sympathetic citizens in Raleigh, they would have to continue to counter the tentative city business and political leaders. On June 12, the same day that protests outside the Sir Walter Hotel attracted nearly five hundred White and Black onlookers, Lyons and the Citizens Coordinating Committee issued a statement claiming that "the biracial committee has been strangely silent since issuing its 'famous' statement that 76 businesses either have integrated or are integrating their facilities. Citizens still want to know— and rightly so—the identity of these businesses." The committee also said it was "likewise disappointed at the strange and loud silence of the office of the mayor."[66]

Mayor Enloe's tentative dance on the issue of integration was being challenged by students from Shaw University and Saint Augustine's College and others in Raleigh. In my survey asking respondents to rate individuals on a scale of 1–10 based on their contributions to improving conditions for African Americans in the city, the average response was 2.5 for Enloe. As previously mentioned, protestors viewed Enloe as a "symbol" rather than a "target" for the protests. And Enloe was symbolic of the type of North Carolina politician who sought to find a way to end the demonstrations but either cared not or dared not to take a strong stance in favor of integration.[67]

Meanwhile, students from Shaw and Saint Augustine's took a strong stand against segregation and demonstrated a clear sense of leadership that most students viewed as part of their education.[68] For many students, their actions during the demonstrations came at a seminal period in their lives

---

[66] Jonathan Friendly, "76 Business Firms Here Integrating," *News and Observer*, 5 June 1963, 1, 3; "Negro 'Sit-In' Group at Hotel Draws Crowd of 500 Spectators," *News and Observer*, 13 June 1963, 38.

[67] "Enloe 'Symbol,' Not Target of Protests," *News and Observer*, 11 April 1963, 31. See appendix for survey results.

[68] See survey (students) in appendix.

that established a precedent for leadership opportunities later. An editorial by a University of Florida professor appeared just as accurate in 1963 as it did in 1960 when he wrote it during the first wave of the sit-in movement. He pointed out that the sit-ins demonstrated that African Americans were "developing skill in taking political and social action. Negro youths are moving into leadership roles. On the other hand, white youths are kept in the background. Action to preserve segregation is in the hands of older people, who are watched, sometimes cynically, by the young."[69] The protestors' actions were part of a broader challenge to the moral concerns posed by segregation. But the actions of student demonstrators also had a tangible impact on their lives. By challenging segregation, they were part of the process of opening societal opportunities, including leadership roles, that were previously denied to African Americans. Civil rights activism was the ultimate course in leadership, one that extended well beyond the classroom.

Civil rights activism in Durham in the early 1960s shared many similarities with Raleigh, but there were also features that made Durham unique. For one, Durham had an individual who stood out as the most significant civil rights leader in the city. By 1963, Floyd McKissick had not only become a highly respected leader in the city but was also earning a nationwide reputation. Raleigh had respected activists as well, but none had the level of name recognition that McKissick had. After serving in World War II, McKissick participated in the 1947 Journey of Reconciliation, a predecessor to the more widely known Freedom Rides of the early 1960s. Though initially denied admittance due to his race, McKissick became the first African American to attend the UNC Law School after a successful appeal led by the NAACP. Like Elwyna and Joseph Holt, and June and Ralph Campbell, McKissick and his wife Evelyn made the courageous decision to attempt to enroll their children in previously all-White schools. Joycelyn McKissick became the first African American female to graduate from Durham High School in 1960.[70]

---

[69] Kimbal Wiles (editorial), "The High Calling of Non-Violent Protests," *Carolina Times*, 7 May 1960, 2.

[70] Christina Greene, *Our Separate Ways: Women and the Black Freedom Movement in Durham, North Carolina* (Chapel Hill: The University of North Carolina Press, 2005), 25, 42; Denique Prout, "Symposium Honors Women," *Campus Echo*

By 1963, Floyd McKissick was a crucial figure in the civil rights movement in Durham. While most protestors remained nonviolent, McKissick was forced to pull protestors with weapons off the picket lines. He represented CORE at the meeting with President John F. Kennedy on the day of the March on Washington for Jobs and Freedom, filling in for the incarcerated CORE national director, James Farmer. There is little doubt that McKissick was a towering figure in the movement in Durham, but that should not obscure the reality that he relied heavily on college and high school students in Durham in his efforts to push for integration. Likewise, students relied on McKissick for guidance and legal advice. He had reinvigorated NAACP youth chapters in Durham in the late 1950s, and his support of student activism in the early 1960s throughout the state had a major impact on the student movement.[71] Although McKissick had developed connections in high places in the civil rights movement by 1963, he continued to recognize the power of students and other young people to push the movement forward.

NCC student activists played a major role in the demonstrations. Guytana Horton was one of the most significant student activists in 1963. Horton was the president of the state NAACP intercollegiate division. In 1962, she and Joycelyn McKissick had been arrested for requesting service at a Durham Howard Johnson's restaurant, which had been a target of CORE and NAACP demonstrations during the Freedom Highways Project. Both women refused to pay their trespass fines and were ordered to work as maids for elderly patients at the county work home. The Freedom Highways Project was successful in bringing about the desegregation of about half of the Howard Johnson's restaurants in North Carolina. But the Durham Howard Johnson's remained segregated and became a primary target for demonstrations in 1963.[72]

Jane Phillips, who was from Los Angeles and in town initially as part of the National Student Association's voter registration efforts, took part

---

Online 100, no. 11 (22 April 2009), available online at issuu.com/campusecho/docs/print_edition_april_22_2009.

[71] August Meier and Elliott Rudwick, *CORE: A Study in the Civil Rights Movement* (New York: Oxford University Press, 1973), 172; Greene, *Our Separate Ways*, 96.

[72] Greene, *Our Separate Ways*, 86, 87.

in a sit-in at the Raleigh Howard Johnson's that ultimately landed her in the Wake County jail. In her trial, she was represented by McKissick, whose objections were repeatedly denied by the justice of the peace while those of the prosecutor were consistently sustained. Phillips recollects that "I had to bite my lip to suppress laughter at this mockery of justice."[73] Phillips, a light-skinned African American, was initially taken to a White cell and told the guard that she was Negro. One of the Black inmates began to ridicule Phillips for her role in the integration effort at the swimming pool at Pullen Park. She was angry at Phillips because those actions led to the city closing that pool as well as the Black-designated pool at Chavis Park, where the woman's children liked to swim. Phillips recalls that an older woman, Rosa, who had been convicted of murder, came to her defense and gave the woman harassing Phillips a "hard and colorful tongue-lashing and a lesson in civil rights, telling her that what we had done was a good thing; that we were helping Negroes in Raleigh, including her and her children, but she was too short-sighted and uninformed to understand; and if she laid a finger on me she'd have hell to pay."[74]

Mid-May 1963 was a historic period in Durham, as massive demonstrations gripped the city, and a new mayor was elected. The demonstrations were like those in several cities throughout North Carolina and throughout the South. To a large extent, the rise in demonstrations was a response to civil rights campaigns taking place in Birmingham, Alabama. The Southern Christian Leadership Conference undertook a major program to further mobilize citizens to confront segregation in the city that Martin Luther King Jr. called the "belly of the beast."[75] Project "C" (for Confrontation) directly challenged segregated practices in the city and took the controversial step of utilizing young students in the protests in early May. The demonstrations in Birmingham also effectively utilized the power of media to expose the darkest aspects of a segregated society. Commissioner of Public Safety Eugene "Bull" Connor's response to the demonstrations provided enduring images to the rest of the country and

---

[73] Phillips, "Night Train to Raleigh."

[74] Phillips, "Night Train to Raleigh."

[75] Jerry Sutton, *A Matter of Conviction: A History of Southern Baptist Engagement with the Culture* (Nashville: B&H Publishing Group, 2008), 167.

the world. The images of fire hoses and police dogs as methods to control protests were perhaps the most iconic evidence of the response to civil rights protests in the United States.[76]

The presence of Martin Luther King Jr. and other prominent SCLC activists such as Ralph Abernathy and Andrew Young clearly brought excitement to local protestors and dramatically increased media coverage in Birmingham. But Project "C" was far from the beginning of civil rights activity in Birmingham. In response to the state of Alabama banning the NAACP, Birmingham's Reverend Fred Shuttlesworth took the lead in creating the Alabama Christian Movement for Human Rights in 1956. He was also a seminal figure in SCLC. Shuttlesworth risked the ultimate sacrifice in the push for integration by attempting to enroll his children in all-White schools. His efforts resulted in a severe beating by segregationists in 1957. At the hospital, the doctor told Shuttlesworth that he must have a hard head, to which Shuttlesworth replied, "Doctor, the Lord knew I was in a hard town, so He gave me a hard head."[77]

Shuttlesworth was among the advocates encouraging high school students to participate in demonstrations. One advantage to utilizing students was their relative immunity to economic reprisals, although those with parents who worked for White employers certainly put their parents' jobs at risk and exposed them to possible charges of contributing to the delinquency of minors. United Press International termed King the "mastermind" of the strategy, but King was concerned that the strategy could backfire. It took tremendous courage for SCLC leadership to embrace the strategy of utilizing children. But the bold approach of the SCLC leaders should not overshadow the courage hundreds of parents displayed by allowing their children to participate or, in other cases, the courage displayed by the children to disobey their parents and school administrators and protest against their wishes. There is no question that King played a crucial role in the Birmingham campaign in the spring of 1963. But the protestors themselves carried the movement and helped to shape King's approach. As historian Thomas F. Jackson cogently argues, "The mass marchers

---

[76] Diane McWhorter, *Carry Me Home: Birmingham, Alabama: The Climatic Battle of the Civil Rights Revolution* (New York: Simon and Schuster, 2001), 308.

[77] McWhorter, *Carry Me Home*, 127–28.

made up the mastermind's mind."[78]

The efforts of King and the SCLC leadership, in addition to the actions of activists in Birmingham, were an inspiration to activists throughout the nation. They provided a further spark to a movement in Durham that had already achieved many victories in the previous three years but that recognized there was much work left undone. On May 18, activists in Durham staged a plethora of demonstrations, including sit-ins at a variety of locations. Police arrested 130 protestors for trespassing at Holiday Inn, S&W Cafeteria, Harvey's Cafeteria, University Grill, Palms Restaurant, and Oriental Restaurant. A typical scene occurred at the Oriental Restaurant. A protest leader spoke with a manager, and the leader told the other protestors they would not be served and were free to leave or stay and wait for police to come. Hundreds of protestors cheered the arrested demonstrators in front of the county courthouse as they were led to jail.[79]

The most significant mass demonstration in Durham occurred on Sunday, May 19, 1963. At Saint Joseph's A.M.E. Church, activists listened to speeches by CORE national director James Farmer and NAACP national director Roy Wilkins. Later that day, protestors crowded around the Howard Johnson's restaurant on the Durham-Chapel Hill Boulevard. Nearly five hundred protestors, mostly high school students and NCC students, marched around the restaurant singing, "We're going to eat at Howard Johnson's one of these days." NAACP voting drive director John Brooks and Saint Joseph's A.M.E. pastor Melvin Swann entered the restaurant and were arrested for trespassing. The demonstrators sat down in the parking lot of the restaurant, and some crowded around parked cars. They refused to leave even after police threatened to utilize tear gas. More than four hundred demonstrators were arrested and taken by five Trailways buses to the county jail, where they continued singing freedom songs.[80]

---

[78] Thomas F. Jackson, *From Civil Rights to Human Rights: Martin Luther King, Jr., and the Struggle for Economic Justice* (Philadelphia: University of Pennsylvania Press, 2007), 160.

[79] Howard Jones, "130 Arrested as Negroes Stage Sit-In Protest Here," *Durham Morning Herald*, 19 May 1963, 1.

[80] Howard Jones, "400 Negroes Are Arrested as Protests Continue Here: Police Break Up Scuffles," *Durham Morning Herald*, 20 May 1963, 1.

The events of May 19, 1963, were indicative of so many of the characteristics of the movement in Durham. First and foremost, NCC students and high school students provided the backbone of the movement, but they received significant support from various people in the community and civil rights leaders who did not live in Durham. The NAACP-CORE efforts in Durham were among the most significant campaigns supported by the two civil rights organizations in 1962 and 1963. The events in May also displayed the willingness of local African American preachers to lead by example, evidenced in Swann's willingness to face arrest.[81]

Among the most important local leaders were NCC students, including Quinton Baker, NAACP college chapter president. Even as a college junior, Baker was a veteran activist who had participated in sit-ins and other forms of protest since 1960. He carried on the tradition of protest that had been enhanced by student leaders like Lacy Streeter, whom Baker knew from their youth in Greenville, North Carolina.[82] Baker's leadership was on display in the parking lot at Howard Johnson's as he urged fellow protestors to remain despite the threats of tear gas (which police ultimately did not use). As a crowd of nearly three hundred White onlookers watched the demonstration develop, Baker told the White crowd, "Look out, all you people who feel I'm an animal, because I am going to prove that I am a man."[83] Baker and the protestors attacked the social traditions that had treated them at best as second-class citizens and at worst as less than human.

On May 20, 1963, Baker and Walter Riley were among the student leaders who gave a petition to the Durham City Council asking for fair employment for African Americans in city jobs and for a law requiring businesses licensed by the public to serve customers without regard to race. Riley, a Hillside High School graduate, was the president of the Durham chapter of the NAACP, despite being only nineteen years old. He had recently married Candida Lall, a White woman from Oakland, California,

---

[81] Meier and Rudwick, *CORE*, 170–72.

[82] Quinton E. Baker, interview by Chris McGinnis, 23 February 2002, Documenting the American South, Southern Oral History Program Collection #4007, Southern Historical Collection, Wilson Library, University of North Carolina at Chapel Hill.

[83] Jones, "400 Negroes Are Arrested as Protests Continue Here," 1.

whom he had met while working with the Freedom Highways Project. They had to get married in Washington, DC, as interracial marriage in North Carolina was prohibited until the US Supreme Court effectively struck down anti-miscegenation laws in *Loving v. Virginia* in 1967. Riley and Baker sought to counter the city and state leadership that had failed to take a strong stance in favor of equal opportunities for African Americans.[84]

The targeting of Howard Johnson's in Durham had added significance since one of North Carolina's US Senators, B. Everett Jordan, was part owner of the Durham restaurant. Much as was the case with Mayor W. G. Enloe in Raleigh, Jordan showed no tendency to take a leadership role in pushing for integration of the business over which he had influence. Jordan was in a position to influence the manager of the store to integrate, but he did not do so. Then the manager of the store, Harold Makepeace, began to receive pressure from the president of the restaurant chain, Howard B. Johnson himself. In late May, Johnson wrote a letter to Makepeace stating that it was a "source of embarrassment in that members of the public confuse your position with that of the company."[85] Like many other restaurant, theater, and hotel owners in the city and throughout the state, Makepeace did not want to integrate unless all the businesses agreed to do so. He would not take a stand for integration unless pressured. For businessmen and politicians like Makepeace, Mayor Enloe, and Senator Jordan, their feet seemed to be stuck in a past that tolerated racial discrimination. This was Tar Heel hospitality at its worst.

By May 1963, civil rights activists in Durham had a new ally in recently elected Mayor R. Wensell "Wense" Grabarek. Unlike in Raleigh where the city council voted for the mayor, the mayor of Durham was elected by popular vote. During his campaign, Grabarek did not speak ambiguously on the issue of race relations as so many North Carolina politicians had. In the week prior to the election, he bluntly stated that "unity of purpose is the first thing we need. Treat each of us exactly alike, we're

---

[84] Jon Phelps, "Grabarek, Negro Leaders Parley," *Durham Morning Herald*, 21 May 1963, 1B; Walter Riley, interview by the author.
[85] New York AP, "Reprimand for Durham Restaurant," *News and Observer*, 1 June 1963, 1.

all equal." As a Pennsylvania native, Grabarek was not raised in a segregated society. He was popular among African Americans in Durham, and his margin of victory was roughly equivalent to the number of voters in predominantly Black districts. In the Hillside High School district, Grabarek outpaced his opponent 853 to 88.[86] His election not only demonstrated the power of the African American vote but also showed that many White voters in Durham were willing to support a candidate who did not appeal to racial discrimination.

Grabarek took office at the peak of civil rights demonstrations in Durham. The protests at Howard Johnson's and other segregated businesses led to overcrowded jails. NCC student Vannie Culmer recalled that more than one hundred people were placed in a jail cell designed for about a dozen people. The cell was hot and crowded, and the jailer told the group that he would close the window if they continued singing. But his threat did not deter the protestors, as they fittingly sang "No more Mr. Charley" and continued with their freedom songs. Fellow NCC student Fay Bryant (Mayo) recalled the excitement and the singing of freedom songs but also the hunger that beset the protestors while in jail. The sandwiches that arrived from campus were a welcome sight.[87]

Grabarek's first few days as mayor of Durham made it clearer that the city faced a committed movement that would not be deterred by arrests. Unlike most other political leaders in North Carolina and throughout the South, Grabarek did not criticize the means that protestors utilized to achieve integration in public accommodations. On May 21, he addressed a mass rally of mostly African Americans held at Saint Joseph's Church and vowed to oppose segregation in exchange for a cessation of the protests. He referred to the civil rights demonstrations as "valuable tools" for getting Whites to understand the "seriousness and sincerity" of the

---

[86] "Carr, Grabarek Give Programs: Railroad Industry 'Fair Deal,'" *Durham Sun*, 10 May 1963, 5A; Charles Barbour, "Grabarek Elected Mayor of Durham: Three Incumbents Among 6 Council Members Chosen," *Durham Morning Herald*, 19 May 1963, 1; "How Durham Voted in Saturday's Municipal Elections," *Durham Morning Herald*, 19 May 1961, 1.

[87] Vannie C. Culmer, phone interview by the author, digital recording, 26 January 2017; Fay Bryant Mayo, phone interview by the author, digital recording, 1 February 2017. "Mr. Charley" was a slang term that essentially referred to an overbearing White man.

protestors.[88] Civil rights activists pressured Grabarek to take a strong stand in favor of integration from an early point in his time as mayor, and for the most part he responded favorably. In his first week as mayor, the Durham youth and college chapters of the NAACP and CORE thanked Grabarek for his efforts.[89] The mayor established the eleven-man biracial Durham Interim Committee to help negotiate further desegregation of businesses in the city. By June 4, 1963, all eleven of the city's motels, its leading hotel, and 55 of the 103 eating establishments had integrated. Just two weeks later, 90 percent of the eating establishments in the city had been integrated.[90]

Grabarek played an important role in bringing about further integration in Durham, but his role should not be overstated. Walter Riley maintains that "Grabarek would like to be known as the one who brought integration to Durham. But it is not true."[91] The reality is that civil rights demonstrators had forcefully pushed for integration using mass protests. They put city political and business leaders in a position where they could no longer take a tentative approach to the issue of segregation. "Moderate" politicians who attempted to walk the fine line between appeasing segregationists and opponents of segregation were put in an untenable position by activists in Durham in the late spring and early summer of 1963. Sit-ins, pickets, and boycotts created an environment in which no logical businessperson could assume the protests would fade away. Grabarek came to the mayor's office in a historic moment in the city and was up to the challenge of providing leadership for integration in an era when many state political leaders equivocated. But it was the civil rights activists, especially those from NCC and Hillside High School, encouraged by veteran activists such as James Farmer and Floyd McKissick, who had provided the impetus for such a historic moment.

---

[88] "Interim Committee Set to Meet Today," *Durham Sun*, 24 May 1963, 5A.

[89] Pat Carter, "Grabarek Given Thanks, Warning by Negro Groups," 23 May 1963, 1.

[90] Paul Fogleman, "More Racial Bars Fall in Durham: Sleeping, Many Eating Facilities Now Integrated," *Durham Morning Herald*, 5 June 1963, 1; Jon Phelps, "90 Pct. of Durham Eating Facilities Now Desegregated," *Durham Morning Herald*, 19 June 1963, 1.

[91] Walter Riley, phone interview by the author.

By late spring 1963, there was increasing pressure on Governor Terry Sanford to take a stronger stand in favor of integration, especially evident in the march on the governor's mansion in Raleigh on May 11. When a protestor shouted that Sanford "should have known our troubles," Sanford replied, "I'm not a dictator, son. You're in a democracy."[92] His response was emblematic of his approach to demonstrators. He was civil and respectful to them but opposed their means of pushing for change. He implied that there was little he could do to force integration. While it might have been wishful thinking to expect Sanford to issue an executive order calling for desegregation in state-licensed businesses, Kentucky Governor Bert Combs did just that in June 1963. Combs ordered all discrimination to end in businesses licensed by the state.[93]

Sanford took a more cautious approach. As protests continued in several North Carolina cities and towns in mid-June, Sanford appealed for an end to demonstrations and called for a meeting with African American leaders on June 25. Fayetteville Mayor Wilbur Clark, whose city had seen massive demonstrations largely led by students from the historically Black Fayetteville State College, claimed that Sanford's call was "the kind of talk we need from people in high places."[94]

The governor's approach at the meeting at the old house chamber was classic Sanford. He exhibited some concern for the goals of the protestors and African American leaders. He acknowledged that "the demonstrations have shown just how unhappy and discontent[ed] you are, how anxious you are to remove, and remove right now, the indignities and injustices which have been visited upon your parents and their parents. The demonstrations brought the message, and the message, in its truth and fullness, stirred action which brought your progress."[95] Thus, he recognized the impact the demonstrations had already made in producing changes in

---

[92] Bob Lynch and Roy Parker Jr., "Negroes Boo Gov. at Mansion," *News and Observer*, 11 May 1963, 1.

[93] Frankfort, Kentucky, AP, "Sweeping Order by Governor: Kentucky Ends Discrimination," *News and Observer*, 27 June 1963, 1.

[94] Roy Parker Jr., "Calls Negro Leaders to Conference: End Marches—Sanford," *News and Observer*, 19 June 1963, 1.

[95] Roy Parker Jr., "Negro Leaders Reject Plea by Sanford: Plan Protests," *News and Observer*, 26 June 1963, 1.

various places throughout the state. He ostensibly acknowledged that protest leaders were no longer willing to wait for further changes regarding desegregation and improved job opportunities. In this sense, Sanford was much more progressive than most other Southern politicians.

However, Sanford's actions at the meeting also demonstrated the tentative dance that plagued his leadership, or in many cases lack thereof, on the issue. Sanford left the June 25 meeting after his short speech and did not remain to hear the comments made by civil rights leaders. This arrangement was apparently worked out with Floyd McKissick, and Sanford believed it to be a time for venting among the civil rights leaders. To prevent the session from spiraling into verbal attacks on the governor's office, Sanford arranged for his most trusted race relations troubleshooter, Capus Waynick, and Good Neighbor Council chairman David S. Coltrane to remain at the meeting.[96] At this historic meeting, Sanford could have listened to the impressive array of civil rights leaders and faced their concerns head on. Waynick and Coltrane were trusted surrogates, but Sanford's arrangement to leave the meeting did not exactly demonstrate strong leadership.

The impressive group of civil rights leaders at the meeting included Floyd McKissick, state NAACP president Kelly Alexander, and Golden Frinks, the SCLC leader who had led several demonstrations in Williamston. It also included student protest leaders, including North Carolina A&T's Jesse Jackson, who played a critical role in demonstrations in Greensboro. Overall, the leaders were not content with Sanford's call for an end to demonstrations. One NAACP official called Sanford's speech "brainwashing," and he urged those in attendance to "go home and plan bigger and better demonstrations." McKissick told the group, "We fear the governor misunderstands the situation. It is utterly necessary that the people see the point of the demonstrations, not just the governor. And every indication is that the majority of the white people in North Carolina have not begun to grasp the point of the demonstrations."[97]

After the meeting, McKissick's daughter Joycelyn asked Waynick to

---

[96] Howard E. Covington Jr. and Marion A. Ellis, *Terry Sanford: Politics, Progress, and Outrageous Ambitions* (Durham: Duke University Press, 1999), 320.

[97] Covington and Ellis, *Terry Sanford*, 321, 322.

join her for lunch at the Sir Walter Hotel. He declined and told her he was afraid management might tell him something to the effect of, "Why, we'll have to feed this Negro, but you white so-and-so get the hell out of here."[98] Waynick should be remembered overall for his efforts to bring about positive changes in race relations and for improving opportunities for African Americans in North Carolina. But his circular logic in response to Joycelyn McKissick's invitation was confounding. He believed that improving race relations required changes in attitudes, not just changes in laws.[99] He and other important figures such as Sanford were in a perfect position to take a lead in challenging attitudes. He was willing to sit down with African American leaders to discuss their concerns. But to sit with an African American at a table or lunch counter was a different story. The racist underpinnings of Tar Heel hospitality and Tar Heel politics remained intertwined in the summer of 1963, but the challenges to both were getting stronger.

Ultimately, the civil rights leaders at the June 25 meeting rejected Sanford's plea to end demonstrations. They recognized the importance of keeping pressure on business and political leaders to enact change. Walter Riley recalls that "anything that came from Sanford [in the way of race relations] was forced. It was not led."[100] Great progress had already been made by the summer of 1963, and civil rights activists realized the significant role that the protests played in bringing about change. Sanford had already proven that he was not a diehard defender of segregation. But by that summer, he was in a position in which he could have taken a strong stand against segregation, even if it was politically unpopular.

At a July 5 meeting, approximately two hundred mayors unanimously adopted a resolution commending Sanford's leadership in the racial crisis in the state. He indeed had made some efforts in encouraging desegregation. He called on the mayors of North Carolina's cities to set an example for the rest of the nation in dealing with the racial crisis. He asserted that the only way to solve the problem was by "removing the injustices and

---

[98] Covington and Ellis, *Terry Sanford*, 322.

[99] Covington and Ellis, *Terry Sanford*, 322.

[100] Roy Parker Jr., "Negro Leaders Reject Plea by Sanford: Plan Protests," *News and Observer*, 26 June 1963, 1; Walter Riley, interview by the author.

indignities long suffered by the Negro race." At the meeting, Greensboro
city councilman Forrest Campbell asked the governor if he planned on
following the lead of Governor Bert Combs of Kentucky in issuing such
an order. Sanford responded that such an approach "is not viewed as a
solution to the problem."[101]

Sanford's approach was to appeal to business leaders to voluntarily
desegregate. In this sense, he was much more of an ally to civil rights activists than nearly all other Southern governors, and certainly more of an
ally than I. Beverly Lake would have been if he had won the 1960 gubernatorial election. In this limited sense, he lived up to his promise of the
"new day" in North Carolina that he had declared in his inauguration
speech.[102] But his refusal to issue an executive order similar to that of Kentucky's governor or to attempt to assert his political authority in favor of
desegregation revealed the tentative dance that characterized Sanford's approach to race relations. In some respects, Sanford had one foot inching
toward a "new day" in race relations in the state, and he was bolder than
most state political leaders in encouraging desegregation. But the activists
pushing for immediate changes in social and economic opportunities for
African Americans could not ignore the reality that the governor seemed
to have one foot in the past that tolerated the customs of a segregationist
vision of Tar Heel hospitality.

Perhaps the most troubling aspect of Sanford's cautious leadership
regarding desegregation and the social and economic opportunities for African Americans was his failure to fully comprehend the connection between education and civil rights activism among students from Black colleges. He seemingly failed to recognize that many Black students viewed
their participation in civil rights demonstrations as part of their education.
Although by 1963, he appeared to sympathize with the general goals of
the demonstrators, he repeatedly demeaned the protests. At the meeting
with the mayors of several cities, Sanford declared, "So long as I am governor, the state is not going to take its cue from the fear of masses or

[101] Greensboro AP, "Sanford Asks Mayors for Racial Crisis Aid: Calls Towns
and Cities to Set Example," *News and Observer*, 6 July 1963, 1.

[102] Memory F. Mitchell, ed., *Messages, Addresses, and Public Paper of Terry
Sanford, Governor of North Carolina, 1961–1965* (Raleigh: Council of State, State of
North Carolina, 1966), 3.

mobs."[103] The governor's bluster betrayed the reality that nearly every demonstration had been peaceful. More significantly, by implying that the demonstrators were actually mobs that inspired fear, he obscured the reality that most of the protestors were well-dressed, educated people who had goals ostensibly similar to Sanford's: quality education and the improved opportunities that resulted.

There is no doubt that Sanford lived up to his campaign promises to improve public education. In his inaugural address in 1961, Sanford declared that "we are on the move because we have put our fundamental faith in universal education."[104] Sanford pushed for major increases in teacher pay to make the state more competitive in obtaining and retaining quality teachers. In his first year as governor in 1961, teacher pay (including bonuses) at public schools was raised approximately 17 percent. By 1963, Sanford had pushed forward plans to dramatically improve higher education in the state, which helped secure legislative approval for a system of community colleges and the establishment of four-year colleges in Charlotte, Wilmington, and Asheville that had previously operated as two-year colleges. The director of the Southern Regional Education Board termed North Carolina a "pace-setter" and maintained that the state's major breakthrough in higher education "is based on the creed that educational opportunity and educational equality must advance hand in hand—that they are inseparable, not inconsistent, but mutually dependent."[105] Sanford had led the push for better public education in the state. In doing so, he opened further economic opportunities for many of the state's citizens. Meanwhile, African Americans throughout the state experienced limits in their opportunities, even for those who were highly educated. The pressure that Black colleges students continued to exert on Sanford and the state leadership indicated that they believed their social and economic opportunities were not equivalent to what they should receive, given their level of education.

Sanford nonetheless demonstrated some willingness to push for

---

[103] Greensboro AP, "Sanford Asks Mayors for Racial Crisis Aid," 1.

[104] Mitchell, ed., *Messages, Addresses, and Public Papers of Terry Sanford*, 5.

[105] Winfred Godwin, "North Carolina Pace-Setter for Southern Education," *News and Observer*, 30 June 1963, 4.

further cooperation among races and for improving conditions for African Americans in the state. On January 18, 1963, he called for the establishment of the North Carolina Good Neighbor Council. According to the council's first chairman, David S. Coltrane, the twenty-four-member council had a twofold mission: "1) to encourage the employment of qualified people without regard to race, and 2) to encourage youth to become better trained and qualified for employment."[106] Sanford asked all mayors to establish local good neighbor councils. He also revealed that his administration had issued memoranda to heads of state agencies and institutions to end discriminatory hiring practices if they had not already done so. Thus, Sanford pushed for the end of official state discrimination in hiring practices. In his speech he argued that "the time has come for American citizens to quit unfair discriminations and to give the Negro a full chance to earn a decent living for his family and to contribute to higher standards for himself and all men."[107] The following excerpt from the January speech was classic Sanford, in which he made a moral and economic appeal for the end of discriminatory practices but qualified it with the reality that he would not utilize his power to actively force such changes:

> We can do this, we should do this, we will do it because we are concerned with the problems and welfare of our neighbors. We will do it because our economy cannot afford to have so many people fully or partially unproductive. We will do it because it is honest and fair for us to give all men and women their best chance in life. We are just going to have to open up jobs for all people on the basis of ability and training, and promotions on the basis of performance. I do not intend to try to force anybody. I do not believe in force. In fact, this is a voluntary, low-pressure program. I do believe the conscience of North Carolinians will get the job done.[108]

Sanford deserves credit for helping to bring about increased opportunities for African Americans in state jobs. He also displayed a level of encouragement for desegregation that was rare among Southern politicians.

---

[106] Capus M. Waynick, John C. Brooks, Elsie W. Pitts, eds., *North Carolina and the Negro* (Raleigh: Mayors Cooperating Committee, 1964), 255.

[107] Waynick, Brooks, and Pitts, eds., *North Carolina and the Negro*, 256.

[108] Waynick, Brooks, and Pitts, eds., *North Carolina and the Negro*, 256.

Yet he fell short of being a true ally to those who sought immediate changes to the policies of discrimination that had plagued private business in the state for so long. His contention that the Good Neighbor Council was a "voluntary, low-pressure program" was emblematic of his cautious approach. There were some potential advantages to this approach from a political standpoint, as any effort by the governor to force integration would have been met with a backlash from conservative state legislators and local politicians. William Chafe points out that Sanford's strategy depended on the voluntary cooperation of local leaders to be effective. He argues that "although Sanford's leadership proved more enlightened and more imaginative than that of any other Southern governor, his strategy for change foundered on its own premise of voluntarism."[109]

By the summer of 1963, protestors had created a scenario in which local good neighbor councils or other biracial committees were forced into becoming more effective and taking a stronger stand toward integration. The statewide Good Neighbor Council established in January did not hold its first formal meeting until July 3, 1963, which came after extensive desegregation in restaurants, theaters, hotels, and motels had already occurred in Raleigh and Durham. Even though the North Carolina Good Neighbor Council had been established prior to the mass demonstrations of the spring and summer of 1963 in many North Carolina cities, the council's efforts were more of a response to protest demonstrations throughout the state rather than vice versa.[110]

Civil rights activists in Raleigh and Durham challenged the traditional customs that preserved a segregated vision of Tar Heel hospitality. That year did not represent the advent of civil rights activism utilizing direct-action tactics in the two cities but rather its zenith. "Protest Triangle" activists had several dedicated allies, including students and faculty from the Research Triangle schools as well as committed citizens in the community. Together they countered the forces of segregation. But they also challenged their reluctant allies like Terry Sanford and certain business

---

[109] William Chafe, *Civilities and Civil Rights: Greensboro, North Carolina and the Black Struggle for Freedom* (Oxford: Oxford University Press, 1980), 150.

[110] AP, "Racial Outlook Uncertain in State," *News and Observer*, 30 June 1963, 11; Roy Parker Jr., "Gov. Pledges No Barriers to State Jobs," *News and Observer*, 4 July 1963, 1.

leaders to take a stronger stand in favor of desegregating public accommodations and opening job opportunities.

As similar movements in other cities grew, the impetus for national change became overwhelming. In the spring and summer of 1963, activists like Mack Sowell had not only witnessed some of the changes in segregated practices in Raleigh but had also been active participants in bringing them about through leading demonstrations and mobilizing the community in support of desegregation. And by the late summer, it became clear that "local pressure combined with a national fervor for change" made it increasingly difficult for politicians and business leaders with their feet stuck in the past to thwart that change.[111]

---

[111] Mack Junior Sowell, interview by the author.

Chapter 7

Local, National, and International Connections

Shaw University alumna Angie Brooks entered the Sir Walter Coffee House in Raleigh on April 30, 1963, with her nephew Joseph Outland, who was enrolled at Shaw, and North Carolina State College (NC State) assistant professor Allard Lowenstein, as well as two NC State students. Because Brooks was Black, she was denied service but not before the manager asked her, "Are you looking for a job?" But Brooks was looking for a place to eat, and she certainly did not need a job at a coffee house. She was the Liberian Ambassador to the United Nations and the Assistant Secretary of State of the West African nation. The group was also denied service at the S&W Cafeteria. The incidents prompted US Secretary of State Dean Rusk to send Brooks an apology letter.[1]

The "Brooks Affair" revealed many of the contradictions of Tar Heel hospitality addressed in previous chapters, not the least of which was the reality that business leaders viewed Brooks as a potential employee but not a patron. The incident demonstrated the central role that Shaw students and alumni played in the drama over desegregation in Raleigh. With Lowenstein's presence, the episode also signified the increasing involvement of Whites in the movement to end segregation in the city. Lowenstein's

---

[1] "Seeks Meal: UN Official Turned Away," *News and Observer*, 1 May 1963, 1, 2; "U.S. Agency Apologizes for Incident Here," *News and Observer*, 2 May 1963, 1.

involvement brought to the forefront the issue of whether faculty members at state-supported institutions should be disciplined or terminated for their involvement in civil rights demonstrations. Many segregationists called for Lowenstein to be fired, while others defended his right to protest.[2] Lowenstein's rights to peaceful protest were part of his civil liberties as an American citizen. But for a scholar who devoted much of his attention to studying race relations and the impact of discriminatory policies in the United States and in Africa, any attempt to remove him from his position at NC State for his involvement in protests could reasonably be considered an infringement on his academic freedom.

The incidents at the Sir Walter Coffee House and S&W Cafeteria illuminate one of the central themes of this chapter. Local movements for desegregation had regional, national, and international connections. In some cases, those connections were literal and practical. In other cases, the connections were rhetorical and ideological, but they were always significant in bringing about the impetus for change. In a practical sense, some activists in Raleigh and Durham formed connections with regional and national civil rights leaders. In an ideological sense, some activists viewed their participation as an international struggle for the rights of non-White persons. Additionally, responses to local demonstrations by state and national politicians were often impacted by Cold War sensibilities, which could be used to support or discredit the demonstrations.

This chapter further explores the connection between civil rights activism and academic freedom in a local, regional, and national context. My primary argument is that in North Carolina in 1963, the advocates of academic freedom were generally also the advocates of civil rights for African Americans. Contrarily, the opponents of academic freedom were the opponents of civil rights activism. This was made further evident in the North Carolina General Assembly's enactment of what became known as the Speaker Ban Law, which was ostensibly aimed at banning Communist speakers at state-supported colleges but which many activists believed was an attempt to thwart civil rights activism.[3] Just as college students and

---

[2] William H. Chafe, *Never Stop Running: Allard Lowenstein and the Struggle to Save American Liberalism* (New York: Basic Books, 1993), 179.

[3] William J. Billingsley, *Communists on Campus: Race, Politics, and the Public*

faculty in the Triangle had taken the primary leadership role in civil rights protests, they also led the opposition to the Speaker Ban Law. Meanwhile, those in favor of the 1963 law were the most ardent supporters of segregation, including many state legislators. The connections between academic freedom and civil rights activism were not unique to the Triangle, but they rang truer in a region of the state containing the heart of higher education in the South.

The Speaker Ban Law represented an example of how certain state legislators and other defenders of segregation reacted to local civil rights protests by framing the demonstrations in Cold War rhetoric. Thus, local events led to reactions that were perceived in both local and international terms. The president of the segregationist North Carolina Defenders of States' Rights declared that a "Communist conspiracy to mongrelize the race" was responsible for the civil rights demonstrations in the state.[4] Yet the primary reason for the enactment of the Speaker Ban Law emanated from local protests and some members of the General Assembly's desire to thwart liberalism and civil rights activism, especially among those at the University of North Carolina at Chapel Hill (UNC). One legislator opposing the law contended that a "spirit of fear and distrust" made UNC the "real object" of the law.[5] Yet it is important to note that the support for civil rights activism in the Triangle among some UNC faculty and students was largely a result of the demonstrations primarily carried out by African Americans.

The year 1963 was pivotal in the debate over which visions of freedom and democracy would prevail in the United States. The sit-ins and other forms of protest in North Carolina sought the end of segregated practices on the local level but were also part of a broader struggle that had wide appeals to securing ideals of freedom for all Americans, including African

---

University in Sixties North Carolina (Athens: University of Georgia Press, 1999), 3; Mack Junior Sowell, interview by the author, digital recording, 20 April 2016, Raleigh, NC; Louis Powell, interview by the author, digital recording, 13 April 2016, New Hill, NC.

[4] Asheville AP, "Rector Blames Reds in Racial Strife," *News and Observer*, 28 June 1963, 29.

[5] William A. Link, *William Friday: Power, Purpose, and American Higher Education* (Chapel Hill: University of North Carolina Press, 1995), 115.

Americans. The civil rights protests in Raleigh and Durham and cities throughout the nation were a precursor to the March on Washington in August 1963, an event largely inspired by the activism of that year. The demonstrations were also a driving force for the eventual passage of the 1964 Civil Rights Act.[6]

Lowenstein's effort to eat at the Sir Walter Coffee House and S&W Cafeteria with Angie Brooks was at once a local, regional, national, and international event. It was a direct challenge to customs against which he continued to agitate in the spring and summer of 1963. Lowenstein denied that the incident had been staged. William Chafe asserts that "Lowenstein, of course, knew exactly what he was doing." The incident itself, and the response by the US State Department that implicitly disavowed North Carolina customs, was an embarrassment for North Carolina's "liberal governor," Terry Sanford. As Chafe points out, "How better to underline the stupidity of Jim Crow."[7]

Lowenstein's previous experiences had helped him to view segregation and racism in America in an international context. In 1958, he traveled to South Africa and spoke at the non-White Fort Hare University College, where he attacked apartheid but said the United States could not be blamed since Americans were ignorant of South Africa's policies. A man from South West Africa (modern Namibia) responded that things were so bad in his native land that "I must come *here* [South Africa] to get a breath of fresh air."[8] Prior to World War I, South West Africa was a German colony under which the indigenous people suffered through a campaign of genocide in the first decade of the twentieth century, which led to the deaths of thousands of Nama and Herero.[9] But since the Versailles Treaty in 1919, the area had been under an international mandate. By 1958, South West Africa was nominally under the supervision of the

---

[6] For analysis of the ways in which demonstrations impacted the 1964 Civil Rights Act, see Kenneth T. Andrews and Sarah Gaby, "Local Protest and Federal Policy: The Impact of the Civil Rights Movement on the 1964 Civil Rights Act," *Sociological Forum* 30 S1 (June 2015): 509–27.

[7] Chafe, *Never Stop Running*, 179.

[8] Chafe, *Never Stop Running*, 134.

[9] Adam Hochschild, *King Leopold's Ghost: A Story of Greed, Terror, and Heroism in Colonial Africa* (Boston: First Mariner Books, 1999), 281–82.

United Nations but was actually under the control of the South African government. Lowenstein traveled to South West Africa the following year and witnessed the horrendous conditions that Black Africans faced. He gave testimony to the United Nations on the conditions and the oppressive system operating there. In 1962, the same year that he became a professor at NC State College, his book *Brutal Mandate* was published. Emory Bundy, who had traveled with Lowenstein to South West Africa, noted that "I witnessed large numbers of South-West Africans who had never been given cause to trust any white man place their complete trust in Al on the basis of a few hours acquaintance." Bundy also pointed to some of the most ominous warnings in Lowenstein's book, which argued that "the present state of affairs in southern Africa is as immoral as in the world today...that a change of direction must be achieved quickly if there is to be any hope of avoiding the frightful consequences of a denouement by blood."[10] Lowenstein also recognized the critical role that the United States could play in ending, or at least curtailing, the unfair system in South Africa. Furthermore, some of his contentions seemed to apply to race relations in the American South as well as South Africa: "If the explosion is violent it will be because the world outside, and especially the United States, permitted nonviolence to fail."[11]

Lowenstein made significant contributions to the movement in Raleigh during his short time in the city. In July, he left to participate in the civil rights movement in Mississippi and played a role in what became known as the Freedom Vote. He also helped lay the foundation for the Freedom Summer Project of the following year. Regarding life and opportunities for African Americans, there was some truth to Malcolm X's assertion that "Mississippi is anywhere south of the Canadian border."[12] But by going from Raleigh to Mississippi, Lowenstein entered more hostile territory for civil rights advocates. Lowenstein expected Mississippi would be "only somewhat worse" than North Carolina but found it was more

---

[10] "Emory Bundy to 'Friends,'" 23 August 1962, Series 1, Box 8, Folder 258, Allard Lowenstein Papers, Southern Historical Collection, Wilson Library, University of North Carolina at Chapel Hill.

[11] "Emory Bundy to 'Friends.'"

[12] Thomas Borstelmann, *The Cold War and the Color Line: American Race Relations in the Global Arena* (Cambridge: Harvard University Press, 2001), 4.

"like South Africa, only a little better."[13]

The crucial period of the civil rights movement in the United States in the 1950s and 1960s coincided with increased efforts among Africans to achieve independence from European powers. Historian Thomas Borstelmann argues that "the movements for racial equality and self-government that arose among the world's non-white majority during the Cold War were destined to succeed or fail, for the most part, together."[14] Many Black activists were inspired by African independence leaders such as Ghana's (Gold Coast before independence from Britain in 1957) Kwame Nkrumah. American civil rights leader, historian, and Pan-Africanism advocate W. E. B. Du Bois left the United States to live in Ghana at Nkrumah's urging. In a symbolic coincidence, Du Bois died in his sleep in Ghana the night before the March on Washington.[15]

Nkrumah attended the historically Black Lincoln University in Pennsylvania in the mid-1930s. Like the American civil rights movement, the independence movement in what became Ghana was primarily nonviolent. Additionally, both movements were influenced by education in their own ways. African Americans at historically Black colleges increasingly felt that the quality education they received was not commensurate with their opportunities in a segregated society. Their training gave them confidence to strive for better opportunities, but a different effect came from education in the Gold Coast. Historian David Birmingham points out that a school education "created a unified stratum of school-leavers who identified with the Gold Coast, rather than with any one ethnic or regional section of it. Education therefore unwittingly and ironically kindled a hotbed of nationalism in which seeds of independence germinated."[16]

Although the connections between Africa and African Americans could sometimes be peripheral to the daily lives of students in Raleigh,

---

[13] Richard Cummings, *The Pied Piper: Allard K. Lowenstein and the Liberal Dream* (New York: Grove Press, Inc., 1985), 231.

[14] Borstelmann, *The Cold War and the Color Line*, 6.

[15] David Birmingham, *Kwame Nkrumah: The Father of African Nationalism* (Athens: Ohio University Press, 1998), 95; David Levering Lewis, *W. E. B. Du Bois: The Fight for Equality and the American Century, 1919–1963* (New York: Henry Holt and Company, 1993), 569–70.

[16] Birmingham, *Kwame Nkrumah*, 4, 31.

there were some tangible connections. For instance, several African students attended Shaw University. Shaw student Carrie Gaddy (Brock) recalled a time when an African student at Shaw decided to head back to campus instead of proceeding with a group going downtown to participate in the sit-ins in February 1960. According to Brock, the student said half-jokingly, "I can't stand to see my African blood spilled."[17]

One of the notable African students at Shaw in the early 1960s was Edward Reynolds, and his experiences reveal some of the regional and international connections of the movement for integration in North Carolina. Reynolds was born in a small town near Accra, Ghana. In his youth, he was heavily influenced by Christian missionaries from Europe and the United States. In the late 1950s, he attended Achimota School in Accra, from which Nkrumah was an alumnus. Most of his teachers were from European countries. The piano keys that formed the crest of Achimota School symbolized the interaction between the races. As Reynolds points out, "You could play a tune with the black keys, you could play a tune with the white keys, but together for the harmony you need the black and white."[18] Reynolds was at Achimota in 1957, the year in which Martin Luther King Jr., A. Philip Randolph, and other civil rights leaders met Nkrumah and celebrated Ghana's independence. This was not only a momentous occasion for Ghanaians but also an inspirational moment for King and other African Americans. According to Taylor Branch, King's experiences in Ghana "helped secure his belief that the *Zeitgeist*, or spirit of the age, was rising to the defense of oppressed peoples."[19]

Reynolds witnessed the historic occasion of Ghana's independence in 1957. In 1961, he began his journey as a participant in an era of historical change in North Carolina. That year, students from Wake Forest College (now Wake Forest University) in Winston-Salem sought an African student to integrate the Baptist school. The push for integrating the school dated back to the previous decade, but the sit-in movement created further

---

[17] Carrie Gaddy Brock, interview by the author, digital recording, 2 March 2016, Raleigh, NC.

[18] Edward Reynolds, phone interview by the author, digital recording, 20 July 2016.

[19] Edward Reynolds, phone interview by the author; Taylor Branch, *Parting the Waters: America in the King Years* (New York: Simon and Schuster, Inc., 1988), 214.

pressure. One Wake Forest student who played a role in bringing an African student to the school stated that "the whole topic of civil rights and integration was all over the campus that spring [1960]."[20] A small group of Wake Forest students had participated in sit-ins primarily orchestrated by students from the historically Black Winston-Salem State Teachers College (now Winston-Salem State University). A group of students formed the African Student Program, and with financial support of some college faculty, they paid for Reynolds to come to North Carolina. Yet the Board of Trustees would not be moved, and Edwards was denied entrance to Wake Forest.[21]

Instead of attending the state's preeminent White Baptist college in 1961, Reynolds enrolled at the historically Black Shaw University. The presence of an African student at Shaw was nothing new, but Reynolds's time at Shaw gave him an opportunity to interact with the Black community in the American South. He was warmly welcomed by students and faculty, and he got to know President William Strassner. He received occasional visits from Wake Forest students, especially those working to get him accepted at the school. One of the most consistent visitors was Pullen Memorial Baptist Church (Raleigh) pastor and Wake Forest graduate W. W. Finlator, an outspoken integration advocate.[22]

On April 27, 1962, the Board of Trustees voted 17–9 to end segregation in the school's undergraduate programs, and Reynolds attended the school in the fall semester of 1962. He experienced some instances of discrimination, such as the few times when someone hung a picture of a gorilla or lion with his likeness. Yet he did not suffer from any threats of violence, and many people made a concerted effort to welcome him. Fellow worshippers at local Black churches gave him money, and some of the custodial staff at Wake Forest gave him cookies. He was warmly welcomed by several students and faculty, especially those who had fought so hard to

---

[20] Lisa O'Donnell, "First Black Student at Wake Forest: 'I Didn't View It as Bravery,'" *Winston-Salem Journal,* 16 September 2012, available at http://www.journalnow.com/news/local/first-black-student-at-wake-forest-i-didn-t-view/article_177493fa-2d2d-5de5-aa77-6cfd252ea38e.html.

[21] O'Donnell, "First Black Student at Wake Forest."

[22] Edward Reynolds, phone interview by the author.

gain his acceptance.[23]

Reynolds was not only a witness but also a participant in historical change. Although he did not participate in any direct-action tactics such as sit-ins, he nonetheless played an important role in integration in the state by becoming the first of two Black undergraduate students at Wake Forest. Student activists had largely paved the path for his acceptance. The sit-in movement led primarily by Black college students had created an impetus for change that was part of the inspiration for White students at Wake Forest to actively pursue acceptance of an African student. His experiences also demonstrate the connection between education and the push for the rights of Black people. Just as highly educated people like Nkrumah led the push for independence in Ghana, so too did Black and White students play a crucial role in challenging the segregated society in the American South.

Reynolds's experiences and the Board of Trustees' vote in favor of integrating undergraduate programs at Wake Forest demonstrated that White North Carolinians were not a monolithic group when it came to race relations and ideas about segregation and integration. The Board of Trustees' members were not a monolithic group themselves, and some had been influenced by the growing push for integration in the years prior to 1962. For those who sought to preserve segregation, it apparently mattered not that Reynolds was a fellow Christian. For them, race trumped religion and humanity. Those who wanted to continue segregated practices stood in stark contrast with fellow White Baptist W. W. Finlator, who challenged segregation not only through his words but through his actions. His visits to a Black African at a historically Black college demonstrated that Tar Heel hospitality could be defined in a way that extended hospitality to all races. The Raleigh pastor and White students and faculty who visited Reynolds treated the African man as a fellow human being, a courtesy that many White Southerners refused to give to fellow American citizens due to the color of their skin.

In Durham, activists made connections with the movement for integration in Chapel Hill, which had an image of being a liberal college town.

---

[23] Lisa O'Donnell, "First Student at Wake Forest"; Edward Reynolds, interview by the author.

A longtime Black resident reflected that "Chapel Hill had an image of being very liberal outwardly. But underneath it, it was different."[24] Restaurants and other places of business in Chapel Hill remained segregated in 1963. In *Game Changers: Dean Smith, Charlie Scott, and the Era that Transformed a Southern College Town*, Art Chansky maintains, "Much of the liberal image was a fraud because little of what was being argued and proposed about ending segregation resulted in voluntary action."[25] In the summer of 1963, as more businesses began desegregating in Raleigh and Durham, Chapel Hill remained segregated. The movement in Chapel Hill involved a mix of college and high school students and community members. The movement received strong support and leadership from a group of UNC students, most notably John Dunne and Pat Cusick.[26]

Just as some UNC students became involved in the protests in Raleigh and Durham, some students from North Carolina College (NCC) played a role in the movement in Chapel Hill. Quinton Baker, a student leader in Durham, also became heavily involved in Chapel Hill in 1963. Baker and Cusick taught young demonstrators in Chapel Hill about Gandhi and nonviolent resistance. They showed the eager protestors how to go limp when arrested and how to protect themselves in a fight. As the two college students trained the young group in the field outside of the Black recreation center on Roberson Street, local police came to the fence surrounding the field and asked Cusick and Baker what kind of army they were training.[27] It was not an army but a group of mostly young people, eager to challenge segregation directly in a nonviolent way, preparing to protect themselves from potential violence.

In mid-1963, Baker lived with Cusick in his rental home on Spring Lane, but Cusick was eventually evicted. According to Cusick, "I was kicked out for having trash in my house—namely that's a synonym for

---

[24] Art Chansky, *Game Changers: Dean Smith, Charlie Scott, and the Era that Transformed a Southern College Town* (Chapel Hill: University of North Carolina Press, 2016), 25.

[25] Chansky, *Game Changers*, 26.

[26] Chansky, *Game Changers*, 57, 60.

[27] Jim Wallace and Paul Dickson, *Courage in the Moment: The Civil Rights Struggle, 1961–1964* (Mineola, NY: Dover Publications, Inc., 2012), 19; John Ehle, *The Free Men* (New York: Harper and Row Publishers, 1965), 76–77.

black people."[28] The resistance to integration in Chapel Hill emboldened Cusick, as did his interaction with Black activists such as Baker and Harold Foster, editor of the *Campus Echo* at NCC and a leader of anti-segregation demonstrations at the Carolina Theater. Cusick recalls that when he first decided to challenge integration, he opposed picketing: "When we started picketing, I wasn't that much in favor of marching. When we started marching, I was not in favor of civil disobedience. The events swept us along."[29]

For Cusick (who attended UNC on the GI Bill and was a decade or so older than most UNC students), his inspiration came not so much from his occasional interactions with some of the leading figures in the regional and national movement (including Floyd McKissick and Martin Luther King Jr.) but from the young people, including some UNC students and the Black teenagers from Lincoln High School.[30] Like many of the other demonstrators, Cusick was jailed for his involvement in sit-ins at the Merchants Association and local restaurants. But as the primary leaders of the movement in Chapel Hill, and for charges related to blocking traffic and resisting arrest (a charge applied to those who went "limp" when arrested), Cusick and Baker were sentenced to prison. Cusick initially received one year in jail and a suspended two-year sentence, although he ultimately served less than a year. In addition to his prison sentence, Baker received a hundred-dollar fine. Meanwhile, the co-owner of Watts Grill, who pulled her dress up and urinated on a demonstrator, and the owner of Carlton's Rock Pile, who doused demonstrators with ammonia, faced no such punishment.[31]

The interaction among activists like Cusick, Dunne, and Baker was at once personal and based on issues of social justice. Their relationship demonstrated the interaction between students from the Protest Triangle

---

[28] Pat Cusick, interview by Pamela Dean, 19 June 1989, interview L-0043, Southern Oral History Program Collection (#4007), Southern Historical Collection, Wilson Library, University of North Carolina at Chapel Hill, available at http://docsouth.unc.edu/sohp/L-0043/menu.html.

[29] Cusick, interview by Dean.

[30] Cusick, interview by Dean.

[31] Chansky, *Game Changers*, 60–64; Capus M. Waynick, John C. Brooks, Elsie W. Pitts, eds., *North Carolina and the Negro* (Raleigh: North Carolina Mayors' Cooperating Committee, 1964), 49; Wallace and Dickson, *Courage in the Moment*, 68.

and Research Triangle schools. By living together, Cusick and Baker demonstrated that they believed in integration on a personal level, in addition to the impact integration would have on society and economic opportunities. Their experience also highlighted some of the differences in challenging segregation in a city with a historically Black college (Durham) and in a small town with the state's most liberal, predominantly White public university. Baker had been a crucial figure in bringing significant desegregation in public accommodations in Durham. In Chapel Hill, he and other activists faced mostly frustrating results, despite the support of some White liberals in the community and at the university.[32]

A primary goal among activists in Chapel Hill was to secure a local public accommodations agreement outlawing racial segregation. In Baker's view, "We knew in order for us to get a civil rights law that would eliminate segregation...we needed to point out that Chapel Hill was never going to voluntarily desegregate, which is what everybody was calling for at that time. Voluntary desegregation of the South, and we were saying, 'It ain't gonna happen.' And the way to demonstrate that was to target Chapel Hill, to make it a focal point of activity."[33] The decision was in the hands of the town's Board of Aldermen, who received pressure from activists to pass the measure but also pressure from local businesspersons to oppose it. One of the most significant demonstrations occurred when James Farmer from CORE led nearly two hundred protestors on a thirteen-mile "Walk for Freedom" in the rain from Durham to Chapel Hill on June 12, 1963. The next day, the Board of Alderman delayed voting on the agreement and approved a measure to negotiate further. The public accommodations bill never passed, and it was not until the 1964 Civil Rights Act was passed that Chapel Hill's remaining segregated places of business were forced to integrate.[34]

While support for demonstrations in Chapel Hill was far from universal among the UNC faculty, several professors participated and offered

---

[32] Pat Cusick, interview by Pamela Dean.

[33] Quinton Baker, interview by Chris McGinnis, 23 February 2002, Interview K-0838, Southern Oral History Program Collection (#4007), Southern Historical Collection, Wilson Library, University of North Carolina at Chapel Hill, http://docsouth.unc.edu/sohp/K-0838/K-0838.html.

[34] Chansky, *Game Changers*, 58.

encouragement, and a few were arrested for their participation. Law professor Dr. Dan Pollitt was among the most supportive, and he had been involved in creating the campus NAACP. He was outspoken in his support for integration in Chapel Hill. Perhaps his most significant contribution came in the form of offering his legal opinion that a potential public accommodations bill would hold up in the courts.[35] Pollitt was among the professors at the Research Triangle schools who gave their moral encouragement and utilized their knowledge and experiences to challenge segregation in the Tar Heel state.

Pollitt's experiences in the 1950s and 1960s demonstrated the connections between civil rights activism and academic freedom. Pollitt had taken a position teaching law at the University of Arkansas in 1955 but was relieved of his duties in 1957 after refusing to sign a loyalty oath. The oath required him to sign a disclaimer that he had never been a member of any subversive organization, including the NAACP, a group with which he was involved. His dismissal demonstrated how institutions in Southern states attempted to connect civil rights organizations with Communism. His refusal to sign the oath also demonstrated a commitment to academic freedom that extended beyond his activities on the campus. That same year, Pollitt accepted a job at UNC. Pollitt later recalled that "I came to Carolina for its record of academic freedom" and because the school administration seemed "receptive to my position."[36]

As civil rights activism reached new heights in 1963 in North Carolina, it became clear that the most ardent defenders of segregation were also those who sought to attack academic freedom. In late June, the North Carolina General Assembly quickly passed the "Act to Regulate Visiting Speakers," which came to be known as the Speaker Ban Law. The legislation barred known Communists, people who advocated the overthrow of the US government, or those who had pled the Fifth Amendment in respect to subversive activities. The bill was essentially railroaded through the House and Senate in the waning days of the summer legislative session

---

[35] David Dansby, phone interview by the author, 14 June 2016; "Desegregation Law Shelved by Alderman," *News and Observer*, 26 June 1963, 3.

[36] "Civil Liberties Champion Dan Pollitt Dies," *Carrboro Citizen*, 5 March 2010, http://www.ibiblio.org/carrborocitizen/main/2010/03/05/legal-giant-dan-pollitt-dies/.

with minimal debate. After the bill quickly passed in the House, Senate president Clarence Stone stifled debate, and the measure passed in about fifteen minutes. State Senator Ralph Scott of Alamance County called it "the most outrageous abuse of the legislative process I have ever seen."[37]

There is a clear correlation between those who supported the Speaker Ban Law and those who most forcefully supported racial segregation. Stone was one of the most ardent supporters of segregation and White supremacy. Unlike many North Carolina politicians who cloaked their racism in platitudes and appeals to traditional customs, Stone's commitment to White supremacy was unmistakable in the 1950s and early 1960s. He vehemently opposed the Supreme Court decision in *Brown v. Board of Education* and believed that the South was "still a conquered province." As William Billingsley points out, "Stone's devotion to white supremacy was as pronounced as his fealty to states' rights. These concepts had served as the twin pillars of southern politics: each had informed and reinforced the other to such an extent that they had become inseparable."[38] Billingsley maintains that Stone and other segregationists shared a conviction that civil equality with Blacks threatened White identity.

Another legislator who supported racial segregation as well as the Speaker Ban Law was John H. Kerr Jr. He represented rural Warren County, which contained the highest percentage of African Americans of any county in the state at over 60 percent. For Kerr and other conservatives in the General Assembly, race and power were closely connected.[39] The sit-in movement and direct challenges to segregation by activists as well as federal efforts to protect African American civil rights threatened the power of men like Kerr. His frustrations seemed to boil over on February 19, 1963. In response to North Carolina A&T acting president Lewis C. Dowdy's budget request to the Joint Appropriations Committee, Kerr asked, "Didn't students from your college take part in the sit-in strikes in Greensboro trying to do away with segregation?" When Dowdy answered with a simple "yes," Kerr retorted, "You come down here begging the white

---

[37] Tom Inman, "Anti-Red Measure Quickly Enacted," *News and Observer*, 26 June 1963, 1, 2.

[38] Billingsley, *Communists on Campus*, 68.

[39] Billingsley, *Communists on Campus*, 78.

folks to give more money to your school.... Some of us are getting tired of it. You can strike all you please, but don't come here and beg us."[40]

Kerr's tirade revealed many of the contradictions of the segregated South. His response to Dowdy's request implied that he and the other legislators personally gave money to the school and that Dowdy should be appreciative of any money that came from their apparent benevolence. Kerr's reply demonstrated a paternalistic view of the relationship between White politicians and African American constituents and citizens of North Carolina, some of whom attended NC A&T. Furthermore, his response revealed his belief that the college administrator should have restricted student participation in demonstrations that sought desegregation and more broadly a fuller opportunity for African Americans to participate in American democracy and economic life. Since many Black college students viewed their participation in the demonstrations as part of their education and as a way of opening future opportunities, Kerr's expectation that administrators at Black colleges should restrict student participation in protests revealed his lack of appreciation for the students' expanded vision of academic freedom.

One of the most outspoken supporters of the Speaker Ban Law was I. Beverly Lake, the staunch segregationist who lost to Terry Sanford in the runoff election for governor in 1960. Lake claimed that the law has "caused howls of distress from those who have placed their faith in a welfare state for America and from others who they have tricked into believing that freedom of speech is in danger."[41] Many Lake supporters also defended the Speaker Ban. At a "White" rally in a field next to Wilkins airstrip about ten miles from Durham, approximately 250 White men and women listened to speakers that complained about the "invasion of human rights by Negroes." One speaker claimed that the "NAACP is Communist-backed and supported to divide and defeat the people of America." Another man who directed the local campaign for Lake for governor in 1960 spoke in favor of the Speaker Ban Law and attacked those who

---

[40] Raleigh AP, "Kerr Upbraids Negro Educator," *Durham Morning Herald*, 20 February 1963, 3.

[41] Parkton AP, "Beverly Lake Backs Anti-Communist Law," *Durham Morning Herald*, 5 July 1963, 10A.

criticized it.[42]

Opposition to the Speaker Ban Law was strong among college administrators, professors, and students. Opponents viewed it as an attack on academic freedom, as it limited the professors' ability to bring in certain speakers and the students' ability to engage with the ideas of Communism. NC State Chancellor John Caldwell called the law a "Berlin Wall of the mind."[43] The president of Duke University, whose school was not impacted since it was a private institution, said Duke had no such regulation since "we feel that it is desirable to expose students to as many opinions as possible." UNC Chancellor William B. Aycock called the Speaker Ban Law "the sloppiest bit of legislation I have ever seen."[44] Thus, opposition to the law was unanimous among the presidents of the Research Triangle schools.

The presidents of historically Black colleges in the Triangle also opposed the Speaker Ban Law. Saint Augustine's president James Boyer argued that "students have long repudiated the idea of 'cloistered virtue,' and want to challenge Communism's ideas first hand."[45] Alfonso Elder, president of state-supported NCC said the law "denies individuals the rights and responsibility to explore and develop their own sense of values."[46] Opponents of the Speaker Ban Law viewed it as an example of the type of restriction on freedom of speech and academic freedom that were the hallmarks of Communist societies from the Soviet Union to China to Cuba.

The Speaker Ban Law was not only an attempt to prohibit Communists from speaking on state-supported campuses. It was also an effort to thwart the momentum of the civil rights demonstrations. Mack Sowell recalled, "We felt that it had nothing to do with Communists." Sowell believed it "was a restriction on African American speakers whom they felt were stirring up people to do things...it was an attempt to quell it,

---

[42] Pat Carter, "Negro Invasion of Rights Is Charged at White Rally," *Durham Morning Herald*, 14 July 1963, 1.

[43] Alice Elizabeth Reagan, *North Carolina State University: A Narrative History* (Raleigh: The North Carolina State University Foundation, Inc., 1987), 188.

[44] "Aycock Makes Blistering Attack on Speaker Ban," *News and Observer*, 11 November 1963, 8.

[45] Tom Inman, "School Chiefs Urge Repeal of Gag Bill," *News and Observer*, 20 July 1963, 1.

[46] Inman, "School Chiefs Urge Repeal."

particularly on the state campuses of North Carolina—[the legislators were saying] you're not going to come here and stir up trouble."[47] Sowell also believes that the hastily enacted bill had something to do with the civil rights demonstrations that were taking place at the Sir Walter Hotel, where many of the legislators lodged and dined. Louis Powell, a 1962 graduate of Shaw University, was very much opposed to the law: "I felt it was designed specifically to control some of the changes that we were hoping would take place [regarding desegregation and increasing opportunities for African Americans]."[48]

Many African Americans and Whites who supported Black civil rights believed there was a connection between the Speaker Ban Law and efforts at thwarting civil rights dialogue and protests. Comments made during that period and in subsequent years by members of the General Assembly reinforce the connection. One legislator recollected that the presence of White professors at the demonstrations was a major factor in bringing about the law. Another representative, George Uzell, recalled in 1965 that "the Speaker Ban Law was originally passed more to curb civil rights demonstrations than to stop Communist speakers on state campuses."[49] Uzell introduced an antitrespassing bill in 1963, providing for stiffer fines and jail sentences for trespassing, a response to the sit-ins.[50] Like other legislators, Uzell represented the connection between efforts to preserve segregation and efforts to limit academic freedom and free speech.

One of the most outspoken supporters of the Speaker Ban Law was WRAL editorialist Jesse Helms, who praised the law as a "strong blow for freedom."[51] Herein lies the ultimate irony of those who supported the Speaker Ban Law. It restricted freedom of speech and the ability for college students to think critically to form their own opinions about a competing system of government and economy. In short, the law was the type of restriction on free speech and critical thinking that characterized many Communist regimes. Helms was undoubtedly an anti-Communist, but

---

[47] Mack Sowell, interview by the author.

[48] Louis Powell, interview by the author.

[49] Billingsley, *Communists on Campus*, 62–63.

[50] Billingsley, *Communists on Campus*, 59.

[51] William A. Link, *Righteous Warrior: Jesse Helms and the Rise of Modern Conservatism* (New York: St. Martin's Press), 85.

like many Southern politicians, he conflated Communism with civil rights activism. He also exhibited an anti-intellectual strain that was common among conservative politicians in the state. Both as an editorialist and later as a US Senator, he often targeted UNC liberals. His circular logic appealed to many defenders of segregation. While many supporters of desegregation recognized the connections between academic freedom and civil rights activism, Helms had a much different view. For Helms, the "two-word catechisms of 'academic freedom' and 'civil rights'" were meaningless. Academic freedom had "little to do with freedom," and the "rights we hear so much about are not very civil."[52]

The Speaker Ban Law was amended in 1965 after the Southern Association of Colleges and Schools notified UNC officials that it jeopardized the university's accreditation. The final death blow came in 1968 when a federal court struck down the law as "unconstitutional because of vagueness." Dan Pollitt played a role in the case by filing an amicus curiae brief on behalf of the North Carolina Civil Liberties Union.[53] Pollitt reflected that "the Speaker Ban Law, I thought, was a result of racism." He believed it was largely a response to the sit-ins and protests gripping cities throughout the state, including in the Triangle. He believed that Angie Brooks and Allard Lowenstein attempting to eat at the Sir Walter was part of what precipitated the law. According to Pollitt, the law was "anti-university and it was anti-Chapel Hill and it was anti-Al Lowenstein at State and all the black campuses."[54] For Pollitt, the Speaker Ban Law demonstrated the connection between the opponents of African American civil rights and those who sought to restrict free speech and academic freedom. The connection between civil rights activism and academic freedom was not unique to the Triangle. But in a subregion of the South, which included the most prestigious private institution (Duke), the oldest public university that had traditionally been a staunch supporter of academic freedom (UNC), as well as three historically Black colleges that were

---

[52] Link, *Righteous Warrior*, 86.

[53] Link, *Righteous Warrior*, 88; Billingsley, *Communists on Campus*, 215, 218.

[54] Dan Pollitt, interview by Ann McColl, Interview L-0064-7, 5 April 1991, Southern Oral History Program Collection (#4007), Southern Historical Collection, Wilson Library, University of North Carolina at Chapel Hill, http://docsouth.unc.edu/sohp/L-0064-7/L-0064-7.html.

instrumental in the sit-in movement, the connection was even clearer than in other parts of the South.

Civil rights activists who opposed the Speaker Ban Law did so not because they were in favor of Communism but because they rejected restrictions on free speech and recognized that segregationists often falsely portrayed civil rights leaders as Communists. Student leaders from historically Black colleges in the Triangle did not seek to overthrow the American government but to force it to live up to its professed ideals of democracy and equality. Most "Protest Triangle" students did not have Communist friends and knew of very few Communists in the area. Frank Porter Graham, the former president of the Consolidated University of North Carolina and a United Nations mediator in 1963, stated that civil rights activists "are not trying to overthrow the Republic. Rather, they are trying to fulfill the promise of the Republic made on July 4, 1776, in Philadelphia." Graham denied segregationist claims that "the Southern Youth Movement started in Moscow." In his estimation, "It started in Greensboro at A&T College."[55]

There was no escaping Cold War rhetoric related to race relations in the United States. Both integrationists and segregationists used appeals to Cold War sensibilities to defend their positions. Harsh reactions to some civil rights protests hurt America's image abroad and provided propaganda opportunities for nations such as Cuba, the Soviet Union, and China as well as the countries they sought to influence. The incidents of violence and police brutality in Birmingham in late spring 1963 were powerful symbols of American racism exploited by Soviet propaganda. A group of North Carolina civic leaders, including Chapel Hill mayor Sandy McClamroch Jr. and Fayetteville mayor Wilbur Clark, toured Eastern Europe in September 1963. Upon returning, Clark reflected that "the race question is definitely being used against us in propaganda." But he also said the people in the region did not ask them about the race problem and that "the people we meet either are more concerned with their own problems or they don't believe all they read." Perhaps the most telling comment came from a Russian man in Moscow, who approached them and said,

---

[55] "4-H Hears Graham Back Integration," *News and Observer*, 24 July 1963, 7.

"America good, Alabama bad."[56]

The Russian man's words shed light on the views of some people in the Soviet sphere of influence but also opened a window to the view of many Americans. Many Americans were appalled when they viewed scenes of police utilizing dogs or protestors being knocked down by fire hoses. But some White Americans refused to fully acknowledge the racism and systemic discrimination outside of the South or even the Deep South. Iconic images of violence toward demonstrators, whether by police or ordinary citizens, helped awaken the conscience of some Americans. But those images often gave comfort to racial "moderates" who believed that racial discrimination was not as bad where they lived as it was in Alabama or Mississippi. The visceral response by many citizens and politicians to civil rights activism in states like Alabama and Mississippi was indeed worse than in most other areas of the country. But systemic racism in the form of employment discrimination, housing discrimination, and unequal access to services, as well as informal prejudice, was an American problem, not just a Southern problem.[57]

Cold War concerns about America's image abroad impacted President Kennedy's approach to civil rights issues. But one should not underestimate the impact that several local movements, led by mostly unheralded activists, had in bringing about a change in approach by key government leaders, including Kennedy. Civil rights activists in the Triangle were among the thousands of protestors who pushed Kennedy into a more proactive approach to civil rights for African Americans in 1963. As sociologists Kenneth T. Andrews and Sarah Gaby point out, the Kennedy Administration had taken a mostly reactive or crisis management approach to civil rights issues in his first two years as president.[58] For example, in response to the violence that the Freedom Rides provoked from

---

[56] Warsaw, Poland, AP, "Tar Heels Find Racial Question Seldom Asked," *News and Observer*, 7 October 1963, 3.

[57] For analysis of race relations and the struggle for civil rights in the North, see Thomas J. Sugrue, *Sweet Land of Liberty: The Forgotten Struggle for Civil Rights in the North* (New York: Random House, 2008); Martha Biondi, *To Stand and Fight: The Struggle for Civil Rights in Postwar New York City* (Cambridge: Harvard University Press, 2006).

[58] Andrews and Gaby, "Local Protest and Federal Policy," 510.

hostile Whites in 1961, Attorney General Robert Kennedy sent federal marshals and pressured Alabama Governor John Patterson to deploy the Alabama National Guard to protect the Riders. Yet Robert Kennedy derided the Riders and criticized them for "providing good propaganda for America's enemies."[59] Of course, it was not the Freedom Riders who provided propaganda for enemies like the Soviet Union but rather social practices and a political system in the South that tolerated extreme racial prejudice, which went largely (albeit not completely) unchallenged by the federal government for nearly a century. Ultimately, Robert Kennedy instructed the Justice Department to push the Interstate Commerce Commission to ban segregation and discrimination in interstate travel, which became effective on November 1, 1961. As Adam Fairclough points out, "The Freedom Rides had forced the Kennedy Administration to act against its will."[60]

By the summer of 1963, the Kennedy Administration was pressured into taking a more proactive approach to civil rights issues. Activists throughout the South had staged hundreds of sit-ins, marches, and boycotts in the spring and summer, while activists in other regions of the United States supported desegregation and emphasized economic concerns. With the increasing activism, Justice Department officials began tracking civil rights demonstrations. Between May 20 and August 8, the department noted 978 demonstrations in 29 cities, most of which targeted public accommodations. Throughout much of June and early July, Robert Kennedy and other government officials met with various groups, including governors; hotel, restaurant, and theater owners; educators; and civil rights activists to discuss civil rights issues and desegregation.[61]

The Civil Rights Act of 1964 was not born in the halls of Congress or in the Oval Office. Rather, it was a political and moral response to the activists on the streets and at the lunch counters and restaurants in Greensboro, Raleigh, Nashville, and dozens of other cities in the South and throughout the nation. President Kennedy's June 11, 1963, speech in

---

[59] Adam Fairclough, *Better Day Coming: Blacks and Equality, 1890–2000* (New York: Penguin Books, 2001), 255.

[60] Fairclough, *Better Day Coming*, 255.

[61] Andrews and Gaby, "Local Protest and Federal Policy," 521.

which he called for legislation that, among other things, would mandate desegregation of public accommodations, signified his willingness to take a leadership role in pushing for legislation. But it is important to recognize that he had been pushed into such a stance by the thousands of activists throughout the South and the rest of the nation.[62]

June 11, 1963, was a crucial and symbolic day in the history of race relations in the United States. It was at once sensational, inspiring, and tragic. It revealed the tensions between Southern politicians and federal agencies as well as the willingness among some Southerners to continue to use terror as a tool in preserving segregation. The first major event that day was Alabama Governor George Wallace's dramatic and carefully staged act of standing in the doorway of the auditorium at the University of Alabama to attempt to deny the registration of African Americans. On June 2, Wallace had reiterated his campaign promise to stand in the door and maintained that the issue was more than integration at the university. He claimed that he wanted to stop "the march of centralized government that is going to destroy the rights and freedom and liberty of the people of this country."[63] As Southern politicians had done for generations, Wallace defended the denial of basic rights to African Americans by portraying federal efforts to secure such rights as a restriction on the freedom of Americans.

Wallace's stance in the doorway provided him an opportunity to publicly show his hardline defense of segregation. He understood that he could not officially block the admission of James Hood and Vivian Malone in the wake of a federal judge's decision the previous week that ultimately prohibited Wallace from interfering with their admission. Unlike the thousands of civil rights activists throughout the country, Wallace was ostensibly not willing to risk jail for his own particular vision of American freedom. As Deputy Attorney General Nicholas Katzenbach approached Wallace, he declared, "I have come here to ask now for unequivocal

---

[62] Richard C. Cortner, *Civil Rights and Public Accommodations: The* Heart of Atlanta Motel *and* McClung *Cases* (Lawrence, KS: University Press of Kansas, 2001), 14, 17.

[63] Dan T. Carter, *The Politics of Rage: George Wallace, the Origins of the New Conservatism, and the Transformation of American Politics* (Baton Rouge: Louisiana State University Press, 2000), 137.

assurance that you will permit these students who, after all, merely want an education in the Great University." Wallace interrupted by saying, "Now you make your statement, but we don't need a speech." Ironically, Wallace then gave a four-page speech denouncing "this illegal and unwarranted action by the Central Government." Ultimately, Katzenbach returned to his car and then walked Vivian Malone to her dormitory across the parking lot, while Justice Department officials drove Hood to his dorm. Later that day, Malone (who, like Hood, had already quietly pre-registered at the Birmingham courthouse with the cooperation of the university) went to the cafeteria and sat down. Six students came and sat at the table and introduced themselves.[64] It was an inspiring act of humanity that demonstrated that not every White Southerner could be grouped in the same category as George Wallace.

That evening, President Kennedy addressed the nation on national television. The speech revealed the impact that the civil rights demonstrations throughout the country had on pushing him to advocate for federal legislation. He stated that the nation faced a "moral crisis" that "cannot be left to increased demonstrations in the streets. It cannot be quieted by token moves or talk." He told the American people that in the following week he would ask the Congress to act and "make a commitment that it has not fully made in this century to the proposition that race has no place in American life or law." Kennedy also recognized the connection between education and civil rights activism. He implored the nation to recognize that "we cannot say to 10 percent of the population…that your children can't have the chance to develop whatever talents they have, that the only way they have to get their rights is to go in the streets and demonstrate."[65]

Kennedy's speech demonstrated his commitment to civil rights legislation that had been inspired by activism in several cities throughout the United States. As historian Robert Weisbrot points out, "There could be no turning back. The President had fully committed the authority of his office—and his political future—to continued civil rights progress."[66] The

---

[64] Carter, *The Politics of Rage*, 148–50.

[65] *Public Papers of the Presidents of the United States: John F. Kennedy, 1963* (Washington, DC: US Government Printing Office, 1964), 468–71.

[66] Robert Weisbrot, *Freedom Bound: A History of America's Civil Rights Movement* (New York: Penguin Books, 1990), 76.

speech was perhaps the most significant moment in demonstrating Kennedy's commitment to civil rights issues, but he had been pressured by civil rights activists to do so. By the summer of 1963, it was clear to Kennedy that taking a reactive stance toward civil rights issues was no longer a tenable approach.

Civil rights activists throughout the nation were encouraged by Kennedy's speech. But for many activists the excitement was short-lived, as news of tragedy came from Mississippi. Shortly after midnight (thus, technically on June 12), NAACP organizer and World War II veteran Medgar Evers returned to his home in Jackson after a long strategy meeting, unaware that Byron de la Beckwith waited behind a clump of honeysuckle vines in an empty lot near the house. Historian Dan T. Carter vividly describes the tragic event that followed: "Beckwith peered through the scope of his 30.06 bolt-action Winchester; Evers's white shirt offered a perfect target in the harsh light of the carport's naked bulb. As Evers reached for the handle of the kitchen door, the steel-jacketed bullet ripped through his back between the tenth and eleventh rib; exiting, it left a massive hole just below the sternum. He died within the hour."[67]

The assassination of Medgar Evers was a chilling reminder that some Southerners would continue to utilize terror as a weapon against civil rights activism. But Kennedy's speech earlier that evening was an example that the civil rights demonstrations throughout the nation were having an impact on national political leaders. While activists in Raleigh and Durham sought to bring about changes in segregated practices on a local level, they also understood that their actions had national implications.[68] "Protest Triangle" students recognized that their activism played a role in Kennedy's support for civil rights legislation and in the ultimate passage of the Civil Rights Act of 1964. Vannie Culmer, a 1963 NCC graduate, recalled that throughout the country, student activists "were one of the galvanizing forces" that led to the Civil Rights Act.[69]

President Kennedy's support for civil rights legislation did not begin

---

[67] Carter, *The Politics of Rage*, 153.

[68] See appendix for survey results.

[69] Vannie C. Culmer, phone interview by the author, digital recording, 26 January 2017.

on June 11, 1963. In a February 28 address to Congress, he outlined some of the basic tenets that would ultimately be included in the Civil Rights Act of 1964. He touted actions taken by the federal government, including bringing about the end to discrimination in rail and bus lines in 1961 and Justice Department efforts to bring about desegregation in fifteen airports in 1962.[70] But his June 11 speech represented a clearer commitment to supporting civil rights legislation and a more aggressive effort to appeal to American citizens for support. His continuous references to protest demonstrations reveal the impact that they had on pushing him into a more proactive stance. He realized that "the events in Birmingham and elsewhere have so increased the cries for equality that no city or state or legislative body can prudently choose to ignore them."[71] But it was not just sensational events like the use of fire hoses and police dogs or Wallace's stance in the doorway that forced Kennedy's hand. These were merely iconic images that helped to reveal the ugliest aspects of the response to demonstrations and efforts to achieve integration. The true momentum for civil rights legislation came from the thousands of demonstrators throughout the South and the rest of the country, most of whom never appeared on the front page of newspapers or heard their names on the evening news.

In late June, Senator Hugh Scott (R-PA) asked Katzenbach why President Kennedy had waited for nearly two and a half years to submit the seven-point civil rights bill to Congress. He specifically asked, "Was your hand forced by the demonstrations?" Katzenbach replied that since Kennedy offered his limited civil rights program in February "things had moved very fast," an indicator that the protests had added a sense of urgency.[72] The administration realized mass demonstrations were not an ephemeral phenomenon; significant efforts needed to be taken not merely to quell them but for the nation to live up to its ostensible ideals of equality,

---

[70] "Special Message on Civil Rights," 28 February 1963, *Papers of John F. Kennedy*, President's Office Files, Legislative Files, John F. Kennedy Presidential Library, Boston, MA.
[71] *Public Papers of the Presidents of the United States: John F. Kennedy, 1963*, 468–71.
[72] Washington AP, "Civil Rights at Local Level Described as Best Solution," *Durham Morning Herald*, 1 July 1963, 1.

freedom, and democracy.

Civil rights activists in the early 1960s realized that the struggle for equal opportunities needed to be pursued by every generation. Since the Civil War, African Americans had made many economic, educational, and social advances. But the march toward freedom was not a straight line toward increased opportunities. Indeed, one of the most significant portions of the civil rights bill that was proposed in 1963 and ultimately passed in 1964 sought to reestablish and guarantee some of the rights afforded to all races in the Civil Rights Act of 1875. The 1875 Civil Rights Act held that US citizens of every race and color "shall be entitled to the full and equal enjoyment of the accommodations, advantages, facilities, and privileges of inns, public conveyances on land and water, theaters, and other places of public amusement." Yet it was deemed unconstitutional by the Supreme Court in 1883. Despite the strong dissent from Justice John Marshall Harlan, the majority of the Court held that the 1875 Act had exceeded the power of the Congress to enforce provisions of the Thirteenth and Fourteenth Amendments. The majority opinion held that the Equal Protection Clause in the Fourteenth Amendment was aimed at prohibiting state actions that denied the rights protected by the amendment. The Court specifically stated, "Individual invasion of individual rights is not the subject matter of the Amendment."[73]

Civil rights activists at the "Protest Triangle" schools were acutely aware of both the advances that African Americans had made since the Civil War and the limitations they faced. The sit-ins and other protests were a way of challenging segregated practices in places of public accommodations but also served to make clear that African Americans were not content with hiring discrimination and restrictions in economic opportunities. Floyd McKissick, the recently named national director of CORE and a man in tune with the aspirations of Black college students in Durham, spoke at Duke University in late October and said that many Black youth asked themselves "why bother" to get an education if they could not get a quality job after graduation.[74] But for students attending

---

[73] Cortner, *Civil Rights and Public Accommodations*, 2–3.
[74] Durham AP, "CORE Official Heard in Duke Camps Speech," *News and Observer*, 1 November 1963, 12.

historically Black colleges, their participation in the demonstrations served as a way of promoting the process of making their educational attainment match their opportunities.

Largely due to the sit-ins and other demonstrations, activists had helped achieve some desegregation in Raleigh by the end of 1963. A report of the Mayor's Community Relations Committee stated that Blacks had gained access to all the indoor theaters, two motels, and about one-third of the restaurants in Raleigh. The report cited significant gains in Black employment in both city, federal, and state government, as well as some modest gains in employment opportunities in the private sector. Perhaps the most interesting aspect of the report was its reference to the impact of the demonstrations in bringing about desegregation and increases in employment opportunities. It stated that the pace of desegregation in the city was "stimulated by the crisis created by the street demonstrations in the spring and summer of 1963."[75]

In Durham, even more extensive desegregation had taken place by the summer of 1963, as 90 percent of the gross food business in the city had been desegregated. In addition, on July 9 the Durham Junior Chamber of Commerce accepted its first African American member, Asa T. Spaulding Jr., who was the president of North Carolina Mutual Life Insurance, one of the largest Black-owned companies in the nation. In both Raleigh and Durham, significant desegregation of public accommodations had occurred, and some gains had been achieved in reducing hiring discrimination and increasing economic opportunities prior to the Civil Rights Act of 1964 and even prior to Kennedy's proposal to Congress for legislation on June 19, 1963.[76]

Nonetheless, activists in Raleigh and Durham realized that federal legislation could help solidify gains that they had made as well as secure additional opportunities for the future. Their actions in their respective cities had brought about significant local change, and they were part of a broader movement that sparked change on a regional and national level.

---

[75] Jonathan Friendly, "Negro Gains Cited in Raleigh Report," *News and Observer*, 14 December 1963, 20.

[76] Jon Phelps, "90 Pct. of Durham Eating Facilities Now Desegregated," *Durham Morning Herald*, 19 June 1963, 1; "Jaycees Here Admit Negro as Member," *Durham Sun*, 10 July 1963, 13B.

They had already participated in several historic moments, and in August 1963 many participated in one of the most historic moments in the nation's history.

Scores of citizens from Raleigh and Durham packed into buses headed for the March on Washington for Jobs and Freedom on August 28, 1963, while others drove their own cars to the historic gathering. The Durham bus contingent departed from Saint Joseph A.M.E. Church and arrived in the nation's capital around nine A.M. Students, including those from NCC, made up a significant portion of the Durham group. Like the others, they were participants in, not simply witnesses to, the historic event. They viewed their involvement as a carryover from the protests in Durham and other cities throughout the country. The buses transported both Blacks and Whites to the historic event. Thus, the trip to Washington had been prepared by the prior activism that challenged segregation in the two North Carolina cities and other cities throughout the country.[77]

Floyd McKissick was one of the Durhamites who played a significant role at the March on Washington. He was one of the speakers, among an impressive list including Martin Luther King Jr., A. Philip Randolph, and John Lewis, and he also met with President Kennedy that day. McKissick represented CORE in the absence of its executive director James Farmer, who was in jail for involvement in civil rights protests in Louisiana.[78] McKissick was an example of a prominent civil rights leader who recognized the important role that students from historically Black colleges played in pushing the movement forward in 1963 and in providing momentum for the March on Washington. From the steps of the Lincoln Memorial, McKissick delivered Farmer's address while Bayard Rustin, the man who had been arrested in North Carolina sixteen years prior, stood behind him. Perhaps the phrase that captured the significance of all the

---

[77] Phelps, "McKissick in Key Role: Number from City in March," *Durham Morning Herald*, 29 August 1963, 1B; Fay Bryant Mayo, phone interview by the author, digital recording, 1 February 2017; Millie Dunn Veasey, phone interview by the author, digital recording, 27 June 2016; Mildred (Campbell) Christmas, phone interview by the author, digital recording, 10 September 2016.

[78] Jon Phelps, "McKissick in Key Role," 1B; McKissick had been elected as the national chairman at the national CORE meeting in Dayton, Ohio, on June 29, 1963. See Dayton Ohio UPI, "McKissick Elected CORE Chairman at National Meet," *Durham Morning Herald*, 30 June 1963, 4.

local movements and their representation at the march was "play well your roles in your struggle for freedom. In the thousands of communities in which you have come throughout the land, act with valor and dignity, and act without fear."[79]

The group who came from Raleigh to the nation's capital included some of the most significant figures who challenged segregated practices, including NAACP President Ralph Campbell Sr. and Shaw's Dean of Religion, Grady Davis. Campbell did not bring his youngest son William, who integrated Murphey Elementary School in 1960, but brought his daughter Mildred and son Ralph Jr. Mildred recalled that they were participants, not just witnesses, at the March on Washington. As a student at Ligon High School in Raleigh, she participated in marches, which often began at the Shaw campus. "We were a participant in the civil rights movement, because we participated in the marches and the demonstrations. We were involved in the struggles here in Raleigh, but also to a wider range, the March on Washington, so we were willing to go and participate in that too…it was a continuous struggle."[80]

Another young Raleigh citizen took a less conventional path to the March on Washington. Without his parents' knowledge, Ligon High School student Bruce Lightner packed up his schoolbag with a peanut butter and jelly sandwich and a jar of Kool-Aid and proceeded to hitchhike to the March on Washington. He eventually encountered a group from Raleigh, including Dr. John Fleming of the Raleigh Citizens Association, with whom he rode home. Lightner recalls that when he returned, his father, who operated Lightner Funeral Home and eventually became Raleigh's first Black mayor a decade later, told his son, "I am mad at you. But I'm also proud of you."[81]

The citizens of Raleigh who participated in the March on Washington recognized its importance for furthering a message of justice and

---

[79] Josh Shaffer, "50 Years Later, Local Memories of a March, a Speech, and MLK," *News and Observer*, 25 August 2013.

[80] Mildred (Campbell) Christmas, phone interview by the author; "Capital City Represented in 'March,'" *Carolinian*, 31 August 1963, 1.

[81] Shaffer, "50 Years Later, Local Memories of a March, A Speech and MLK"; "Capital City Represented in 'March,'" 1; Bruce Lightner, interview by the author, digital recording, 16 June 2016, Raleigh, NC.

equality for which many of them had already struggled in their own city. One participant reflected, "It was a mighty fine demonstration and showed that Negroes really believe in the things we are fighting for. I certainly hope the oppressors will catch the message." A Saint Augustine's employee recalled the significance of the experience and included the hope that was reflected in "We Shall Overcome," the anthem of the movement: "I am glad that I could participate in the March on Washington for Freedom and Jobs. It was a reminder of hope, sacrifice and of faith. Deep in my heart I do believe that we shall overcome some day."[82]

The March on Washington was in many ways the zenith of a movement that had already made significant gains in various communities throughout the country, albeit one that recognized there was much work left to be done. The movements in Raleigh and Durham were like those in other cities in that they had regional, national, and international implications. Incidents such as the denial of service to Angie Brooks at the Sir Walter Coffee House in Raleigh demonstrated that local movements could not be neatly separated from national and international conceptions about the role of race in determining how societies and governments should operate. Although some civil rights leaders such as John Lewis remained unimpressed with the civil rights bill that ultimately passed in 1964, the March on Washington nonetheless played a role in drawing further attention to civil rights issues and garnering support for the legislation.[83]

Like the other more than two hundred thousand Black and White Americans who attended the March on Washington, those from Raleigh and Durham listened intently to Martin Luther King's eloquent and moving "I Have a Dream" speech. For many, this was not the first time they had heard him address a crowd. Some heard him address the crowd of over a thousand people at White Rock Baptist Church in Durham in the wake of the first week of sit-ins in February 1960, in which King termed the sit-in protests "one of the most significant developments in the civil rights

---

[82] "'Marchers' Report on Experience," *Carolinian*, 7 September 1963, 1.

[83] Washington AP, "Big 'Freedom' March Is Staged By 200,000," *News and Observer*, 29 August 1963, 1. SNCC leader John Lewis's initial draft speech did not support the Kennedy administration's bill, but he ultimately changed it to say "we support the administration's civil rights bill, but with reservations."

struggle."[84] Others had personally met the civil rights leader, while others saw him speak at Raleigh's Memorial Auditorium on April 16, 1960, as part of the activities of the Youth Leadership Conference on Nonviolent Resistance at Shaw University. At the Raleigh speech, King asserted that the demonstrations by Black college students were part of a "world-wide revolution," and he also pointed out, "These students have made it clear that segregation is a cancer in the body politic."[85]

While the content and theme of King's speech in April 1960 and that of August 1963 were different, they both shared a common characteristic. They both were impacted by a movement that had been carried primarily by Black college students and other largely unheralded individuals in several cities throughout the South and the nation. In one of the most iconic moments in American history, King passionately delivered the message. But activists like David Forbes, Lacy Streeter, Barbara Woodhouse, Joycelyn McKissick, Mack Sowell, and Quinton Baker had prepared the stage.

---

[84] Gene Roberts Jr., "Negro Leader Urges Students to Continue Segregation Protest," *News and Observer*, 17 February 1960, 1, 2.

[85] "At Meeting Here: Negroes Discuss Regional Plans," *News and Observer*, 17 April 1960, 1, 2.

Chapter 8

Conclusion:
The Legacy of the "Protest Triangle" Activists

In early July 1964, Shaw University graduate Albert Sampson entered the Heart of Atlanta Motel in downtown Atlanta and was told by the owner, "I can't accommodate any Negroes." The owner refunded the room deposit, which Sampson had previously wired to the motel. The motel's denial of service to the African American man violated the 1964 Civil Rights Act, which prohibited racial discrimination in public accommodations. Sampson, who was then the executive director of the Atlanta branch of the NAACP, testified in the US Supreme Court case, *Heart of Atlanta Motel v. United States,* that the owner told him that he "had a suit against the federal government on this same basic situation and he said that if the courts decide for me to open up, I'll open up; but until then I can't accommodate any Negroes."[1]

Ultimately, the US Supreme Court ruled against the Heart of Atlanta Motel and sustained the arguments made by government lawyers that the denial of service based on race violated the Civil Rights Act, primarily

---

[1] Richard C. Cortner, *Civil Rights and Public Accommodations: The* Heart of Atlanta Motel *and* McClung *Cases* (Lawrence, KS: University Press of Kansas, 2001), 1, 42–43; Albert Sampson, phone interview by the author, digital recording, 12 July 2016.

based on Congress's right to regulate interstate commerce.[2] John Lewis, the SNCC leader and former Fisk University student who participated in the Youth Leadership Conference on Nonviolent Resistance at Shaw University in April 1960, hailed the ruling as "the landmark in the struggle for complete social, economic, and political equality for all Americans" and said that the case "vindicated the thousands of demonstrators who made the civil rights bill not only possible but imperative."[3]

Sampson's involvement in the effort to integrate the Heart of Atlanta Motel represented a continuation of his civil rights activism in Raleigh during his time as a student at Shaw University. It was also indicative of the ways students from the "Protest Triangle" schools continued the struggle for social justice and improving opportunities for African Americans in the years after their graduation. Sampson, the former Shaw University student body president and campus NAACP president, was appointed by Martin Luther King Jr. as the National Housing Director of SCLC in the mid-1960s. He was also a speaker at the Million Man March in 1995. He has served as a pastor at Fernwood United Methodist Church in Chicago and founded "George Washington Carver F.A.R.M.S. (Farmer's Agricultural Resources Management System)," which assists Black farmers in the South in marketing and selling their crops to customers in the North.[4]

Sampson was among the many activists from the "Protest Triangle" schools who realized that political leaders rarely "bestow" freedom upon minorities and that every generation must struggle for social justice and for government to be responsive to its citizens, regardless of race. Like other student activists, he also viewed his participation in civil rights demonstrations as part of his education and as a way of opening future opportunities. Civil rights activists in Raleigh and Durham helped push for a more open society, which paved the way for impressive accomplishments. William Campbell, the seven-year-old boy who integrated

---

[2] Cortner, *Civil Rights and Public Accommodations*, 171–74.

[3] Linda McClain, "Involuntary Servitude, Public Accommodations Laws and the Legacy of *Heart of Atlanta, Inc. v. United States*," *University of Maryland Law Review* 71, no. 83 (2011): 119.

[4] Albert Sampson, phone interview by the author; National Parks Service, International Civil Rights Walk of Fame, "Rev. Dr. Albert Sampson," nps.gov/features/malu/feat0002/wof/albert_sampson.htm.

Murphey Elementary School in September 1960, recalled that the sit-ins had set a standard and "paved the way for more thoughtful integration."[5] It is unlikely that Campbell would have been elected the mayor of Atlanta in 1993 or that his brother Ralph Jr. would have become the first African American state auditor in North Carolina in the same year if not for the actions of civil rights activists throughout the nation pushing for integration and for Black voter registration.[6]

Some of the 1960s-era student activists returned to work at their respective colleges, where they continued the tradition of promoting quality education while maintaining their advocacy for social justice. One example included David Forbes, who became the Dean of the Shaw University Divinity School in 2014. Fellow Shaw graduate and 1960s-era student protestor Louis Powell recalled Forbes's leadership in civil rights demonstrations. Powell remembers that Forbes's reputation on campus made him an obvious choice as a leader in the movement and that his activism has carried on to this day. Powell compared him to the man who held the same position in the early 1960s. In perhaps the ultimate compliment, Powell pointed out that Forbes was and is an effective leader and very dynamic, asserting, "He was the second Grady Davis."[7]

Forbes's experiences in Raleigh are a powerful reminder of the connection between the past and more recent social, political, and economic issues. He participated in "Moral Mondays" rallies in downtown Raleigh. The demonstrations, largely organized by the North Carolina chapter of the NAACP, opposed what the civil rights group and other activists believed was a regressive agenda by the General Assembly regarding social programs, voting rights, education, and tax policy, which ultimately disproportionately hurt minorities and the poor. The protestors sought to put pressure on lawmakers to expand Medicaid coverage, raise the minimum wage, increase funding for public education, and repeal a law that required

---

[5] Albert Sampson, interview by the author; William Campbell, phone interview by the author, digital recording, 11 September 2016.

[6] William Campbell, phone interview by the author; Mildred (Campbell) Christmas, phone interview by the author, digital recording, 10 September 2016.

[7] David Forbes, interview by the author, digital recording, 13 April 2016, Raleigh, North Carolina; Louis Powell, interview by the author, digital recording, 13 April 2016, New Hill, NC.

people to show state-issued identification in order to vote. On April 29, 2015, the second anniversary of the beginning of the "Moral Mondays" demonstrations, General Assembly police officers arrested twenty protestors after lawmakers complained that they could not conduct business with the chanting outside the assembly building. The arrests brought the total number of arrests related to the protests to more than one thousand since 2013. Forbes was among those taken to the Wake County Detention Center after being arrested for trespassing and violating the fire code on April 29, 2015, more than fifty-five years after he was arrested for participating in civil rights demonstrations at Cameron Village in Raleigh in February 1960. According to Forbes, "My mind went back to 1960 when I heard the jail door clang."[8]

Most student activists at the "Protest Triangle" schools perceived their participation in civil rights protests as part of their education. For many, their experiences in sit-ins and other demonstrations were part of what made their college experience a defining moment not only in their lives but also in the lives of others who benefitted from their sacrifices. Among those students was John T. Avent, whose participation in the sit-ins in Durham ultimately led to a US Supreme Court decision in *John Thomas Avent et al. v. North Carolina* after the North Carolina Supreme Court upheld the convictions for Avent and four other North Carolina College at Durham students, as well as two Duke University students. The highest court in the nation vacated the North Carolina Supreme Court decision and remanded it back to the North Carolina Court to reconsider. Ultimately, Avent never served the fifteen-day sentence that he received in 1960. Avent's experiences demonstrate the commitment that student protestors made toward advancing civil rights for African Americans. Avent believes not only that the sit-ins and the cases they inspired were crucial in getting the Supreme Court to essentially rule on segregation but also that the cases involving sit-ins provided "the pillar of the Civil Rights

---

[8] Mark Binker, "49 Arrested at NC General Assembly 'Moral Monday' Protest," 13 May 2013, http://www.wral.com/49-arrested-at-moral-monday-protest-at-state-legislature-/12441971/; Jorge Valencia, "20 Protestors Arrested at NC General Assembly as 'Moral Monday' Protests Return," WUNC North Carolina Public Radio, http://wunc.org/post/20-protesters-arrested-nc-general-assembly-moral-monday-protests-return#stream/0; David Forbes, interview by the author.

Act."[9]

One of Avent's lesser-known experiences is also significant in understanding the student-led protests and their connection to ideas of academic freedom. After his graduation in 1963, Avent sought to apply to medical school. He decided to take a long shot and ask the recently retired president of NCC for a letter of recommendation, despite his doubts about whether Alfonso Elder knew him. In their brief meeting, Elder agreed to write the letter, and without Avent mentioning the protests, Elder told him about how Mayor E. J. Evans had approached him in 1960 and asked him to reign in the student protestors and Elder had said no. For the college president who had previously emphasized a concept of "student self-direction," Elder was not willing to restrict the students' actions. To do so would have thwarted their right to protest unjust social practices and would have represented a restriction on their academic freedom. In a moment that likely reflected the thoughts of many older Durhamites, Avent recalls that Elder told him, "I'm proud of you students and all that you did."[10]

Student demonstrators at Shaw University, Saint Augustine's College, and North Carolina College at Durham literally proceeded from campus to counter to participate in sit-ins in the early 1960s. But they also countered reactionary politicians and businesspersons, and for some that struggle continues to this day. Mack Junior Sowell, the Shaw student who led protests in Raleigh in 1963, including those at the Sir Walter Hotel, which accommodated many state legislators, asserts, "Without the pressure, there weren't going to be changes. Even so today."[11] There have been powerful recent reminders that the struggle to challenge and encourage legislators and citizens to live up to ostensible American ideals of democracy and equality is not merely the work of a past generation. There are

[9] John Thomas Avent, phone interview by the author, digital recording, 12 July 2017; Chicago-Kent College of Law at Illinois Tech, "Avent v. North Carolina," Oyez, https://www.oyez.org/cases/1962/11.
[10] Alfonso Elder, "The Evolution of a Concept of Student Self-Direction," Folder 28, Series 3, Speeches, 1960–1963, Alfonso Elder Papers, University Archives, Records and History Center in the James E. Shepard Memorial Library, North Carolina Central University, Durham, NC; John Thomas Avent, phone interview by the author.
[11] Mack Junior Sowell, interview by the author.

reasons for skepticism, but the actions of the 1960s-era student protestors provided tangible results and offer hope that the bells of freedom can ring louder than the clang of the jailhouse door.

Appendix

Survey Composite Results—
Responses to Statements

[The underlined number next to each statement represents the average of the response to that statement among those surveyed.]

GENERAL SURVEY COMPOSITE RESULTS
Please rate the following on a scale of 1–10:
1=Strongly disagree
10=Strongly agree

NOTE: You can choose any number between 1 and 10 based on how much you agree with the statement.

5.69 1) The civil rights demonstrations in Raleigh/Durham from 1960–1963 were primarily local and were not primarily reactions to events in Greensboro and other cities in North Carolina.

6.85 2) Teachers at Shaw University/Saint Augustine's College/North Carolina College (whichever you attended) encouraged their students to take part in the demonstrations.

2.33 3) Mayor W.G. Enloe did his best to help Raleigh integrate restaurants, theaters, and other public accommodations.

5.85 4a) Governor Terry Sanford (January 1961–January 1965) provided positive leadership in the civil rights struggle in North Carolina.

3.08 4b) Governor Luther Hodges (November 1954–January 1961) provided positive leadership in the civil rights struggle in North Carolina.

4.58 5) There was one clear local leader of the desegregation demonstrations.

4.85 6) Leaders of the local movement feared for their safety and that of their families.

6.0 7) Demonstrators attempted to get African American bystanders to join the protests.

3.62 8) White men and women played a significant role in the demonstrations in Raleigh.

2.73 9) US military personnel (White or Black) played a significant role in the local demonstrations.

5.77 10a) The primary goals of the demonstrations were achieved (by the end of 1963).

5.85 10b) The primary goals of the demonstrations were achieved (by the end of 1964).

Appendix

SURVEY COMPOSITE RESULTS—PERCEPTIONS OF GROUPS/INSTITUTIONS

[The underlined number next to each group represents the average response among those surveyed.]

Please rank the following institutions/groups in order of importance to the desegregation of public accommodations and to the reduction of discriminatory hiring practices in Raleigh (or Durham).

1=Most important institution/group
8=Least important institution/group

5.9	City Council
2.0	Local NAACP, SNCC, SCLC, or CORE
1.5	Shaw University/Saint Augustine's College (or NC College at Durham) student organizations
2.17	Local Churches
4.36	Federal Government
4.82	Mayor's Biracial Committee
2.25	State and National NAACP, SNCC, SCLC, or CORE
5.0	State Government of North Carolina

SURVEY COMPOSITE RESULTS—IMPORTANT INDIVIDUALS
[The underlined number next to each individual represents the average response among those surveyed.]

Focusing on the period from 1960–1964, please rate the following people on a scale of 1–10 based on the following question: To what extent did the individual do all that was in their power to improve conditions for African Americans in Raleigh and/or in North Carolina? For any individuals that you were unaware of, please leave the line next to their name blank.

1=Individual did not make any effort to improve conditions for African Americans.
10=Individual did everything in their power to improve conditions for African Americans.

4.67   President Dwight D. Eisenhower
8.58   President John F. Kennedy
8.64   Lyndon B. Johnson
8.5   Robert F. Kennedy
3.44   Senator Sam Ervin Jr.
3.0   Senator B. Everett Jordan
3.18   Luther Hodges (Governor, 1954–1961)
6.58   Terry Sanford (Governor, 1961–1965)
1.71   Dr. I. Beverly Lake
2.5   William G. Enloe (Mayor, 1957–1963)
9.5   Reverend W. W. Finlator
8.83   Ella Baker
9.83   Ralph Campbell Sr.
7.86   Dr. William R. Strassner
9.88   Dr. Grady Davis
8.67   Dr. James A. Boyer

SURVEY COMPOSITE RESULTS—STUDENT PERCEPTIONS
[The underlined number next to each statement represents the average
    response among those surveyed.]

Please rate the following on a scale of 1–10:
1=Strongly disagree
10=Strongly agree

9.83 1) You valued the opportunity to participate in the demonstrations
if you chose to do so as part of the academic freedom afforded at
Shaw University/Saint Augustine's College (in other words, you
believed that the college should not tell you whether or not you
could participate).

8.25 2) Students viewed participation in the movement as a part of their
education and as a way of opening societal opportunities.

7.1 3) You viewed student leadership as a counter to established city
leadership.

8.91 4) You believed that Whites would not "bestow" freedom and that
African Americans needed to struggle to earn freedom.

6.5 5) Student athletes played a prominent role in the local movement.

8.92 6) Student demonstrators believed they were participants in creating historical change, not just witnesses to history.

9.25 7) Female students were equally important to the local movement
as men.

8.91 8a) There was a high level of cooperation in regards to the demonstrations between students at Shaw University and Saint Augustine's College.

7.5 8b) There was a high level of cooperation in regards to the demon-
strations between students at Shaw University/Saint Augustine's
College (whichever you attended) and North Carolina College at
Durham.

5.67 8c) There was a high level of cooperation in regards to the demonstrations between students at Shaw University/Saint Augustine's
College and State College (North Carolina State).

4.78 8d) There was a high level of cooperation in regards to the demonstrations between students at Shaw University/Saint Augustine's
College and the University of North Carolina (Chapel Hill).

4.7 8e) There was a high level of cooperation in regards to the demonstrations between students at Shaw University/Saint Augustine's College and Duke University.

6.92 8f) There was a high level of cooperation in regards to the demonstrations between students at Shaw University/Saint Augustine's College and other historically Black colleges in North Carolina such as NC A&T and Fayetteville State (Teachers) College.

4.17 9) The local movement would have thrived even without support from civil rights groups such as the NAACP, SNCC, CORE, and SCLC.

8.83 10) You viewed participation in the demonstrations as potentially enhancing the positive reputation of your college rather than tarnishing its reputation.

3.92 11) There was some social pressure to participate in the demonstrations.

Bibliography

Archives

Atlanta, Georgia
King Library and Archives, Martin Luther King Jr. Center for Nonviolent
    Social Change
Martin Luther King Jr. Papers
Southern Christian Leadership Conference Papers
Student Nonviolent Coordinating Committee Papers

Chapel Hill, North Carolina
Southern Historical Collection, Wilson Library, University of North Carolina at
    Chapel Hill
Allard Kenneth Lowenstein Papers
Floyd B. McKissick Papers

Charlotte, North Carolina
Special Collections and University Archives, J. Murrey Atkins Library,
    University of North Carolina at Charlotte
Harry Golden Papers

Durham, North Carolina
Rare Book, Manuscript and Special Collections Library, Duke University
Black History at Duke Reference Collection, 1948–2001 and n.d.
Evans Family Papers
Rencher Nicholas Harris Papers
University Archives, Records and History, North Carolina Central University
Alfonso Elder Papers

Nashville, Tennessee
Civil Rights Collection, Nashville Public Library
Series II, Civil Rights Ephemera Collection
Series III, Civil Rights Oral History Collection
Series IV, Civil Rights Periodical Collection

Raleigh, North Carolina
Archives and Special Collections, Prezell R. Robinson Library,
    Saint Augustine's University
James A. Boyer Papers
Joseph Holt Jr. Papers
Archives and Special Collections, James E. Cheek Learning
    Resource Center, Shaw University
Miscellaneous Clippings Files
Shaw Journal Clippings
North Carolina Division of Archives and History
Governor's Papers, Luther Hodges
Governor's Papers, Terry Sanford
Governor's Papers, William B. Umstead
Olivia Raney Local History Library
Miscellaneous Clippings

Washington, DC
Manuscript Division, Library of Congress
National Association for the Advancement of Colored People Papers

Newspapers
Campus Echo (North Carolina College at Durham student newspaper)
Carolina Times (Durham)
Carolinian (Raleigh)
Carolinian (Woman's College of the University of North Carolina, Greensboro)
Carrboro Citizen
Charlotte Observer
Chronicle (Duke University student newspaper)
Daily Tar Heel (UNC-Chapel Hill student newspaper)
Durham Morning Herald
Durham Sun
Florida Flambeau (Florida State University student newspaper)
Indy Week (Durham)
New York Times
News and Observer (Raleigh)
Pen (Saint Augustine's College student newspaper)
Raleigh Times
Shaw Journal (Shaw University student newspaper)
Southern Patriot (Southern Conference Education Fund)
Student Voice (Student Nonviolent Coordinating Committee)
Tennessean (Nashville, Tennessee)

Wilmington Daily Record
Winston-Salem Journal

Interviews by the Author
Avent, John T. Phone interview by author, 12 July 2017. Digital recording.
Beatty, Celestine. Phone interview by author, 13 July 2017. Digital recording.
Bullock, Stafford G. Interview by author, 2 March 2016. Digital recording. Raleigh.
Brock, Carrie Gaddy. Interview by author, 2 March 2016. Digital recording. Raleigh.
Camm, Vivian (McKay). Interview by author, 27 April 2016. Digital recording. Lynchburg, VA.
Campbell, William. Phone interview by author, 11 September 2016. Digital recording.
Christmas, Mildred (Campbell). Phone interview by author, 10 September 2016. Digital recording.
Clayton, McLouis. Interview by author, 2 March 2016. Digital recording. Shaw University campus, Raleigh.
Culmer, Vannie C. Phone interview by author, 26 January 2017. Digital recording.
Cunningham, Pete. Phone interview by author, 21 June 2016. Digital recording.
Dansby, David. Phone interview by author, 14 June 2016. Recording in notes.
Dumas, Caroline. Phone interview by author, 13 July 2017. Digital recording.
Forbes, David C. Interview by author, 13 April 2016. Digital recording. Shaw University campus, Raleigh.
Holt, Joseph, Jr. Interview by author, 7 July 2016. Digital recording. Saint Augustine's University campus, Raleigh.
Jhirad (Shwartz), Susan. Phone interview by author. 30 October 2021. Digital recording.
Lightner, Bruce. Interview by author, 16 June 2016. Digital recording. Raleigh.
Mayo, Fay Bryant. Phone interview by author, 1 February 2016. Digital recording.
Merritt, Ben. Phone interview by author, 26 January 2017. Digital recording.
Opton, Edward. Phone interview by author, 11 April 2016. Digital recording.
Othow, Helen Chavis. Phone interview by author, 13 July 2016. Digital recording.
Powell, Louis. Interview by author, 13 April 2016. Digital recording. New Hill, North Carolina.
Raphael, Ray. Phone interview by author, 8 November 2021. Digital recording.
Reynolds, Edward. Phone interview by author, 20 July 2016. Digital recording.
Riley, Walter. Phone interview by author, 14 June 2016. Digital recording.

Sampson, Albert. Phone interview by author, 12 July 2016. Digital recording.

Sowell, Mack Junior. Interview by author, 20 April 2016. Digital recording. Shaw University campus, Raleigh.

Tucker, Otis, Jr. Mail interview by author, received 5 May 2016.

Veasey, Millie Dunn. Phone interview by author, 27 June 2016. Digital recording.

Walker, Wyatt Tee. Phone interview by author, 15 July 2017. Digital recording.

Wyche, LaMonte, Sr. Phone interview by author, 29 June 2016. Digital recording.

Young, Andrew J. Interview by author, 18 May 2016. Digital recording. Atlanta.

Other Interviews

Baker, Quinton E. Interview by Chris McGinnis, 23 February 2002. Interview K-0838. Southern Oral History Program Collection #4007. Wilson Library, University of North Carolina at Chapel Hill.

Cusick, Pat. Interview by Pamela Dean, 19 June 1989. Interview L-0043. Southern Oral History Program Collection #4007. Wilson Library, University of North Carolina at Chapel Hill.

Finlator, William W. Interview by Jay Jenkins, 19 April 1985. Interview C-0007. Southern Oral History Program Collection #4007. Wilson Library, University of North Carolina at Chapel Hill.

Pollitt, Daniel H. Interview by Ann McColl, 5 April 1991. Interview L-0064-7. Southern Oral History Program Collection #4007. Wilson Library, University of North Carolina at Chapel Hill.

Books, Articles, Dissertations, and Other Sources

Anderson, Jean Bradley. *Durham County: A History of Durham County, North Carolina.* 2nd ed. Durham: Duke University Press, 2001.

Andrews, Kenneth T., and Sarah Gaby. "Local Protest and Federal Policy: The Impact of the Civil Rights Movement on the 1964 Civil Rights Act." *Sociological Forum* 30, no. S1(June 2015): 509–27.

Baade, Hans, and Robinson O. Everett, eds. *Academic Freedom: The Scholar's Place in Modern Society.* Dobbs Ferry, NY: Oceana Publications, Inc., 1964.

Baker, Ella. "Bigger Than a Hamburger." *Southern Patriot* 18, no. 5 (June 1960): 4.

Bay, Mia. *Traveling Black: A Story of Race and Resistance.* Cambridge: The Belknap Press of Harvard University Press, 2021.

Billingsley, William J. *Communists on Campus: Race, Politics, and the Public University in Sixties North Carolina.* Athens: University of Georgia Press, 1999.

Birmingham, David. *Kwame Nkrumah: The Father of African Nationalism.* Athens: Ohio University Press, 1998.

Bissett, Jim. "The Dilemma Over Moderates: School Desegregation in Alamance County, North Carolina." *Journal of Southern History* 81, no. 4 (November 2015): 887–930.

Blumberg, Herbert H. "Accounting for a Nonviolent Mass Demonstration." *Sociological Inquiry* 38 (Winter 1968): 43–50.

Borstelmann, Thomas. *The Cold War and the Color Line: American Race Relations in the Global Arena.* Cambridge: Harvard University Press, 2001.

Branch, Taylor. *Parting the Waters: America in the King Years, 1954–1963.* New York: Simon and Schuster, Inc., 1988.

Brinson, Linda Carter. "Edward Reynolds: Courage to Change a Campus." *Wake Forest Magazine* (Spring 2013): 3–9.

Brown, Hugh Victor. *A History of the Education of Negroes in North Carolina.* Raleigh: Irving Swain Press, Inc., 1961.

Brown, Leslie. *Upbuilding Black Durham: Gender, Class, and Black Community Development in the Jim Crow South.* Chapel Hill: University of North Carolina Press, 2008.

Bryan, G. McLeod. *Dissenter in the Baptist Southland: Fifty Years in the Career of William Wallace Finlator.* Macon, GA: Mercer University Press, 1985.

Bynum, Thomas. *NAACP Youth and the Fight for Black Freedom, 1936–1965.* Knoxville: University of Tennessee Press, 2013.

Carson, Clayborne. *In Struggle: SNCC and the Black Awakening of the 1960s.* Cambridge: Harvard University Press, 1981.

Carter, Dan T. *The Politics of Rage: George Wallace, the Origins of the New Conservatism, and the Transformation of American Politics.* Baton Rouge: Louisiana State University Press, 1995.

Carter, Wilmoth A. *The New Negro of the South: A Portrait of Movements and Leadership.* New York: Exposition Press, 1967.

———. *Shaw's Universe: A Monument to Educational Innovation.* Raleigh: Shaw University, 1973.

———. *The Urban Negro of the South.* New York: Vantage Press, Inc., 1961.

Chafe, William H. *Civilities and Civil Rights: Greensboro, North Carolina and the Black Struggle for Freedom.* Oxford: Oxford University Press, 1980.

———. *Never Stop Running: Allard Lowenstein and the Struggle to Save American Liberalism.* New York: Basic Books, 1993.

Chansky, Art. *Game Changers: Dean Smith, Charlie Scott, and the Era that Transformed a Southern College Town.* Chapel Hill: University of North Carolina Press, 2016.

Clift, Virgil A., Archibald W. Anderson, and H. Gordon Hullfish, eds. *Negro Education in America: Its Adequacy, Problems, and Needs.* New York: Harper and Brothers, 1962.

Cortner, Richard C. *Civil Rights and Public Accommodations: The* Heart of Atlanta *and* McClung *Cases.* Lawrence, KS: University Press of Kansas, 2001.

Covinton, Howard E., and Marion A. Ellis. *Terry Sanford: Politics, Progress, and Outrageous Ambitions.* Durham: Duke University Press, 1999.

Cummings, Richard. *The Pied Piper: Allard K. Lowenstein and the Liberal Dream.* New York: Grove Press, Inc., 1985.

Curry, Constance, et al. *Deep in Our Hearts: Nine White Women in the Freedom Movement.* Athens. The University of Georgia Press, 2000.

Deroche, Andrew J. *Andrew Young: Civil Rights Ambassador.* Wilmington, DE: Scholarly Resources, Inc., 2003.

Drescher, John. *Triumph of Good Will: How Terry Sanford Beat a Champion of Segregation and Reshaped the South.* Jackson: University Press of Mississippi, 2000.

Dudziak, Mary L. *Cold War Civil Rights: Race and the Image of American Democracy.* Princeton: Princeton University Press, 2000.

Eagles, Charles W. *Outside Agitator: Jon Daniels and the Civil Rights Movement in Alabama.* Chapel Hill: University of North Carolina Press, 1993.

Ehle, John. *The Free Men.* New York: Harper and Row, 1965.

Ellsworth, Scott. *The Secret Game: A Wartime Story of Courage, Change, and Basketball's Lost Triumph.* New York: Little, Brown and Company, 2015.

Eskew, Glenn T. *But for Birmingham: Local and National Movements in the Civil Rights Struggle.* Chapel Hill: University of North Carolina Press, 1997.

Fairclough, Adam. *Better Day Coming: Blacks and Equality, 1890–2000.* New York: Penguin Books, 2001.

Fairclough, Adam. *To Redeem the Soul of America: The Southern Christian Leadership Conference and Martin Luther King, Jr.* Athens: University of Georgia Press, 1987.

Finkin, Matthew W., and Robert C. Post. *For the Common Good: Principles of Academic Freedom.* New Haven: Yale University Press, 2009.

Fleming, Maria. *A Place at the Table: Struggles for Equality in America.* Oxford: Oxford University Press, 2001.

Forman, James. *The Making of Black Revolutionaries.* New York: MacMillan Company, 1972.

Furgurson, Ernest B. *Hard Right: The Rise of Jesse Helms.* New York: W.W. Norton and Company, 1986.

Gaillard, Frye. *The Dream Long Deferred.* Chapel Hill: University of North Carolina Press, 1988.

Gershenhorn, Jerry. "Hocutt v. Wilson and Race Relations in Durham, North Carolina, During the 1930s." *North Carolina Historical Review* 78, no. 3 (July 2001): 275–308.

Gershenhorn, Jerry. *Louis Austin and the Carolina Times: A Life in the Long Black*

Freedom Struggle. Chapel Hill: University of North Carolina Press, 2018.

Grant, Joanne. *Ella Baker: Freedom Bound*. New York: John Wiley and Sons, Inc., 1998.

Greene, Christina. *Our Separate Ways: Women and the Black Freedom Movement in Durham, North Carolina*. Chapel Hill: University of North Carolina Press, 2005.

Hahn, Steven. *A Nation Under Our Feet: Black Political Struggles in the Rural South from Slavery to the Great Migration*. Cambridge: The Belknap Press of Harvard University Press, 2003.

Hartnett, Kimberly Marlowe. *Carolina Israelite: How Harry Golden Made Us Care about Jews, the South, and Civil Rights*. Chapel Hill: University of North Carolina Press, 2015.

Harvey, Paul. *Redeeming the South: Religious Cultures and Racial Identities among Southern Baptists, 1865–1925*. Chapel Hill: University of North Carolina Press, 1997.

Hochschild, Adam. *King Leopold's Ghost: A Story of Greed, Terror, and Heroism in Colonial Africa*. Boston: First Mariner Books, 1999.

Hofstadter, Richard, and Walter P. Metzger. *The Development of Academic Freedom in the United States*. New York: Columbia University Press, 1955.

Holden, Charles J. *The New Southern University: Academic Freedom and Liberalism at UNC*. Lexington: University Press of Kentucky, 2012.

Hunter, Tera. *To 'Joy My Freedom: Southern Black Women's Lives and Labors after the Civil War*. Cambridge: Harvard University Press, 1997.

Jackson, Thomas F. *From Civil Rights to Human Rights: Martin Luther King, Jr., and the Struggle for Economic Justice*. Philadelphia: University of Pennsylvania Press, 2007.

Jacoway, Elizabeth, and David R. Colburn, eds. *Southern Businessmen and Desegregation*. Baton Rouge: Louisiana State University Press, 1982.

Jaffe, A. J., Walter Adams, and Sandra G. Meyers. *Negro Higher Education in the 1960's*. New York: Frederick A. Praeger, Publishers, 1968.

Jenkins, Clara Barnes. "An Historical Study of Shaw University, 1865–1963." PhD dissertation, University of Pittsburgh, 1965.

Johnson, K. Todd, and Elizabeth Reid Murray. *Wake: Capital County of North Carolina*. Vol. II. Raleigh: Wake County, 1983.

Jonas, Glen. "Two Roads Diverged: The Civil Rights Movement Comes to FBC Raleigh." *Baptist History and Heritage Society* (22 June 2019).

King, Arnold L. *The Multicampus University of North Carolina Comes of Age, 1956–1986*. Chapel Hill: University of North Carolina Press, 1987.

Klarman, Michael J. "The White Primary Rulings: A Case Study in the Consequences of Supreme Court Decision-Making." *Florida State University Law Review* 29, no. 55 (2014): 55–107.

Koopman, G. Robert, Alice Miel, and Paul J. Misner. *Democracy in School*

Administration. New York: D. Appleton-Century Company, Inc., 1943.

Lall Pugh, Candida. "Wouldn't Take Nothing for My Journey Now." *Veterans of the Civil Rights Movement* (2011). http://www.crmvet.org/nars/lall2.htm. Accessed 22 January 2017.

LeLoudis, James L. *Schooling the New South: Pedagogy, Self, and Society in North Carolina, 1880–1920.* Chapel Hill: University of North Carolina Press, 1996.

Lewis, David Levering. *W. E. B. Du Bois: The Fight for Equality and the American Century, 1919–1963.* New York: Henry Holt and Company, 2000.

Link, William A. *Righteous Warrior: Jesse Helms and the Rise of Modern Conservatism.* New York: St. Martin's Press, 2008.

Link, William A. *William Friday: Power, Purpose and American Higher Education.* Chapel Hill: University of North Carolina Press, 1995.

Litwack, Leon. *Trouble in Mind: Black Southerners in the Age of Jim Crow.* New York: Alfred A. Knopf, 1998.

Lowenstein, Allard. *Brutal Mandate: A Journey to South West Africa.* New York: MacMillan, 1962.

MacIver, Robert M. *Academic Freedom in Our Time.* New York: Columbia University Press, 1955.

McAdam, Doug. *Freedom Summer.* Oxford: Oxford University Press, 1988.

McClain, Linda. "Involuntary Servitude, Public Accommodations Laws and the Legacy of *Heart of Atlanta, Inc. v. United States.*" *University of Maryland Law Review* 71, no. 83 (2011): 83–162.

McEntarfer, Heather Killelea. "Catching Hell: The Joe Holt Integration Story." *Terrain.org* 22 (Summer/Fall 2008). http://www.terrain.org/essays/22/mcentarfer.htm. Accessed 1 February 2016.

McGrath, Earl. *The Predominantly Negro Colleges and Universities in Transition.* New York: Bureau of Publications, Columbia University, 1965.

McWhorter, Diane. *Carry Me Home: Birmingham, Alabama: The Climactic Battle of the Civil Rights Revolution.* New York: Simon and Schuster, 2001.

Meier, August, and Elliott Rudwick. *CORE: A Study in the Civil Rights Movement, 1942–1968.* New York: Oxford University Press, 1973.

Miller, Steven Patrick. *Billy Graham and the Rise of the Republican South.* Philadelphia: University of Pennsylvania Press, 2009.

Mitchell, Memory F. *Messages, Addresses, and Public Papers of Terry Sanford, Governor of North Carolina, 1961–1965.* Raleigh: Council of State, State of North Carolina, 1966.

Mitchell, Glenford E., and William H. Peace III. *The Angry Black South.* New York: Corinth Books, 1962.

Morgan, Iwan, and Philip Davies, eds. *From Sit-Ins to SNCC: The Student Civil Rights Movement in the 1960s.* Gainesville: University Press of Florida, 2012.

Moye, J. Todd. *Ella Baker: Community Organizer of the Civil Rights Movement.* Lanham, MD: Rowman and Littlefield Publishers, Inc., 2013.

Payne, Charles M. *I've Got the Light of Freedom: The Organizing Tradition and the Mississippi Freedom Struggle.* Berkeley: University of California Press, 1995.

Perkins, David, ed. *The News and Observer's Raleigh: A Living History of North Carolina's Capital.* Winston-Salem: John F. Blair, 1994.

Phillips, Jane. "Night Train to Raleigh: Summer 1962 Voter Registration, Chased by the Klan, and Going Incognegro Below the Mason-Dixon Line." 2016. https://www.crmvet.org/nars/phillips.htm.

Pincoffs, Edmund L., ed. *The Concept of Academic Freedom.* Austin: University of Texas Press, 1975.

Public Papers of the Presidents of the United States: John F. Kennedy, 1963. Washington, DC: US Government Printing Office, 1964.

Raphael, Ray. *A Life in History.* Unpublished work shared with the author (2021).

Raleigh City Museum. *Let Us March On: Raleigh's Journey Toward Civil Rights.* Raleigh: Raleigh City Museum, 2000.

Ransby, Barbara. *Ella Baker and the Black Freedom Movement: A Radical Democratic Vision.* Chapel Hill: University of North Carolina Press, 2003.

Reagan, Alice Elizabeth. *North Carolina State University: A Narrative History.* Ann Arbor, MI: Edwards Brothers, Inc., 1987.

"Rev. Dr. Albert Sampson." *International Civil Rights: Walk of Fame.* nps.gov/features/malu/feat0002/wof/albert_sampson.htm. Accessed 22 June 2022.

Rogers, Ibram H. *The Black Campus Movement: Black Students and the Racial Reconstruction of Higher Education, 1965–1972.* New York: Palgrave MacMillan, 2012.

Rohe, William H. *The Research Triangle: From Tobacco Road to Global Prominence.* Philadelphia: University of Pennsylvania Press, 2011.

Rosen, Richard A., and Joseph Mosnier. *Julius Chambers: A Life in the Legal Struggle for Civil Rights.* Chapel Hill: University Press of North Carolina, 2016.

Rustin, Bayard, and George Houser. "We Challenged Jim Crow!" Report prepared for CORE and the Fellowship of Reconciliation, April 1947.

Saint Augustine's College Ninety-Third Catalogue, 1959–1960. Raleigh: Saint Augustine's College, 1960.

Shattuck, Gardiner, Jr. *Episcopalians and Race: Civil War to Civil Rights.* Lexington: University Press of Kentucky, 2000.

Stone, Gregory, and Douglas Lowenstein. *Lowenstein: Acts of Courage and Belief.* New York: Harcourt, Brace, Jovanovich, Publishers, 1983.

Stoper, Emily. *The Student Nonviolent Coordinating Committee: The Growth of*

Radicalism in a Civil Rights Organization. New York: Carlson Publishing, Inc., 1968.

Sugrue, Thomas. *Sweet Land of Liberty: The Forgotten Struggle for Civil Rights in the North*. New York: Random House, 2008.

Sutton, Jerry. *A Matter of Conviction: A History of Southern Baptist Engagement with the Culture*. Nashville: B&H Publishing Group, 2008.

Thorpe, Earle E. *A Concise History of North Carolina Central University*. Durham: Harrington Publications, 1984.

Wallace, Jim, and Paul Dickson. *Courage in the Moment: The Civil Rights Struggle, 1961–1964*. Mineola, NY: Dover Publications, Inc., 2012.

Vann, Andre D., and Beverly Washington Jones. *Durham's Hayti*. Charleston, SC: Arcadia Publishing, 1999.

Waynick, Capus M., John C. Brooks, and Elsie Pitts, eds. *North Carolina and the Negro*. Raleigh: Mayors Cooperating Committee, 1964.

Weisbrot, Robert. *Freedom Bound: A History of America's Civil Rights Movement*. Penguin Books, 1990.

Young, Andrew. *An Easy Burden: The Civil Rights Movement and the Transformation of America*. New York: Harper Collins, 1996.

Index

INDEX

INDEX